The Formal Method in Literary Scholarship

The Formal Method in Literary Scholarship

A CRITICAL INTRODUCTION TO SOCIOLOGICAL POETICS

P. N. Medvedev/M. M. Bakhtin

Translated by
Albert J. Wehrle

THE GOUCHER COLLEGE SERIES

The Johns Hopkins University Press   Baltimore and London

Manufactured in the United States of America

Originally published in the USSR under the title *Formal'nyi metod v
literaturovedenii (Kriticheskoe vvedenie v sotsiologicheskuiu poetiku)*, (Leningrad:
"Priboi," 1928).

The Johns Hopkins University Press, Baltimore, Maryland 21218
The Johns Hopkins Press Ltd., London

Library of Congress Catalog Number 77-15529
ISBN 0-8018-2028-6

Library of Congress Cataloging in Publication data will be found on the last
printed page of this book.

Contents

Part Four: The Formal Method in Literary History

Chapter Eight: The Work of Art as a Datum External to
Consciousness   145

Chapter Nine: The Formalist Theory of the Historical Development of
Literature   159

Introduction:
M. M. Bakhtin/P. N. Medvedev

In 1967 the Soviet psycholinguist A. A. Leont'ev drew attention to a "Bakhtin school" which was active in the late twenties, but confined his citations to a book by Valentin N. Voloshinov.[1] The absence of a reference to a work by the school's leader received some explanation in one of the papers read at Moscow University in honor of Bakhtin's seventy-fifth birthday and surveyed in a 1971 issue of the journal *Voprosy iazykoznaniia* [*Problems in Linguistics*].[2] The eminent philologist Viacheslav V. Ivanov, in a paper later published in expanded form and translated into English, refers to (but does not name) witnesses who could support Bakhtin's authorship of three articles and two books that appeared under Voloshinov's name, as well as of *The Formal Method.* Ivanov treats the excerpts he draws from the various texts (for another purpose — a survey of Bakhtin's career) as sufficient to show that all the works cited belong to the same author. The *Problems in Linguistics* report also provided some new information about the "Bakhtin school": a "circle" (in the Russian tradition), it included artists (in the wide sense) as well as scholars like Voloshinov, Medvedev, and L. V. Pumpianskii.[3] About the same time (1926-29) there existed a sort of "inner circle"; Bakhtin and his wife lived communally with a few other couples in Peterhof, the site of a royal residence founded by Peter the Great on the shore of the Finnish Gulf not far from Leningrad. The commune included Medvedev and his wife, but not Voloshinov. To date nothing has been published on this fascinating aspect of Bakhtin's life in Leningrad.[4] It is known that Bakhtin, Medvedev, and Voloshinov met in the Belo-Russian city of Vitebsk (about five hundred kilometers south of Leningrad) in the early twenties. Here they might have already traced the general guidelines for what they set out to accomplish in Leningrad: the elaboration of a science of ideologies based upon Marxism. Systematic steps in this direction were the call for a sociologization of psychology issued in *Freudianism* (1927), the blueprint for sociological linguistics developed in *Marxism and the Philosophy of Language* (1929), and an apparently unrealized plan for a critique of contemporary philosophy that was to be titled *Filosoficheskaia mysl' sovremennogo zapada.*[5] *The Formal Method* was also part of this concerted effort to rethink the study of culture.

Perhaps one day we will obtain inside information about how the
literary criticism section of the Bakhtin circle operated. The few pieces of
the puzzle we have now are hard to put together. Ivanov reports that
Voloshinov and Medvedev "made only small insertions and changes in
particular parts" of the books and articles in question and changed some
titles.[6] V. N. Turbin seems to support Ivanov when he quotes Bakhtin as
saying, with regard to *The Formal Method:* "Pavel Nikolaevich [Medvedev]
added to it, and not always for the better." According to Turbin, this was
as much as Bakhtin ever said about the book. At other times he would
confine himself to the remark that he "helped" with it. Knowing Bakhtin's
reticence about the book, Turbin decided to conduct an experiment. In
1965, on a visit to Bakhtin, Turbin laid a copy of *The Formal Method* on
the table without a word. Bakhtin said nothing, but his wife exclaimed:
"Oh, how many times I copied that!" On the other hand, the latest
published information, provided by Vadim V. Kozhinov, is that the
problematic books and articles were written "on the basis of conversations
with Mikhail Mikhailovich."[7] Taken by itself, this account assigns
Voloshinov and Medvedev a greater role in the actual writing of the
works than Ivanov's version, taken by itself, does. The speculations that
follow are based on the premise that it is less likely that one of these
accounts is erroneous than that both are somehow accurate within the
situation as a whole.

Pushkin's *Tales of Belkin* (1830) can help conceptualize the possibilities
of that situation and some intrinsic aspects of the works involved in it as
well. In this collection of five stories, Pushkin reviews the past of Russian
prose and sets guidelines for its future. He studies the language of prose
fiction by refracting it through a system of multiple narrators; in the
process language is turned back against itself and becomes the object of
its own investigation. Perhaps the story in which language is most aware
of language is "Young Lady/Peasant Girl" ["Baryshnia-krest'ianka"]. The
young hero, upon learning that the peasant girl he loves is, in fact, a
landowner's daughter, still uses her assumed name after he discovers the
deception. That he continues to call her Akulina is language's way of
suggesting that he discovers himself as well: we identify ourselves in the
names we give others. The real Andrei Berestov is not the pale dandy
with the death's head ring, but the simple-hearted young fellow who
meets Akulina in the grove at dawn. There he speaks "the language of
true passion," while Akulina (Liza) speaks a stylized peasant language.
He teaches Akulina to write (Lévi-Strauss's presentation of writing as
exploitation ["A Writing Lesson," *Tristes Tropiques*] provides an interesting perspective here). When Liza (Akulina) meets Andrei in her father's
house, disguised as herself, she speaks only French. When Andrei learns
that he is to marry the heavily powdered and rouged person he takes

for the real Liza, he writes to Akulina "in his neatest handwriting and wildest style." As for the styles of the story as a whole, Viktor Vinogradov numbers these at five.[8] These result from the way Pushkin brings the story to the reader: "Young Lady/Peasant Girl" was related to Ivan Petrovich Belkin by a Miss K. I. T. and prepared for publication by an anonymous editor.

I will continue to use the names under which I first met the works of the Bakhtin school to refer to the authors of those books and articles (cf., "Akulina"/Liza). In this sense, the slash separating the names on the title page of this translation may be taken as the conventional signifier/signified bar (Medvedev/Bakhtin). The Bakhtin school's approach to problems of poetics, linguistics, and psychology parallels Pushkin's approach to prose in its intent to evaluate the past and set guidelines for the future. And, like the *Tales of Belkin*, each of the three books involved has an inner dimension in which what it seeks to demonstrate external to itself finds a place in its argument. In *Freudianism*, Voloshinov remarks (figuratively) that the Oedipus relationship is the family unit "made strange" (p. 91)*; actually, his analysis of the complex can itself be seen as "making *it* strange" (p. 82). Medvedev, of course, deals with this central formalist device ("making it strange"—*ostranenie*), and its influence can be seen in his analysis of other formalist devices: "We are not at all exaggerating the formalist scheme of literary evolution; we are merely giving it logical precision" (p. 163), for instance. *The Formal Method* could even be seen as a formalist analysis of formalism, to the extent that it is the realization of Shklovskii's metaphor that the work of art (here: method) is equal to the sum of its devices. Indeed, one of the charges leveled at Medvedev is that his is a neo-Kantian critique of [neo-Kantian] formalism (see below).[9]

The subject of *Marxism and the Philosophy of Language* also finds an internal parallel: a major theme of the book (I should say "text") is reported speech, which is the basis of Kozhinov's published account of how the text was composed—its composition thus mirrors the phenomena it analyzes. (The problems of reported speech include the editorial changes mentioned by Ivanov, functions belonging to the editor of Belkin's stories in our model.) *Marxism and the Philosophy of Language* is analyzed as "text" by Samuel M. Weber (following Derrida's distinction between "book" and "text") on the basis of Voloshinov's description of "dialogue" in the wide sense. Voloshinov writes:

---

*Page numbers in parentheses after quotations from Voloshinov refer to translations cited in notes 5 and 10 of this introduction. Pages from the present translation of Medvedev are also cited in the body of the text. Page numbers after quotations from Bakhtin refer to the original Russian of articles collected in a volume identified in note 16.

A book, i.e., *a verbal performance in print,* is also an element of verbal communication. It is something discussable in actual, real-life dialogue, but aside from that, it is calculated for active perception, involving attentive reading and inner responsiveness, and for organized, *printed* reaction.... Moreover, a verbal performance of this kind also inevitably orients itself with respect to previous performances in the same sphere, both those by the same author and those by other authors.... Thus the printed verbal performance engages, as it were, in ideological colloquy of large scale.[10]

The works of the Bakhtin school can be seen as the realization of dialogic interaction—from which it follows that to assign the texts to Bakhtin alone is to "monologize" them. To put it another way: we do not want to say that one side of the sign is all there is.[11] So the title of this introduction (Bakhtin/Medvedev), viewed as signifier and signified, will be juxtaposed to the two names on the title page (Medvedev/Bakhtin) in (what at present seems to be) the proper formulation of the text's origin.

The origin of *Freudianism,* like that of *Marxism and the Philosophy of Language* in dialogue, is suggested in aspects internal to the text. Perhaps Voloshinov's misrepresentation of the patient-analyst relationship as taught by Freud—according to Voloshinov the doctor uses his authority to impose the "correct" point of view—was symptomatic of his felt position as Bakhtin's student, of his role in "conversations with Mikhail Mikhailovich." An observation belonging to I. R. Titunik seems relevant here. He notes that *Freudianism* involves a "peculiar 'duplexity' of addressee" —the text seems to be intended for the general reader and the more sophisticated scholar at the same time.[12] It might be that this reflects writing with both the circle and the larger public in mind, Voloshinov writing what he later terms a "popular essay" with the image of Bakhtin before him.

Detailed stylistic analysis of the writings associated with the Bakhtin circle, work similar to that carried out by Vinogradov on the *Tales of Belkin,* could provide insights into the authorship controversy. While there are obvious similarities between the works, there are noticeable stylistic and terminological differences too. Both similarities and differences can arise in a process of editing and reediting. I. R. Titunik discloses traces of the editorial process in *Freudianism:* "Internal evidence makes it fairly certain that the work was actually completed in 1926. The first several chapters contain occasional footnotes by an editor (nowhere identified), obviously added in 1927."[13] It might be noted that Bakhtin's statement that "Pavel Nikolaevich added to it [*The Formal Method*], and not always for the better" implies that Medvedev's editorial contribution was not insignificant. I am hypothesizing that an editing process was an integral part of the work of the Bakhtin school, and that it follows to view this process in interaction with a (verbal) reporting process (Kozhinov's published version). The contradiction between the Ivanov and Kozhinov versions, in this scheme, is only apparent, the result of taking a part for the whole, of taking an excerpt out of the early, middle, or late stages of work.

Certain constants in the approaches Bakhtin, Medvedev, and Voloshinov bring to the problems they deal with could be useful as a framework for the future stylistic analysis of the works of the circle. Voloshinov and Medvedev have the same general objections to Freudianism and formalism: both movements fail to define their theoretical positions with respect to other trends, both are charged with sectarianism, with exclusiveness of jargon, and the habit of quoting only each other. In *Freudianism* Voloshinov stresses the importance of definition: "Objective psychology is a young discipline; it is only beginning to take shape. The way it can best clarify its *point of view* and *methods* is by intelligently criticizing and combating other trends" (p. 23). This is the approach taken in *The Formal Method:* a sociological poetics is worked out against formalism. The idea of struggle is also important in Medvedev's study of the emergence of West European and Russian formalist theories. Not a few of Russian formalism's shortcomings, he finds, arise from the inadequacies of its opposition. Freudianism and formalism are found to evade real ideological struggle in the same way: both simply reverse the "official" doctrine of the dominating movement which preceded them. Everything which was previously considered the most important in literature, its content, the formalists relegate to "material," and treat this material as mere motivation for the device. "Behind 'material' and 'device' there is no difficulty in seeing the old dyad of form and content, moreover, in its most primitive form. The formalists merely turn it inside out" (p. 110). "The basic concepts of formalism—'transrational language,' 'deautomatization,' 'deformation,' 'deliberately-difficult form'—are merely negations corresponding to various indices of practical, communicative language" (p. 87). Similarly, Voloshinov finds it easy to see "the defects of subjective psychology's definition of the consciousness in the Freudian concept of the unconscious, to which they were transferred without the slightest critical qualification" (p. 68). In *Problems of Dostoevskii's Poetics,* Bakhtin identifies negation as one of the only two possibilities available within a monologic world view: "*tertium non datur:* a thought is either confirmed or negated."[14] In all the works of the Bakhtin school, monologue is contrasted to dialogue, the social interaction outside of which meaning does not exist. In *The Formal Method:* "Ideological creation [ideology in the Marxist sense] is not within us, but between us" (p. 8); the study (science) of ideologies proposed on the first page of that book is the study of the "ideological colloquy of large scale" described in *Marxism and the Philosophy of Language.* The latter specifies: "Ideology may not be divorced from the material reality of sign (i.e., by locating it in the 'consciousness' or other vague and elusive regions)" (p. 21). In *Problems of Dostoevskii's Poetics:*

> An idea does not *live* in one's *isolated* individual consciousness—if it remains there it degenerates and dies. An idea begins to live, i.e., to take shape, to develop, to find and renew its verbal expression, and to give birth to new ideas only when it enters into genuine dialogical relationships with other ideas, the ideas of the *other*.[15]

Individualistic subjectivism and abstract objectivism in linguistic philosophy (*Marxism and the Philosophy of Language*), formalism, and Freudianism are similar in that they are found guilty of removing the object of their study from social intercourse, from the interrelationships of dialogue. To this list of offenders Bakhtin adds the adherents of the "official poetics" of the novel ("The Word in the Novel," 1934-35).[16] The distinction between "official" and "unofficial" is important in the works of the circle. In "The Word in the Novel" Bakhtin contrasts the centralizing forces of poetry to the decentralizing movement of the novel and related genres in terms of an "official above" and an "unofficial below," where "all 'languages' were masks and there was no certified and indisputable language identity" (p. 86). The reference to an "unofficial," masked lower culture anticipates Bakhtin's study of the semiotics of medieval and Renaissance carnival in his brilliant doctoral dissertation on Rabelais (rejected in 1946)[17] Perhaps Bakhtin was stimulated to the insights of his analyses of nonverbal sign systems by what Paul de Man would term the "blindness" of *Freudianism*—the failure to recognize that the Freudian unconscious (termed the "unofficial" consciousness by Voloshinov) is structured like language.[18]

Interest in how the writings of the Bakhtin circle were produced has overshadowed the question of why we have this confusing situation to deal with. Vadim Kozhinov says it is "a long story" (correspondence). V. N. Turbin feels that Bakhtin gave *The Formal Method* to Medvedev as a gift, in the communal spirit. This interpretation keeps alive the ethos of the early days of "Marxist romanticism." At the same time, this gift-giving can be viewed in a practical light: only as a movement (a body of texts unified by approach) could Bakhtin's ideas enter the ideological struggle on an equal footing with other trends. The late twenties was the time of the collective, not of the individual, hero.[19] The Bakhtin collective existed in the exchange of articles, books, and names (Lévi-Strauss points out that society *is* the structure of exchange—women, gifts, signs). The larger dimension of the Bakhtin/Medvedev exchange finds a parallel in the (carnivalized) plot of "Young Lady/Peasant Girl." There two feuding landowners decide to cement their reconciliation by the marriage of Liza/Akulina and Andrei. In substance, *The Formal Method* aims at a rapprochement between Marxism and formalism.

A look at the later twenties in the Soviet Union reveals many features of the phenomenon Bakhtin speaks of as "carnival" (in his books on Rabelais and Dostoevskii and elsewhere). Life was "drawn out of its usual rut," "turned inside out." The NEP (New Economic Policy) period was perceived by all as an interlude, a temporary situation, a transition in which "eccentric" relationships were the rule. The capitalist, the bourgeois carnival king, was once again on top—but this was clearly a "mock crowning," in which the idea of "discrowning" was present from the start (the archetypal two-sided carnival image). Perhaps it was Nikolai Zabolotskii (a translator of Rabelais) who best captured the atmosphere of Leningrad at this time in his book of ambivalent and "physiological" poems entitled *Scrolls [Stolbtsy]* (1929). In an unpublished paper, A. Dorogov has observed that, just as the activity of the formalists was connected to the poetic practice of the Russian futurists, Bakhtin's ideas may be linked to the line of poetry which included Zabolotskii's avant-garde group "Oberiu," who studied the word in its social context.[20] Vadim Kozhinov has observed that Bakhtin was associated with other people of the "carnival" type.[21] Perhaps the exchange of identities within the Bakhtin circle owed something to this carnival atmosphere, or at least was stimulated by Bakhtin's attraction to ambivalence, disguises, the "unofficial," and nonwritten popular tradition. At any rate, the result is itself a structure of mystification and reversals that captures the imagination. We return to it, not for that alone, but because Bakhtin is convincing when he writes that "Every genuinely important step forward is accompanied by a return to the beginning...more precisely, to a renewal of the beginning. Only memory can go forward...."[22] We want to remember Bakhtin because, to know where contemporary literary scholarship is going, it is useful to know where Bakhtin was.

* * * *

The Formal Method received a favorable review in the journal *Literature and Marxism* in 1929. M. K. Dobrynin wrote:

> The book accomplishes its task—a critical introduction to sociological poetics—despite a number of shortcomings.
> The formulation of the basic task of literary scholarship as that of specification is absolutely correct. The basic relationship to formalism as to a good enemy, the criticism of it on its own grounds, the attention to the problems it raises, the striving to critically approach their solution and thereby the solution of the essential task of our scholarship—the establishment of a sociological poetics—all these things make the book interesting, valuable, and very necessary today.[23]

In a few short years, however, the accent shifts to the "shortcomings" Dobrynin mentions. The 1934 *Literary Encyclopedia* characterizes

Medvedev as "an eclectic with aspirations to 'sociologism' and material-
ism," and the book as "an interesting systematic criticism of formalism.
However, because of the author's unstable position, close to neo-
Kantianism, this criticism does not always hit the mark." In 1933
Medvedev published a book, entitled *In the Writer's Laboratory*, on the
general subject of the psychology of artistic creativity. This pedestrian
volume, basically a string of quotations about writing culled from classic
European authors, as well as trusty socialist realists like Ol'ga Forsh, is
lacking in all the characteristics of works of the Bakhtin circle.[24] Freud is
not mentioned; Lenin and Engels are quoted, and Medvedev makes sure
to talk about the class struggle. In 1934 he published a revised edition of
The Formal Method entitled *Formalism and Formalists*. The content was cut
somewhat and fleshed out with antiformalist rhetoric and a less favorable
attitude to West European formalism.[25] But this was not enough. Or, in
any case, Medvedev was "illegally repressed" (*Short Literary Encyclopedia*,
1967) and died in 1938.[26] Here Bakhtin's gift of *The Formal Method* acquires
a fateful aspect; and what happened to Voloshinov after 1934 is unknown.

In 1929 Bakhtin's ground-breaking study of Dostoevskii's "poly-
phonic novel" appeared. The book was controversial, drawing an article
from Lunacharskii, the commissar of education, himself.[27] Soon after,
Bakhtin left Leningrad. He spent about six years in Kustanai, on the
border of Kazakhstan and Siberia, in uncertain circumstances.[28] In 1936
he was teaching at the Pedagogical Institute in Saransk, Mordovian
A.S.S.R., about five hundred fifty kilometers southeast of Moscow. The
next year he was allowed to return to Moscow, perhaps for health
reasons—from 1923 he had been suffering from chronic osteomyelitis.
The reader of his book on Rabelais will be struck by the fact that this
celebration of the body was written by a sick man. Bakhtin's disease led to
the amputation of one leg in 1938. We may imagine the amputee's
sensation of his missing limb—present/absent, his/no longer his—as
similar to his feeling for *The Formal Method*, and that this sensation was
intensified by Medvedev's death in the same year that the leg was lost.

Bakhtin taught at various secondary schools outside of Moscow
through the war years and returned to Saransk in 1945. In 1957 the
Pedagogical Institute became a university, and Bakhtin became head of
the Department of Russian and Foreign Literature, a position he held
until his retirement in 1961. The end of his teaching career almost
coincides with his return to print in more than local publications. In 1963
a revised and expanded version of his study of Dostoevskii's poetics was
published by a major press in Moscow.[29] This event might be viewed as
an official endorsement of semiotic research in that Iurii M. Lotman's
Lectures on Structural Poetics was printed the next year as the first issue in
the series *Studies in Semiotic Systems* of Tartu (Estonian S.S.R.) University.[30] The reappearance of Bakhtin's book could also be seen as an

acknowledgment that his approach is not inconsistent with Marxism. In this regard, *Problems of Dostoevskii's Poetics* could even have been intended as a measure of forthcoming structuralist studies. This hypothesis receives some support from the appearance of the Moscow annual *Context* in 1972, which some see as balanced against the work being done at Tartu. The 1974 volume contains an article by Bakhtin (dated 1940, 1974) in which he criticizes contemporary structuralism in basically the same terms he uses to characterize scholars who "monologize" Dostoevskii.[31] The current "*Context*" position on Tartu probably follows that of the leading literary scholar D. S. Likhachev as expressed in an interview in *Literaturnaia gazeta* (11 August 1976, no. 32). Likhachev, who has fruitfully applied Bakhtin's approach to European carnival to the Russian tradition, finds that the Tartu structuralists have gone from the one extreme of exclusive synchrony to the other of "opening" the text to such an extent that literary scholarship may be turned into the study of culture.

In 1965 the journal *Voprosy literatury* (*Problems in Literature*) published some material from Bakhtin's research of the mid-thirties. This journal intermittently continued to bring out fragments from his unpublished work on the nature and history of the novel. Finally, in 1975, the year of Bakhtin's death, these works were published in more complete form in one volume, *Problems in Literature and Esthetics. Studies from Various Years.* The earliest of these studies, "The Problem of Content, Material, and Form in Literary Art," was written in 1924 for the journal *Russkii sovremennik,* but the journal went out of existence before it could appear.

This essay, about eighteen thousand Russian words long, may be considered a preface to *The Formal Method.* Or, *The Formal Method* could be considered a preface to the essay, not only because the earlier work appeared later but because the essay is at times more detailed, as, for instance, in its treatment of "The Problem of Distancing and Isolation." And it might have been the elements of *Isolationsontologie* present in this section of the essay that first drew attention to Bakhtin, that marked him as someone to watch in the sharpening ideological struggle—despite the explicit antiformalist direction of the work. It begins in a typical way: Bakhtin identifies the two poles of abstract (symbolist) philosophizing and scientific *Kunstwissenschaft.* Concentrating on formalism as representative of the latter in literary scholarship, Bakhtin calls it to task for ignoring problems of general esthetics, for lacking a philosophical basis: "Without a systematic concept of the esthetic, both as distinct from the cognitive and ethical, and together with them in the unity of culture, one cannot even separate the object of poetics—the artistic work in the word [*khudozhestvennoe proizvedenie v slove*]—from the mass of other writing."[32] In *The Formal Method* the "unity of culture" (later in the essay "the unity of nature") will be the unity of the "ideological environment," and the fundamental ground for the study of ideologies will be Marxism. The phrasing "artistic work in the word" is indicative of Bakhtin's equation of the two as crossroads of evaluations. The author goes on to identify the five basic errors of "materialist esthetics" (i.e., formalism). Materialist esthetics is not capable of establishing a ground for artistic form—it can only treat the work hedonistically, as a stimulator, or as a thing of utilitarian value. Second (and third), materialist esthetics cannot distinguish between the esthetic and the technical (external) aspects of the work, cannot separate the purely linguistic from the poetic. Fourth, materialist esthetics cannot deal with the esthetic vision outside of art. Included in this "outside of art" is myth and social and political activity —the regions of the (later) "unofficial." Fifth, materialist esthetics cannot be the basis for *Kunstgeschichte* because it isolates its object from the unity of cultural generation. Materialist esthetics "at best is only capable of substantiating a chronological listing of the changes in technical devices of a given art form, for an isolated technique cannot have a history" (p. 23). This introductory section is followed by sections respectively dealing with literary content, material, and form, sections which need to be studied in relation to *The Formal Method*. Perhaps the most important principle of these parts is the pervasiveness of evaluation. Most basically: when literature is opposed to life or reality, that reality is not neutral, but evaluated life (p. 27). This principle is elaborated in the closing sections of Part III, Chapter Two of the Bakhtin/Medvedev book.

Pavel Nikolaevich Medvedev was born in 1891, four years before Bakhtin and a few years before the advent of Russian symbolism. By the time he had finished his law degree at the University of Petrograd (Leningrad), symbolism had given way to other schools. Velimir Khlebnikov published his transrational poem "Incantation to Laughter" in 1910, and the Russian futurists issued their manifesto "A Slap in the Face of Public Taste" in 1912. In the same year the acmeists proclaimed that they were breaking with the symbolists for the sake of "beautiful clarity." By this time, or soon after, Medvedev may have been in Vitebsk. He was there for certain at the start of the Revolution. He conducted military and civilian propaganda courses and taught at the pedagogical institute there. In 1921 he published a short tribute on the death of Aleksander Blok. Subsequently, Medvedev was to be one of the first Soviet scholars to study Blok's archives, concentrating on his dramatic works. Upon moving to Leningrad in 1922, Medvedev became the editor of a theater journal which included the formalists Boris Tomashevskii and Viktor Zhirmunskii among its contributors. He also worked in the artistic literature section of the State Publishing House (Gosizdat') at this time, the beginning of the NEP period.[33]

In 1921 the Soviet Union was near exhaustion following world war, revolution, and civil war. Lenin adopted the New Economic Policy as a tactical retreat, to give the country a chance to recover. The revolutionary pressures of "War Communism" were eased in most areas of Russian life. In the economic sector, for instance, this meant a return to some private ownership and to the use of capitalist management. Developments on the "economic front" found their parallel in literary life, in a return to free competition among literary groups, private publishing houses, and the toleration of nonproletarian "literary specialists." Proletarians were angered by this toleration; the name of one of their journals, *On Guard* [*Na postu*], symbolized their adherence to War Communism. One of the essays in Trotskii's *Literature and Revolution* (1923) provided a name for their enemies: "fellow travelers," those who, while not overtly against the Revolution, were not committed to it either. The literature of the years 1921-24 was dominated by fellow travelers who were bitterly opposed by those demanding engagement. In 1924 the struggle reached a decisive point, and the decision went in favor of the fellow travelers. In 1925 the Central Committee of the Party declared that, while there can be no neutral literature in a class society, tolerance would be shown to transitional ideological forms. This pronouncement further stimulated the revival of literature and literary scholarship.

Literary scholarship was dominated by formalism. The main opposition came from those favoring a sociological approach to literature, not all of whom were orthodox Marxists. Therefore, the orthodox, among whom Medvedev counted himself, had to divide their attention between problems within the sociological approach and the external challenge of formalism. Medvedev addressed himself to a problem within sociological criticism in a 1926 review of P. N. Sakulin's book *The Sociological Method in Literary Scholarship* (1925). Marxism, wrote Medvedev, is a monistic system. But for Sakulin the study of the literary work follows two methods, a formal method for the immanent study of literature, and a sociological method for "causal," historical study. Sakulin's method is dualistic, even pluralistic, not Marxist, and, therefore, as the title of the review underscores, is "Sociologism without Sociology."[34]

Medvedev uses another eye-catching title in a 1925 article that is his first confrontation with formalism: "Scholarly Sal'erism." As might be expected, the famous lines from Pushkin's *Mozart and Sal'eri*, in which the latter claims to have dissected music like a cadaver and "verified harmony with algebra," serve as an epigraph. But, except for a closing phrase ("Sal'erism fully developed and absolutized leads to the murder of Mozart"), the metaphor is not developed. In fact, Medvedev agrees that the "morphological" (his preferred term) study of the literary work as material object is "not only possible, but even necessary." The problem, he goes on to state, is that formalism presumes to more than that. It has developed into an esthetic dogma, a world view. Formalism, objects Medvedev, is only acceptable as a descriptive method. It is not fit to be the basis for a truly scholarly historical or theoretical poetics and cannot be considered a poetics in itself. This argument reappears in *The Formal Method.*

Another position that reappears in the book is developed in a postscript to Medvedev's article in which he responds to Boris Eikhenbaum's statement (*Press and Revolution*, 1924, no.5) that formalism is not a single method. Medvedev writes:

> But, if there is no formal method, there is formalism as a principle, there is a formalist world view [*mirovozrenie*]. It's like robbing Peter to give to Paul. Even Eikhenbaum writes: "The problem does not concern the methods of literary study, but the principles of the formulation of literary scholarship—its content, basic object of study, and the devices that make it a special science.... The recognition that the basic problem of literary scholarship is the specific form of literary works and that all the elements of its construction have formal functions as constructive elements is, of course, a principle, not a method."
>
> Thus, "formalism" is once again declared to be a principle of literary scholarship (poetics)....
>
> One more note: not without bravado does B. M. Eikhenbaum declare: "We have as many methods as you like." Look at us, he seems to say, aren't we grand!
>
> This bravado is out of place. Method should arise from the object being studied. Only this can prevent its being fastened on from outside or haphazardly being made to fit its object. If "literary scholarship" has a "basic object of study," then it can hardly be that "as many methods as you like" are what is required to study it. A position of methodological monism is dictated by the very essence of the task. And this position should be more than obligatory for those who are thinking about "the formulation of the theory and history of literature as an independent science."[35]

Eikhenbaum restates his position on this point in his important article "The Theory of the Formal Method" (1926, 1927), and Medvedev confronts him on it once again in *The Formal Method.* I. R. Titunik describes that confrontation in these terms:

> Medvedev did not hesitate to construe formalist working hypotheses as invariable principles and formalist focuses of attention as value judgments. Thus the history of the formal method was viewed, not in evolutionary terms, as Eikhenbaum had insisted it should be, but as the systematic filling in of a preconceived program. Anything in formalist writings not consistent with this "program" was taken as evidence of "betrayal" of their own doctrine on the part of this or that formalist. The picture of the formal method obtained by this procedure does not reflect the way the formalists actually

operated. They did, of course, have a general theory; only it was a general theory in (to crib a phrase) a continuous process of generation.[36]

It is true that Medvedev finds certain principles, such as the one he calls "the law of perceptibility-automatization," to be invariable—but one of the other constants of the formal method as he sees it is its fortuitousness, its accidental nature. He presents the formalist as a *bricoleur* who rummages through the grab-bag of world literature for parts that can be adapted to the needs of his method. He does not consider the development of formalism as "the systematic filling in of a preconceived program" as much as an unsystematic elaboration of a haphazardly conceived program—albeit one that follows an inner necessity. For instance: "The last problem the formalists encountered was that of genre. This problem was inevitably last because their first problem was poetic language" (p. 129). Here inevitability is the result of an unsystematic initial approach to the problem. Compare Bakhtin's analysis of the Greek adventure novel: "This logic [of events] is that of accidental coincidence (i.e., accidental simultaneity) and accidental asynchronism (i.e., accidental difference in time). And the 'earlier' or 'later' of this accidental simultaneity and asynchrony have an essential and decisive meaning. If something were to happen a minute earlier or later, that is, if there were no accidental simultaneity or discontinuity, there would be no plot, nothing to write a novel about."[37] Similarly, formalism would not be itself, Medvedev argues, without its fatal, but accidental, nature.

Medvedev's preference is for an *engineer* (the other term of Lévi-Strauss's pair), one who *would* consciously follow a strict procedure toward set objectives. The relationship between these two terms has been convincingly formulated by Jacques Derrida: "The engineer is a myth produced by the *bricoleur.*"[38] It is a necessary myth, as is, in Bakhtin's work, the "official." For instance, difference from an "official poetics of the novel" is all that really defines Bakhtin's poetics of the novel. In "The Epic and the Novel" (1941) he writes:

> The "novelization" of literature does not mean that other genres are stuck with a strange and unusual genre canon. The novel is noncanonical by nature. It is moldability [plastichnost'; L. *plasticus*] itself. It is eternally searching, eternally researching itself and revising all its former forms. It can only be thus for a genre which is constructed in the zone of immediate contact with generating reality.[39]

This movement of forms reviewing themselves and replacing themselves in chains of "eternal" substitutions calls to mind the notion of "free play," the structure of language which depends on the difference situated in the sign. The major themes of Bakhtin's work originate in such differences as those between the "centrifugal force" of the novel and the "centripetal" direction of poetry, between "popular" culture and "official" culture, between "pure linguistics," which disregards meaning, and sociological linguistics. The zone of contact between such relationships is generally presented as one of ambivalence, most spectacularly, ambivalent laughter (Rabelais, Gogol). Those who find "ahistoricism" in Bakhtin's thought are reacting to the mythical aspect of "free play," and "ambivalence."[40] This reaction calls the whole enterprise into question. Specifically: if Medvedev were to abandon the myth of the *engineer*, the basis for a dialogue with formalism would be prohibitively narrowed.

Voloshinov's article "The Word in Life and the Word in Poetry" (1926) can be used to identify the major components of Medvedev's discourse in *The Formal Method*.[41] His writing is shaped as much by what he is against as by what he affirms. Viktor Shklovskii's importance as propagandist and theoretician of formalism can almost be estimated from the orientation of Medvedev's book, which is directed toward the reader, the third component of Voloshinov's scheme. The speaker seeks to accommodate himself to the reader, to approximate his level.[42] Shklovskii's texts, on the other hand, implicitly call for the reader to model himself after the speaker, to read Shklovskii in Shklovskii's terms. One indication of this is his way of citing formalist works and theories by author only, presuming that the reader is as well acquainted with the body of formalist texts as he himself is. More specifically, orientation toward the speaker is typically Shklovskian in passages such as the following:

> The rhythm of prose is, on the one hand, the rhythm of the work song, the "dubinushka," and replaces the order to "heave-ho"; but, on the other hand, it makes work easier, automatizes it . . . . But the rhythm of poetry is different. There is "order" in art, but no column of a Greek temple precisely fulfills the requirements of a particular order; artistic rhythm is prosaic rhythm disrupted. (Cited by Medvedev, p. 90).

Here the word "order" is used in the sense of "organization" in general, and, with the meaning of "heave-ho," related to the ictus of the Russian syllabo-tonic line, which is compared to a sequence of temple columns, none of which fulfill the requirements of a particular "order" (Doric, Ionic, etc.). Another example of Shklovskii's sender-oriented style is his hyperbole, his appreciation of his own extremes, as: "The juxtaposition of world to world or cat to stone—all are equal." Medvedev himself remarks on the literariness of this writing: "This statement, of course, is not a scholarly principle, but a paradox of the feuilleton variety, that is, a little work of art" (p. 123). The argument of Medvedev's book, on the other hand, makes no pretensions to art in moving deliberately through a stiff framework of categories. The metaphoric flashes which occasionally light up passages in theoretical works like "The Word in the Novel" are absent here. The style of *The Formal Method* has been referred to as, among other things, sharp and stabbing. It is also *inter alia* clumsy and repetitous. Medvedev often uses the club in his argument, but can be sarcastic, and at other times simply "pulls out," as Victor Erlich puts it.[43]

One can often observe (in general reading) that transitional points, the movements from one topic to another, are more stylistically marked, more idiosyncratic than more contentful passages of a given work. The sectioned chapter structure of *The Formal Method* is suited to the combination of styles and the concealment of such idiosyncrasies. One recalls the practice of the Renaissance studio: the master would work out the over-all plan of the canvass and assign certain sections or figures to his apprentices. There are numerous instances in which the work of the master cannot be distinguished from that of his students. Bakhtin himself comments on a somewhat analogous circumstance in medieval literature: "In the Middle Ages...the boundaries between the other's word and one's own discourse were flexible, ambiguous, often intentionally devious and tangled. Certain types of works were constructed like mosaics, from the texts of others."[44] *The Formal Method* is apparently such a text. And even if we someday obtain facts which can help unriddle the operations of the Bakhtin circle and the nominal ambiguities of the authorship question, these will not touch the actual origin of this (or any) text in dialogue, will not mean the monologization of Bakhtin.[45]

A Note on the Translation

I undertook this translation at the suggestion of Renate Horlemann of The Johns Hopkins University Humanities Center, herself responsible for Voloshinov, *Marxismus und Sprachphilosophie*, ed. and intro. Samuel M. Weber (Frankfurt/M and Berlin, 1975). The reader of English probably learned of the existence of Medvedev's book from Victor Erlich's essential *Russian Formalism. History—Doctrine*, 2nd, revised edition (The Hague, 1965). There *The Formal Method* is described as "the most extended and scholarly critique of OPOIAZ ever undertaken by a Marxist" (p. 114). This would have been interesting to many Soviet readers too, for *The Formal Method*, like the names of those connected with it, had not been mentioned in cyrillic print for many years. Vadim Kozhinov cites *The Formal Method* in a note to his 1965 article "Vozmozhna li strukturnaia poetika?" ["Is Structuralist Poetics Possible?"] *Voprosy literatury* 6 (1965): 88-107, but still finds it necessary, seven years later, to remind readers that a detailed and comprehensive analysis of formalism had "long since been carried out." Kozhinov identifies Medvedev as Bakhtin's "very close confederate in thought [*blizhaishii edinomyshlennik*]" and goes on to say: "This book, which can presently be found in only the largest libraries, is now somewhat out of date in form and terminology. But its essentials retain the most vital significance and its republication would, without question, be extremely useful" ("Istoriia literatury v rabotakh OPOIAZa," *Voprosy literatury* [1972], no.7, 100). To make the translation more useful I have correlated Medvedev's references to formalist texts with translations when possible, relying primarily on Tzvetan Todorov, ed. and trans., *Théorie de la littérature* (Paris, 1965) and *Texte der russischen Formalisten,* Jurij Striedter and Wolf-Dieter Stempel eds. and trans., 2 vols. (Munich, 1972). Two other useful translation collections are by Ladislav Matejka and Krystyna Pomorska, *Readings in Russian Poetics* (Cambridge, Mass., 1971) and Lee T. Lemon and Marion J. Reis, *Russian Formalist Criticism* (Lincoln, Neb., 1965). I have added references to the Todorov, Striedter, and Stempel volumes to Medvedev's footnotes, and have sometimes used later editions or different collections of articles and books cited in the original. These will be obvious from the dating, and such changes are not specially indicated. When square brackets appear, they enclose a translator's addition. The paragraphing is that of the original Russian text. Explanatory notes have for the most part been limited to the identification of Russians mentioned in the text. The transliteration system is basically that of the Library of Congress without *any* diacritical marks, as illustrated by the following citation of the original: Pavel Nikolaevich Medvedev, *Formal'nyi metod v literaturovedenii (Kritscheskoe vvedenie v sotsiologicheskuiu poetiku)* (Leningrad: "Priboi," 1928).

Some European, American, and Soviet scholars do not find the texts sufficient to take the place of a documented explanation of why the names on the original title pages of books by Voloshinov and Medvedev should be changed to Bakhtin. Vadim Kozhinov, Bakhtin's executor, says that he has known about Bakhtin's authorship for fifteen years and has informed me that not long before his death Bakhtin signed a document which says that if the listed works are republished, they should be in his name, with a note that Voloshinov or Medvedev only made some changes or additions. This paper, which is now held by VAAP (The All-Union Copyright Agency) is apparently the basis for Ivanov's 1971 statement. In my introduction I have discussed Ivanov's statement (and, consequently, the VAAP document) in an attempt to show some of the complexity of the matter in relation to the names that appear on the title page of this translation and to the way in which they appear. To attempt to do more would be to try to simplify and close a case that has not yet been opened. Finally, and apart from that, I believe that until Kozhinov and any others who may have the facts make them known, the names under which the books and articles appeared originally should be given preference for that historical reason alone, regardless of the personal opinion of the translator or scholar who deals with them.

Special acknowledgment is due Vadim Liapunov, Indiana University, for his many valuable suggestions. I also want to express my appreciation to Michael Holquist, The University of Texas at Austin, who read the manuscript, and I thank V. N. Turbin, Moscow University, who was helpful in a number of ways. I have appreciated the interest of William P. Sisler, humanities editor at The Johns Hopkins University Press, the support of Richard Macksey, of The Johns Hopkins Humanities Center, and Dean James Billet, Goucher College. The publication itself was generously supported by a grant from Goucher College.

PART ONE

The Object and Tasks of Marxist Literary Scholarship

CHAPTER ONE
The Study of Ideologies
and Its Immediate Tasks

Specification as the
Basic Problem of the Study of Ideologies

Literary scholarship is one branch of the study of ideologies. On the basis of the single principle it uses to understand its object, and the single method it uses to study it, the study of ideologies embraces all areas of man's ideological creativity.

The bases of the study of ideologies (in the form of a general definition of ideological superstructures, their function in the whole of social life, their relationship to the economic base, and some of their interrelationships as well) have been profoundly and firmly established by Marxism. However, the detailed study of the distinctive features and qualitative individuality of each of the branches of ideological creation — science, art, ethics, religion, etc. — is still in the embryonic stage.

Between the general theory of superstructures and their relationship to the base and the concrete study of each specific ideological phenomenon there seems to be a certain gap, a shifting and hazy area through which the scholar picks his way at his own risk, or often simply skips over, shutting his eyes to all difficulties and ambiguities. The result is that either the specificity of the phenomenon suffers, for instance, the specificity of the work of art, or an "immanent" analysis which takes account of specificity but has nothing to do with sociology is artificially fitted to the economic base. And it is precisely a developed sociological doctrine of the distinctive features of the material, forms, and purposes of each area of ideological creation which is lacking.

Of course, each area has its own language, its own forms and devices for that language, and its own specific laws for the ideological refraction of a common reality. It is absolutely not the way of Marxism to level these differences or to ignore the essential plurality of the languages of ideology.

The specificity of art, science, ethics, or religion naturally should not obscure their ideological unity as superstructures of a common base,

3

or the fact that they follow the same sociological laws of development. But this specificity should not be effaced by the general formulas of these laws.

On the basis of Marxism itself a specific sociological method should be developed which could be adapted to the characteristics of the different ideological areas in order to provide access to all the details and subtleties of ideological structures.

But if this is to be accomplished, the characteristics and qualitative peculiarities of ideological systems must first be understood and defined.

Marxism can hardly borrow these definitions from the idealist "philosophy of culture" [*Kulturphilosophie*] or from the various branches [*-wissenschaften*] of positivist research, for this would be to adjust the base to fit the definitions when, in fact, the definitions must be deduced from the base.

The definitions formulated by West European scholarship do not pretend to be sociological. They are either understood naturalistically, mainly on the basis of biology, or they are atomized into insipid and positivistic empirical data which are lost in a wilderness of senseless detail. Or, finally, these definitions are estranged from all empiricism and locked into a self-contained idealist kingdom of "pure ideas," "pure values," and "transcendental forms," and therefore rendered completely helpless before the concrete ideological phenomenon, which is always material and historical.

West European scholarship does, of course, include extensive factual material which Marxism can and should use (critically, to be sure), but Marxism cannot accept the principles, methods, and sometimes even the concrete methodology by which that material was obtained. (Exceptions to the latter include manuscript methodology, paleography, methods in the philological preparation and analysis of texts, etc.)

The Crises of the Idealist "Philosophy of Culture" [*Kulturphilosophie*] and Humanistic Positivism

Even in West European scholarship and philosophy there is presently deep dissatisfaction with both idealist disengagement from reality and the absurdities of positivism and naturalism, which are incapable of any sort of synthesis. There is a growing desire to unite wide philosophical synthesis (the previous idealist "philosophy of culture") with concrete study of the living variability, variety, specificity, and material embodiment of ideological phenomena (which, in opposition to idealism, positivism had suggested for various areas of the humanities).

In accord with this desire, European formalism began to take shape in the last years of the previous century (Fiedler, Hildebrand, Meier-Graefe). It was equally hostile to the positivism of the previous epoch and to the idealist philosophical esthetics, with its gross generalizations and disinterested view of the concrete phenomena of art.

The battle was simultaneously waged on the two fronts of positivism and idealist esthetics by the most authoritative representatives of art scholarship at the turn of the century, Alois Riegl and August Schmarzow.[1] At present the tendency toward wide synthesis on the concrete basis of art history is most vividly represented by the works of Wölfflin and Worringer.

The Vossler school is an analogous philological movement (*Idealistische Neufilologie*) which attempts to adapt idealist philosophy to concrete problems of linguistics and the history of language.

In literary history there is the same tendency toward mastering the concrete and specific reality and historicity of the literary phenomenon without forfeiting general principles and ties wth a unified world view. It is sufficient to name Gundolf, Ermatinger, Hefele, and Walzel. Part of the philosophical basis for these tendencies is provided by phenomenology (Husserl, Scheler, Moritz Geiger), but the intuitive philosophy of life is more important (Bergson, Simmel).

Simultaneous with the crisis of neo-Kantian cultural philosophy, enthusiasm for philosophy has deeply infiltrated the humanities, which until recently were the refuge of positivism.

Typical manifestations of this "philosophy from below"[2] were such books as Dessoir's *Ästhetik und allgemeine Kunstwissenschaft*, Utiz's *Grundlegung der allgemeinen Kunstwissenschaft*, and Hamann's *Ästhetik*.

These books are quite different from the usual esthetics. They are infused with the desire to proceed from the concrete and specific problems and requirements of art scholarship itself, rather than from the general requirements of a philosophical system. But at the same time they are not positivistic works of the usual type.

All of the above distinguishes the present trends in Western philosophy and scholarship from the striving for a philosophy "systematic at all costs" which was characteristic of the preceding period and was particularly evident in neo-Kantianism.

In the previous period the ruling tendency was to systematize principles and self-sufficient methods. Now the desire is to penetrate, by means of a single concept, into the world of concrete things and living historical events in their uniqueness and individuality. Previously the desire was to make ends meet in abstract thought about the world; now it is to comprehend the concrete facts of life and history in all their variability and diversity.

The "will to system" has obviously been replaced by the desire to master the concrete world of things and events without losing their living and meaningful unity.

The Problem of
Synthesizing Philosophical
World View and the Concreteness
and Objectivity of Historical Study

Contemporary European thought is suffering keenly from the simultaneous crises of idealism and positivism. Is there a basis for a positive solution?

We believe that only dialectical materialism can be this basis. The task of uniting a wide synthesis and general philosophical orientation with a mastery of the material diversity and historical generation of ideological phenomena is insolvable and even contradictory on any other basis. Between the insipid empiricism of positivism and the abstract disinterestedness of idealism *tertium non datur* for the bourgeois world view. A semi-mystical "philosophy of life," which only exists because it is enigmatic and incomplete, can only provide a seeming solution to the crisis.

The desired synthesis of philosophical world view and the concrete historical study of specific phenomena of art, science, ethics, religion, etc., is only possible on the basis of the solid principles of dialectical materialism.

But it is necessary to go beyond the declaration and endless repetition of these principles and apply them to concrete problems of art scholarship, scientific research, and so on. It is necessary to fill the gap between the general doctrine of ideological superstructures and the concrete elaboration of particular problems. It is necessary to overcome once and for all the naive apprehension that the qualitative uniqueness of, say, art, could suddenly turn out to be something other than sociological. It is precisely within the sociological system that there can be no deep qualitative differences!

There is no doubt that specification is often used to hide from sociology. For this reason it is all the more necessary for Marxism to apply itself to specification, ignoring neither the special problems that result, nor the special methodological orientations which correspond to them and which are ramifications of a unified sociological method.

The Concreteness and
Materiality of the Ideological World

All the products of ideological creation—works of art, scientific works, religious symbols and rites, etc.—are material things, part of the practical reality that surrounds man. It is true that these are things of a special nature, having significance, meaning, inner value. But these meanings and values are embodied in material things and actions. They cannot be realized outside of some developed material.

Nor do philosophical views, beliefs, or even shifting ideological moods exist within man, in his head or in his "soul." They become ideological reality only by being realized in words, actions, clothing, manners, and organizations of people and things—in a word: in some definite semiotic material. Through this material they become a practical part of the reality surrounding man.

The connection of all ideological meaning, no matter how "ideal" or "pure," with concrete material and its organization is much more organic, essential, and deep than it previously seemed. Philosophy and the humanities were too fond of purely conceptual analyses of ideological phenomena and the interpretation of their abstract meanings to properly evaluate problems connected with their direct reality in things and their genuine realization in the processes of social intercourse.

Scholarship to the present has been interested only in the individual physiological and, in particular, psychological processes of the creation and comprehension of ideological values, overlooking the fact that the individual, isolated person does not create ideologies, that ideological creation and its comprehension only take place in the process of social intercourse. Each individual act in the creation of ideology is an inseparable part of social intercourse, one of its dependent components, and therefore cannot be studied apart from the whole social process that gives it its meaning.

Bourgeois scholarship sets ideological meaning which has been abstracted from concrete material against the individual consciousness of the creator or perceiver. The complex social connections of the material environment are replaced by an invented connection between the individual consciousness and the opposing meaning.

"Meaning" and "consciousness" are the two basic terms of all bourgeois theories and philosophies of culture. Idealist philosophy, in addition, posits a "transcendental consciousness" or "general consciousness" (*Bewusstsein überhaupt*) between the individual consciousness and meaning, the role of which is to preserve the integrity and purity of abstract ideas from disturbance and dissolution in the living generation of material reality.

On the basis of this approach to ideological creation certain habits of thought and research have formed that are not easy to overcome. A persistent deafness and blindness to concrete ideological reality has become established, involving both the reality of things and social actions and the complex material relations which interpenetrate this reality. We are most inclined to imagine ideological creation as some inner process of understanding, comprehension, and perception, and do not notice that it in fact unfolds externally, for the eye, the ear, the hand. It is not within us, but between us.

Two Sets of Immediate
Problems in the Study of Ideologies

The first principle from which Marxist study of ideology must proceed is the principle of the material and completely objective nature of ideological creation as a whole. Ideology exists completely in the external, objective world and is completely accessible to a unified and essentially objective method of cognition and study.

Every ideological product and all its "ideal meaning" is not in the soul, not in the inner world, and not in the detached world of ideas and pure thoughts, but in the objectively accessible ideological material—in the word, in sound, in gesture, in the combination of masses, lines, colors, living bodies, and so on. Every ideological product (ideologeme) is a part of the material social reality surrounding man, an aspect of the materialized ideological horizon. Whatever a word might mean, it is first of all materially present, as a thing uttered, written, printed, whispered, or thought. That is, it is always an objectively present part of man's social environment.

But the material presence of the ideological phenomenon is not a physical or completely natural presence, and the physiological or biological individual should not be set against it.

Whatever a word's meaning, it establishes a relationship between individuals of a more or less wide social environment, a relationship which is objectively expressed in the combined reactions of people: reactions in words, gestures, acts, organizations, and so on.

There is no meaning outside the social communication of understanding, i.e., outside the united and mutually coordinated reactions of people to a given sign. Social intercourse is the medium in which the ideological phenomenon first acquires its specific existence, its ideological meaning, its semiotic nature. All ideological things are objects of social intercourse, not objects of individual use, contemplation, emotional experience, or hedonistic pleasure. For this reason subjective psychology cannot approach the meaning of the ideological object. Nor can physiology or biology.

The above presents the Marxist study of ideology with two sets of basic problems: (1) problems of the characteristic features and forms of organized ideological material as meaningful material; (2) problems of the characteristics and forms of the social intercourse by which this meaning is realized.

Only a thorough working out of both sets of problems will bring the necessary completeness and precision to the Marxist doctrine of the reflection and refraction of reality in ideologies.

The Problem of
Organized Ideological Material

The primary problem in the first set is the problem of the general characteristics of organized ideological material, i.e., the problem of the characteristics of ideological objects as opposed to (1) physical, natural bodies and (2) to the instruments of production and (3) to consumer goods.

Naturalistic positivism and mechanical materialism did not appreciate or even simply ignored differences of the first type, those between ideological objects and physical ones, and above all strove to reveal a natural mechanical regularity at work everywhere. It is clear that consistent naturalism lacks access to not only the more sophisticated formulations, such as science and literature, but to any other substantial aspects of ideological creation as well. Examples of the most consistent naturalism of this type are the neogrammarian theory of "sound laws" (*Lautgesetze*) and the pragmatic doctrine of culture as the adaption of the human organism to a purely natural environment.

Utilitarian positivism, which was sometimes even capable of infiltrating Marxism, ignored differences of the second type and thought of ideological objects by analogy with instruments of production (and partly with consumer goods).

But instruments of production lack any special meaning. They do not express or reflect anything. They have only an external purpose, and the technical organization of their physical form is adapted to that purpose.

Utilitarian positivism made a sturdy nest for itself in the art scholarship of the second half of the nineteenth century (particularly in classical archeology). Here it mainly relied on the authority of Gottfried Semper, whose following definition is characteristic: a work of art is "a mechanical product, consisting of a particular purpose, raw material, and technique" (*ein mechanisches Produkt aus Gebrauchszweck, Rohstoff, und Technik*).[3]

This is a fine and complete definition of an instrument of production, but fits no ideological product of any kind.

This conception of the work of art gave rise to all sorts of theories explaining the origin of various artistic forms and styles on the basis of the techniques of particular industries (textiles, pottery, and so on). All of these theories were subjected to devastating criticism by Alois Riegl and August Schmarzow.[4]

The formula Riegl opposed to Semper's is fundamental for the whole of contemporary Western art scholarship: "The work of art is the result of a definite and purposeful artistic volition, which manifests itself in a struggle with practical purpose, raw material, and technique. (*Ein Kunstwerk ist das Resultat eines bestimmten und zweckbeurissten Kunstwollens, das sich im Kampfe mit Gebrauchszweck, Rohstoff und Technik durchsetzt.*")

The concepts of artistic volition (*Kunstwollen*) and the "resistance of the material," to which are added utilitarian purpose (if there is one) and technique, are presently the basic concepts of West European formalist art scholarship. Technique has no creative role. Ability (*können*) has no formative influence on "artistic volition." All change and development in the history of the arts is due to changes in "artistic volition" and has nothing to do with the growth and perfection of artistic "ability." Worringer, for instance, in his book *Abstraktion und Einfühlung,* finds the explanation for certain forms of ancient sculpture (arms not differentiated from torso, legs stuck together) not in a lack of ability (which would actually be absurd for the examples just cited) but in a definite artistic volition: the striving for an inorganic compactness and integrity for the body, the preference for inorganic form over organic.

Utilitarian positivism, which conceives of ideological objects by analogy with instruments of production, is completely discredited in contemporary European art scholarship. The specificity of the ideological object and ideologically organized material is everywhere understood and acknowledged.

The very concept of "artistic volition" is, of course, unacceptable to Marxism. The opposition of this "volition" to technical ability is also unacceptable, although it is undeniably absurd to understand art history as the history of the perfection of technical ability. But Marxism should completely accept the critical aspect of contemporary art scholarship which is directed against positivism in both its forms (naturalism and, especially, utilitarianism).

The difference between ideological objects, which signify, reflect, and refract reality, from instruments of production should be assimilated and conclusively proved. It is necessary to understand and study the special forms taken by ideological material, forms which sharply differ from and cannot be reduced to any production technique whatsoever.

Finally, theories which see ideological objects through analogy with consumer goods are extremely widespread. It is true that there are no plans to pursue this analogy to its end. No consistent utilitarian positivism is involved here. Nevertheless, in a concealed form, the approach to ideological objects as if they were consumer goods is quite widespread and is presently beginning to penetrate practically all the works of decadent bourgeois criticism.

Especially pertinent here are all hedonistic theories of ideology and, in particular, of art. The conception of a work of art as an object of individual pleasure and experience is essentially the expression of a tendency to equate an ideological phenomenon to a product of individual consumption.

Meanwhile, the work of art, like every other ideological product, is an object of intercourse. It is not the individual, subjective psychic states it elicits that are important in art, but rather the social connections, the interactions of many people it brings about. Everything that is realized within a closed-off, psychophysiological organism and does not go beyond its confines is equal to zero in terms of ideology. All these subjective psychic and physiological processes are merely dependent ingredients of social processes.

Food is ingested by the individual organism, and clothing warms the individual organism. When several people consume products, they remain separate entities as far as the process of consumption is concerned. But participation in the perception of an ideological product presupposes special social relationships. Here the very process is intrinsically social. Special forms of social intercourse are established for the plurality perceiving the ideological product.

The poet's audience, the readers of a novel, those in the concert hall—these are collective organizations of a special type, sociologically distinctive and exceptionally important. Without these distinctive forms of social intercourse there are no poems, no odes, no novels, no symphonies. Definite forms of social intercourse are constituent to the meaning of the works of art themselves.

The doctrine by which the work of art is an object of individual consumption, whatever subtle and ideal forms it assumes (artistic pleasure, intellectual enjoyment of truth, bliss, esthetic ecstasy, and so on), is completely unacceptable to Marxism, for it is inadequate to the specific social nature of the ideological phenomenon. And no matter how elevated and subtle the formulas provided by the versions of the doctrine might be, in the final account they are all based on gross hedonism. And, incidently, we will see later that our formalists did not escape digressions into such hedonism in their conception of artistic form.

Meaning and Material:
The Problem of Their Interrelationship

After the first problem has been solved; i.e., after the specific features of ideological objects as opposed to natural objects, instruments of production, and consumer goods have been established, the process of specification should continue within the ideological world itself. It is necessary to establish precise and concrete distinctions between separate ideologies: science, art, etc. However this specification should not be from the point of view of their abstract meanings, as was the case with the idealist "philosophy of culture," but from the standpoint of their concrete material reality, on the one hand, and their social meaning as realized in forms of concrete intercourse, on the other.

Concrete material reality and social meaning should always be the primary criteria of specification.

Before all else, we see in ideological objects various connections between meaning and its material body. This connection may be more or less deep and organic. For instance, the meaning of art is completely inseparable from all the details of its material body.

The work of art is meaningful in its entirety. The very constructing of the body-sign [*telo-znak*] has a primary importance in this instance. Technically auxiliary, and therefore replaceable, elements are held to a minimum. The individual reality of the object, with all the uniqueness of its features, acquires artistic meaning here.

The relationship of science to the material embodying it is somewhat different. Although there is not and cannot be meaning apart from material here either (as is true of all ideological material), this material is basically relative and replaceable in nature. Scientific meaning is easily transferred from one material to another and is easily reproduced and repeated. Isolated, unique features in the material organization of a scientific work are in most cases unimportant. In scientific work there are many supplementary features of only a technical significance which are therefore completely replaceable and often even indifferent.

In addition to this relationship to the material, to its separate aspects and characteristics, meaning itself varies among the separate ideologies. That is, ideological works have different functions within the unity of social life. In this regard, the social connections which implement meaning are also varied. That is, the aggregates of all the actions and interactions elicited and organized by ideological meaning are also different. This explains the various relationships of ideologies to the surrounding reality and the special laws for the refraction of reality that are proper to each ideology.

The Problem of the
Forms and Types of Ideological Intercourse

The problem of the implementation or realization of meaning brings >
us to the second set of problems encountered in the study of ideologies.

The forms and types of ideological intercourse have hardly been
studied. Particularly pernicious reasons for this are incorrect habits of
thinking fostered by idealism, with its stubborn tendency to conceive of
ideological life as a single consciousness juxtaposed to meaning.

However it is no less harmful to understand ideological intercourse
simplistically, as a number of people gathered in one place, as in a
concert hall or at an art exhibition. Such direct intercourse is just one
variety of ideological intercourse and, at present, perhaps not even one
of the most important. Forms of direct intercourse are constitutive to
only some genres of art.

It would be absurd to imagine scientific intercourse as constitutive to
such forms of science as the scientific meeting or conference. The forms
of cognitive intercourse are exceptionally complex and subtle, and very
deeply lodged in the economic base. Of course, the organized collective
response to nature that is fundamental to humanity determines the forms
by which nature is known, from those of simple daily life to the complex
methods of scientific study. The mutual orientation of people defines
each act of cognition, and the more complex, differentiated, and organized
this mutual orientation is, the deeper and more important is the resulting
comprehension.

The forms of artistic intercourse are no less complex and subtle.
They are extremely varied and differentiated, from the intimate "audience" of the drawing room lyric to the immense "multitude" of the
tragedian or novelist.

We know of only one work of West European art scholarship which
takes account of how the forms of artistic intercourse determine the
structure of artistic works. This is Paul Bekker's *Die Symphonie von
Beethoven bis Mahler.* According to Bekker, the audience, as a defined
collective organization, is a constitutive aspect of the determination of
the symphonic genre itself.[5]

The Concept of the
Ideological Environment and Its Meaning

The basic problems we have enumerated do not, of course, exhaust
the pressing problems of the Marxist study of ideologies today. There is
yet another very important problem, which we will call the problem of
the ideological environment.

Social man is surrounded by ideological phenomena, by objects-signs [*veshch'-znak*] of various types and categories: by words in the multifarious forms of their realization (sounds, writing, and the others), by scientific statements, religious symbols and beliefs, works of art, and so on. All of these things in their totality comprise the ideological environment, which forms a solid ring around man. And man's consciousness lives and develops in this environment. Human consciousness does not come into contact with existence directly, but through the medium of the surrounding ideological world.

The ideological environment is the realized, materialized, externally expressed social consciousness of a given collective. It is determined by the collective's economic existence and, in turn, determines the individual consciousness of each member of the collective. In fact, the individual consciousness can only become a consciousness by being realized in the forms of the ideological environment proper to it: in language, in conventionalized gesture, in artistic image, in myth, and so on.

The ideological environment is the environment of consciousness. Only through this environment and with its help does the human consciousness attain the perception and mastery of socioeconomic and natural existence.

The ideological environment is constantly in the active dialectical process of generation. Contradictions are always present, constantly being overcome and reborn. But for each given collective in each given epoch of its historical development this environment is a unique and complete concrete whole, uniting science, art, ethics, and other ideologies in a living and immediate synthesis.

Man the producer is directly oriented in the socioeconomic and natural environment of production. But every act of his consciousness and all the concrete forms of his conduct outside work (manners, ceremonies, conventional signs of communication, etc.) are immediately oriented in the ideological environment, are determined by it, and in turn determine it, while only obliquely reflecting and refracting socioeconomic and natural existence.

It seems to us that the concept of the concrete ideological environment has an enormous significance for Marxism. Aside from a general theoretical and methodological significance, the concept has great practical importance. For, in addition to purely ideological creation, a whole series of very important social acts are directly aimed at the development of this environment in its concrete totality. The politics of social upbringing and education, cultural propaganda, and educational work are all forms of organized influence on the ideological environment which presuppose a knowledge of its laws and concrete forms.

Here too, in the conceptualization of the ideological environment, the idealist philosophy of culture played a sorry role. This philosophy replaced the living connections between all ideological formations in the concrete and materially expressed ideological horizon with systematic extraspatial and extratemporal connections of abstract meanings.

For the positivist humanities there was no such thing as a unified ideological environment. It was atomized into a trivial empiricism of separate and unconnected facts. And the more isolated and meaningless the individual fact, the more solid and positive it seemed. To be convinced of this it is sufficient to recall positivist linguistics and the neogrammarians' history of language or positivist classical archeology. The futile and incorrect desire to reduce ideological creation to natural laws necessitated disregard for the social unity of the ideological world and its laws of development.

Naturalism and pragmatism ignored the ideological environment in its various forms, just as they ignored the socioeconomic environment and made the human organism adapt itself directly to the biological environment.

Marxists often do not fully appreciate the concrete unity, variety, and importance of the ideological environment, and move too quickly and too directly from the separate ideological phenomenon to conditions of the socioeconomic environment. This is to lose sight of the fact that the separate phenomenon is only a dependent part of the concrete ideological environment and that it is directly determined by this environment in the most immediate way. It is just as naive to think that separate works, which have been snatched out of the unity of the ideological world, are in their isolation directly determined by economic factors as it is to think that a poem's rhymes and stanzas are fitted together according to economic causality.

Those are the sets of immediate problems confronting Marxist ideological study. We have cited only the main lines of their formulation and solution. It is our purpose to approach the concrete tasks of just one branch of this study: the tasks of literary scholarship.

Only an exhaustive and deep elaboration of all the problems we have cursorily mentioned will lead to the required differentiation within the unity of the Marxist sociological method and will allow scholarship, with the help of this method, to master all the details of the specific structures of ideological phenomena.

CHAPTER TWO
The Immediate
Tasks of Literary Scholarship

The Reflection
of the Ideological Environment
in the "Content" of the Literary Work

On the one hand, the unity of all the branches of literary scholarship (theoretical poetics, historical poetics, literary history) is based on the unity of Marxist principles for the understanding of ideological super-structures and their relationship to the base. On the other hand, this unity is based on the specific (also social) characteristics of literature itself.

Literary scholarship is one of the branches of the study of ideologies. All the major tasks of this study surveyed in the preceding chapter pertain to literary scholarship as well and are likewise its immediate tasks. But the proper formulation and elaboration of these tasks is complicated by one particular circumstance.

The characteristics of literature include one that is very important, one which has played and continues to play a fateful role in the history of the scholarly study of literary phenomena. It has led historians and theoreticians away from literature and its direct study and has interfered with the proper formulation of literary problems.

This characteristic concerns the relationship of literature to other ideologies, its unique position in the totality of the ideological environment.

Literature is one of the independent parts of the surrounding ideological reality, occupying a special place in it in the form of definite, organized philological works which have their own specific structures. The literary structure, like every ideological structure, refracts the generating socioeconomic reality, and does so in its own way. But, at the same time, in its "content," literature reflects and refracts the reflections and refractions of other ideological spheres (ethics, epistemology, political doctrines, religion, etc.). That is, in its "content" literature reflects the whole of the ideological horizon of which it is itself a part.

Literature does not ordinarily take its ethical and epistemological content from ethical and epistemological systems, or from outmoded ideological systems (as classicism did), but immediately from the very process of the generation of ethics, epistemology, and other ideologies. This is the reason that literature so often anticipates developments in philosophy and ethics (ideologemes), admittedly in an undeveloped, unsupported, intuitive form. Literature is capable of penetrating into the social laboratory where these ideologemes are shaped and formed. The artist has a keen sense for ideological problems in the process of birth and generation.

He senses them in *statu nascendi*, sometimes better than the more cautious "man of science," the philosopher, or the technician. The generation of ideas, the generation of esthetic desires and feelings, their wandering, their as yet unformed groping for reality, their restless seething in the depths of the so-called "social psyche"—the whole as yet undifferentiated flood of generating ideology—is reflected and refracted in the content of the literary work.

Literature always represents man, his life and fate, his "inner world," in the ideological purview. Eveything takes place in a world of ideological quantities and values. The ideological environment is the only atmosphere in which life can be the subject of literary representation.

Life, the aggregate of defined actions, events, or experiences, only become plot [*siuzhet*], story [*fabula*],[1] theme, or motif once it has been refracted through the prism of the ideological environment, only once it has taken on concrete ideological flesh. Reality that is unrefracted and, as it were, raw is not able to enter into the content of literature.

Whatever plot or motif we choose, we always reveal the purely ideological values which shape its structure. If we disregard these values, if we place man immediately into the material environment of his productive existence—that is, if we imagine him in a pure, absolute, ideologically unrefracted reality—nothing of the plot or motif will remain. No concrete plot (for instance the plot of *Oedipus the King* or *Antigone*), but every plot as such is the formula of ideologically refracted life. This formula is composed of ideological conflicts, material forces which have been ideologically refracted. Good, evil, truth, crime, duty, death, love, victory, etc.—all are ideological values without which there can be no plot or motif.

All these values are quite different, of course, depending on whether they belong to the ideological purview of a feudal lord, a member of the big bourgeoisie, a peasant, or a proletarian. Differences in plot follow from differences in values. But if the world is to be represented in literature, ideological refraction, cognitive, esthetic, political, or religious refraction, is an obligatory and irrevokable preliminary condition for the world's entrance into the structure and content of literature.

Not only plot, but the lyric motif, various problems, and in fact every meaningful element of content is subordinate to this basic law: in them reality that has already been ideologically refracted is shaped artistically.

The Three
Basic Methodological Errors
of Russian Criticism and Literary History

The content of literature reflects the ideological purview, i.e., other nonartistic, ideological formations (ethical, epistemological, etc.). But, in reflecting these other signs, literature creates new forms, new signs of ideological intercourse. And these signs are works of art, which become a real part of the social reality surrounding man. Reflecting something external to themselves, literary works are at the same time in themselves valuable and unique phenomena of the ideological environment. Their role cannot be reduced to the merely auxiliary one of reflecting other ideologemes. Literary works have their own independent ideological role and their own type of refraction of socioeconomic existence.

Therefore, when speaking of the refraction of reality in literature, these two types of reflection should be strictly separated: (1) the reflection of the ideological environment in the content of literature; (2) the reflection of the economic base that is common to all ideologies. Literature, like the other independent superstructures, reflects the base.

This double reflection, this double orientation of literature in reality, makes the methodology and concrete methods of literary study extremely complex and difficult.

Russian literary criticism and literary history, (Pypin, Vengerov, and others[2]), in studying the reflections of the ideological environment in literary content, committed three fatal methodological errors:

1) It limited literature to reflection alone; that is, it lowered it to the status of a simple servant and transmitter of other ideologies, almost completely ignoring the independently meaningful reality of the literary work, its ideological independence and originality.

2) It took the reflection of the ideological purview to be the direct reflection of existence itself, of life itself. It did not take into account the fact that the literary reflects only the ideological horizon, which itself is only the refracted reflection of real existence. To reveal the world depicted by the artist is not to penetrate into the actual reality of life.

3) It finalized and dogmatized basic ideological points reflected by the artist in his work, thus turning active and generating problems into ready theses, statements, and philosophical, ethical, political, religious, etc. conclusions. It did not understand or consider the vital fact that the essential content of literature only reflects generating ideologies, only reflects the living process of the generation of the ideological horizon.

The artist has nothing to do with prepared or confirmed theses. These inevitably show up as alien bodies in the work, as tendentious prosisms. Their proper place is in scientific systems, ethical systems, political programs, and the like. Such ready and dogmatic theses have at best only a secondary role in the literary work; they never form the nucleus of its content.

Almost all critics and historians of literature committed these same mistakes with varying degrees of crudeness. The result was that literature, an independent and unique ideology, was equated with other ideologies and vanished in them without a trace. Analysis squeezed the literary work for poor philosophy, superficial sociopolitical declarations, ambiguous ethics, and short-lived religious doctrines. What remained after this squeezing, i.e., the most essential thing, the artistic structure of the literary work, was simply ignored as mere technical support for other ideologies.

And the ideological squeezings themselves were profoundly inadequate in terms of the real content of the works. What had been presented in the living generation and concrete unity of the ideological horizon was put in order, isolated, and developed into a finished and always disreputable dogmatic structure.

Literary Criticism and "Content"

That the critic, particularly the critic-contemporary, would react this way is quite understandable and in part natural. The critic, like the reader he represents, is frequently drawn into the flood of generating ideology the artist has revealed to him. If the work is really deep and timely, then the critic and reader will recognize themselves, their problems, their own personal ideological process of generation (their "quest"), and will recognize the contradictions and conflicts of their own constantly active and involved ideological horizon.

For in the ideological horizon of any epoch and any social group there is not one, but several mutually contradictory truths, not one but several diverging ideological paths. When one chooses one of these truths as indisputable, when one chooses one of these paths as self-evident, he then writes a scholarly thesis, joins some movement, registers in some party. But even within the limits of a thesis, party, or belief, one is not able to "rest on his laurels." The course of ideological generation will present him with two new paths, two truths, and so on. The ideological horizon is constantly developing—as long as one does not get bogged down in some swamp. Such is the dialectic of real life.

And the more intensive, impetuous, and difficult this process of generation is, and the more substantially and deeply it is reflected in a genuine work of art, the more ideological, interested, and attentive the reaction of the critic and reader will be. This is inevitable and good.

But it is bad if the critic imposes a thesis on the artist, a thesis in the sense of the "last word," and not as the generation of an idea. It is bad if the critic forgets that there is no philosophy in literature, only philosophizing, no knowledge, but only the process of cognition. It is bad if he dogmatizes the extraartistic ideological composition of the content. It is bad, furthermore, if, because of the latter, merely reflected generation of the extraartistic ideological purview, the critic does not notice and does not appreciate the real generation of art in the given work, does not notice the independence and unquestionably dogmatic and assertive nature of the purely artistic position of the author.

For the artist only asserts himself in the process of the artistic selection and shaping of the ideological material. And this artistic assertion is no less social and ideological than epistemological, ethical, political, etc. assertions are.

Sensible and serious literary criticism will not ignore these facts.

The Tasks of Literary
History with Regard to "Content"

But for scholarly history and literary theory the above is not enough. The critic can remain within the bounds of the ideological environment as it is reflected by the artistic content, as well as within the actual artistic ideological horizon. But the historian must reveal the very mechanics of ideological generation.

Beyond the generation of the reflected and actual ideological horizon (which must be strictly differentiated because the methods used to study their elements are different), the historian must reveal the class struggle. He must penetrate the ideological horizon to the real socioeconomic being of the given social group.

For the Marxist literary historian the reflection of being in the forms of literature as such is most important. That is, social life must be expressed in the specific language of literature. The Marxist prefers to study the language of other ideologies on the basis of more direct documents and not on the basis of their secondary refraction in the structure of the literary work.

It is least of all permissible for a Marxist to draw direct conclusions about the social reality of a given epoch from secondary ideological reflections in literature, as quasi sociologists have done and continue to do, being ready to project any structural element of the artistic work, for instance, the hero or plot, directly into real life. For a genuine sociologist, of course, the hero of a novel or an event of plot tell much more as elements of the artistic structure (i.e., in their own artistic language) than can be learned from naively projecting them directly into life.

The Reflection
of the Ideological Horizon
and Artistic Structure in the Literary Work

Let us look a bit closer at the interrelationship between the reflected ideological horizon and the artistic structure within the unity of the literary work.

The hero of a novel, for instance, Bazarov of Turgenev's *Fathers and Sons*, if taken out of the novelistic structure, is not at all a social type in the strict sense, but is only the ideological refraction of a given social type. Socioeconomic historical scholarship defines Bazarov as a *razno-chinets*.[3] But he is not a *raznochinets* in his actual being. He is the ideological refraction of a *raznochinets* in the social consciousness of a definite social group, the liberal nobility to which Turgenev belonged. The ideologeme of a *raznochinets* is basically ethical and psychological, and partly philosophical.

The ideologeme of a *raznochinets* is an inseparable element of the unified ideological horizon of the social group to which Turgenev belonged. The image of Bazarov is an oblique document of this ideological horizon. But this image is already a detached and practically worthless document for the socioeconomic history of the fifties and sixties, i.e., worthless as material for the actual study of the historical *raznochinets*.

That is the situation if Bazarov is removed from the artistic structure of the novel. Of course, as a matter of fact, Bazarov is presented to us as a structural element of a literary work and not as an ethical and philosophical ideologeme. And in this is his essential reality for the sociologist.

Bazarov is first of all the "hero" of a Turgenev novel, i.e., an element of a definite genre type in its concrete realization. The nobleman's ideologeme of a *raznochinets* has a definite artistic function in this realization, first in the plot, then in the theme (in the wide sense of the word), in the thematic problem, and, finally, in the construction of the work in its totality. Here this image is constructed completely differently and has a different function than, say, the image of the hero in classical tragedy.

It is true that this ideologeme of a *raznochinets*, upon entering the novel and becoming a dependent structural element of the artistic whole, in no wise ceases to be an ethical, philosophical ideologeme. On the contrary, it brings to the structure of the novel all its extraartistic ideological meaning, all its seriousness, and the fullness of its ideological responsibility. An ideologeme deprived of its direct meaning, of its ideological bite, cannot enter the artistic structure, for it does not provide precisely what is necessary and constituent to the poetic structure—its full ideological acuity.

But, without losing its direct meaning, the ideologeme, in entering the artistic work, enters into a chemical, not mechanical, relationship with the features of artistic ideology. Its ethical, philosophical spirit becomes an ingredient of poetic spirit, and its ethical-philosophical responsibility is absorbed by the totality of the author's artistic responsibility for the whole of his artistic statement. The latter, of course, is as much a social statement as an ethical, philosophical, political, or any other ideological statement is.

A specific method and concrete methodology is needed if the isolation of extraartistic ideologemes from artistic structures is to be at all careful and precise. In most cases such work is baseless and futile.

The purely artistic intentions of the novel completely permeate the ethical-philosophical ideologeme that is Bazarov. It is very hard to separate it from plot. Plot, with its specific laws of development and its specific logic, determines the life and fate of Bazarov to a much greater extent than the reflected extraartistic ideological conception of his life as a *raznochinets*.

It is no less difficult to separate the ideologeme from the thematic unity of the work, which, in Turgenev, is lyrically embellished, and from the thematic problem of the two generations.

The hero is generally an extremely complex literary formation. The hero is constructed at the point where the major structural lines of the work intersect. That is why it is so difficult to separate the extraartistic ideologeme which underlies the hero from the purely artistic material in which he is enmeshed. There are many methodological problems and difficulties involved. We will intentionally simplify them somewhat and will not develop them to their full extent.

We will use a crude analogy from the natural sciences. Oxygen, precisely as oxygen, i.e., in all its chemical uniqueness, is part of the composition of water. But a definite chemical method and laboratory procedure (i.e., the techniques of chemical analysis) are needed to extract oxygen from water.

Similarly, in the Turgenev example, the unquestioned presence of the ethical-philosophical ideologeme in the composition of the artistic whole far from guarantees its correct and methodologically pure extraction. It is in a chemical combination with the artistic ideologeme.

Furthermore, once the ideologeme has been extracted, a special method is required to relate it to the ideological horizon of the corresponding social group. Of course, this ideologeme, which was a dependent element of the work, becomes a dependent element of the general ideological horizon when separated from the work.

In connection with the above it is necessary to take still stricter account of the fact that the ideologeme itself and the ideological horizon which enfolds it are in the process of generation. The ideologeme of the *raznochinets* in the image of Bazarov is not at all an ethical-philosophical statement in the exact sense of the word, but rather the contradictory generation of such a statement. This cannot be overlooked.

But, we repeat, the major task of the Marxist historian or theoretician of literature does not involve the isolation of the extraartistic ideologeme, but the sociological definition of the artistic ideologeme itself, i.e., the sociological definition of the work of art.

It is possible to obtain oxygen from water if necessary. But oxygen is not adequate to water as a whole. Water is necessary to life precisely as water. In the same way, a novel figures and is active in social life precisely as a novel, as an artistic whole. The basic task of the literary historian and theoretician is to study the novel as such. Extraartistic ideologemes are studied from the standpoint of their artistic functions in the novel.

Both the artistic structure of the novel and the artistic function of each of its elements are in themselves no less ideological and sociological than the esthetic, philosophical, or political ideologemes present in it. But the artistic ideology of the novel is primary and more immediate for the scholar than its reflected and twice-refracted extraartistic ideologemes.

The extraartistic ideologeme, in chemical combination with the artistic construction, forms the thematic unity of the given work.

Thematic unity is a particular mode of orientation in reality, proper only to literature, which allows it to control aspects of reality which are inaccessible to other ideologies. All this admits of special study following special methods.

The "Content" of Literature
as a Problem of Esthetics and Poetics

The characteristic of the artistic structure we have surveyed—its inclusiveness [*soderzhatel'nost'*], i.e., the organic inclusion of other ideologies in the process of generation—is the general property of almost all esthetics and poetics, with the exception of esthetics oriented on decadent theories of artistic creation.

In the most recent literature on esthetics this characteristic inclusiveness receives a detailed and principled examination and substantiation in the esthetics of Hermann Cohen, admittedly in the idealistic language of his philosophical system.

Cohen understands "the esthetic" [*das Ästhetische*] as a kind of superstructure over other ideologies, over the reality of cognition and action. Thus, reality enters art already cognized and ethically evaluated. However, this reality of cognition and ethical evaluation is for Cohen, as for any consistent idealist, the "ultimate reality." The real existence which determines cognition and ethical evaluation is unknown to Cohen. The ideological horizon, deprived of concreteness and materiality and synthesized into an abstract systematic unity, is Cohen's ultimate reality.

Given such idealist presuppositions, it is completely understandable that Cohen's esthetics could not master the full concrete plenitude of the artistic work and its concrete connections with other ideological phenomena. Cohen replaces these concrete connections with systematic ties between three areas of philosophy: logic, ethics, and esthetics. It is also completely understandable that Cohen does not examine or analyze the artistic functions performed by extraartistic ideologemes—cognition and ethical evaluation—in the concrete structure of the work.

The inclusion of extraesthetic values in the artistic work is also developed in the idealist esthetics of Jonas Cohn[4] and Broder Christiansen,[5] although less fundamentally and distinctly. These ideas are still less distinct in the psychological esthetics of Lipps and Volkelt (*Einfühlungsästhetik*). Here the concern is not with the inclusion of ideologeme in the concrete structure of the artistic work, but with various combinations, within the psyche of the artist and observer, of cognitive and esthetic acts, feelings, and emotions, on the one hand, and esthetic material on the other. Everything is dissolved in a sea of experiences in which these authors vainly try to perceive some stable connections and laws. It is, of course, impossible to formulate concrete problems of art scholarship on such an unstable, subjective basis.

One finds a more concrete formulation of the problem in the methodological work of Max Dessoir and Emile Utitz, based on the phenomenological method in the latter. However, the degree of methodological precision and concreteness that would be able to satisfy the Marxist study of ideologies is lacking here too.

The esthetic constructions of Richard Hamann brought great confusion to the problem. Under the influence of nonobjective arts, or, more precisely, nonobjective trends in art, and influenced by expressionism in the visual arts, this esthetician and scholar overestimated the "thing-like nature" [*veshchnost'*] and "constructive formedness" of the artistic work.[6] In his early works he overestimated the generally correct but purely negative and formalistically empty principle of esthetic distancing and isolation.[7]

The Problem of Distancing and Isolation

In view of its significance for general esthetics, we will pause to discuss the principle of distancing and isolation in a bit more detail. For it might seem that the distancing and isolation of the work of art and its content contradict the feature of the poetic structure we have just examined, the inclusiveness of art.

Such is not the case. If the principle is correctly understood, there is no contradiction. What is, in fact, distanced and isolated in art? And what is distanced from what?

Clearly it is not abstract physical qualities which are distanced, but ideological values, the various phenomena of social reality and history. But ideological meaning is not distanced. On the contrary, this meaning immediately enters the distanced existence of art. A phenomenon enters art exactly as good or evil, worthlessness or greatness, and so on.

We already know that without ideological evaluations (in abstraction from them) neither plot, nor theme, nor motif can be realized. And, in fact, the phenomenon is not distanced from ideological value, but from its reality and everything connected with it—emotional attraction, individual need, fear, and so on. The phenomenon enters the distanced world of art with all its value coefficients, not as a naked and meaningless physical body, but as social meaning.

But while distanced from reality and isolated from its pragmatic connections, the social meaning of the artistic content, from another standpoint and in a different social category, rejoins reality and its connections. It does so precisely as an element of the artistic work, the latter being a specific social reality no less real and active than other social phenomena.

Returning to our example, we see that Turgenev's novel is no less real and no less tightly and inseparably woven into the social life of the 1860s as a real factor than a real live *raznochinets* could be, not to mention the nobleman's ideologeme of a *raznochinets*. Its reality as a novel is merely different than the reality of a real *raznochinets*.

So, social meaning which enters the content of a novel or other work, while distanced from reality in one way, compensates by becoming part of social reality in another way, in a different social category. And one must not lose sight of the social reality of the novel due to the reflected and distanced reality of the elements it contains.

The reality of a novel, its contact with actuality, and its role in social life cannot be reduced to the mere reflection of reality in its content. It is part of social life and active in it precisely as a novel and, as such, sometimes has an extremely important place in social reality, a place sometimes no less important than that of the social phenomena it reflects.

The fear of losing touch with the immanent reality of literature for the sake of another reality which is merely reflected in it need not lead to the denial of the latter's presence in the artistic work, as in Russian formalism, or to an underestimation of its structural role in the work, as was the case in European formalism. This is destructive not only from the standpoint of general methodological and sociological interests (relatively) extrinsic to art but also from the standpoint of art itself, for one of its most important and essential structural elements is not fully appreciated, which results in the distortion of its whole structure.

Only Marxism can bring the correct philosophical direction and necessary methodological precision to the problems we have raised. Only Marxism can completely coordinate the specific reality of literature with the ideological horizon reflected in its content, i.e., with other ideologemes. And only Marxism can do so in the unity of social life on the basis of the socioeconomic laws which totaly permeate all ideological creation.

Marxism, given the totally sociological nature of all ideological phenomena, including poetic structures, with their purely artistic details and nuances, removes the danger of the fetishization of the work, the danger that the work might be transformed into a meaningless object and artistic perception into the hedonistic "sensation" of the object, as in our formalism, and also avoids the opposite danger that literature might be made a servant of the other ideologies, the danger of losing touch with the work of art in its artistic specificity.

The Object, Tasks, and Methods of Literary History

In addition to being reflected in the content of the artistic work, the ideological horizon exerts a shaping influence on the work as a whole.

The literary work is an immediate part of the literary environment, the aggregate of all the socially active literary works of a given epoch and social group. From a strictly historical point of view the individual literary work is a dependent and therefore actually inseparable element of the literary environment. It occupies a definite place in this environment and is directly determined by its influences. It would be absurd to think that a work which occupies a place in the literary environment could avoid its direct influences or be an exception to its unity and regularity.

But the literary environment itself in its turn is only a dependent and therefore actually inseparable element of the general ideological environment of a given epoch and a given sociological unity. Both in its totality and in each of its elements literature occupies a definite place in the ideological environment, is oriented in it, and defined by its direct influence. In its turn the ideological environment in its totality and in each of its elements is likewise a dependent element of the socioeconomic environment, is determined by it, and is permeated from top to bottom with socioeconomic laws of development.

We thus have a complex system of interconnections and mutual influences. Each element of the system is defined within several unique but interrelated unities.

The work cannot be understood outside the unity of literature. But this whole unity and the individual works which are its elements cannot be understood outside the unity of ideological life. And this last unity, whether it is taken as a whole or as separate elements, cannot be studied outside the unified socioeconomic laws of development.

Thus, in order to reveal and define the literary physiognomy of a given work, one must at the same time reveal its general ideological physiognomy; one does not exist without the other. And, in revealing the latter, we cannot help revealing its socioeconomic nature as well.

The genuine concrete historical study of the artistic work is only possible when all these conditions are observed. Not one of the links of this complete chain in the conception of the ideological phenomenon can be ommitted, and there can be no stopping at one link without going on to the next. It is completely inadmissible to study the literary work directly and exclusively as an element of the ideological environment, as if it were the only example of literature instead of an immediate element of the literary world in all its variety. Without understanding the place of the work in literature and its direct dependence on literature, it is impossible to understand its place in the ideological environment.

It is still more inadmissible to omit two links and attempt to understand the work immediately in the socioeconomic environment, as if it were the only example of ideological creation, instead of being primarily oriented in the socioeconomic environment as an inseparable element of the whole of literature and the whole ideological purview.

The extremely complex aims and methods of literary history are defined by all of the above.

Literary history is concerned with the concrete life of the literary work in the unity of the generating literary environment, the literary environment in the generating ideological environment, and the latter, finally, in the generating socioeconomic environment which permeates it. The work of the literary historian should therefore proceed in unbroken interaction with the history of other ideologies and with socioeconomic history.

The Marxist historian need not fear eclecticism or the substitution of the history of culture for the history of literature. Such eclecticism and substitution are only to be feared by positivism, where unity is always bought at the price of confusion and every sort of substitution. The concrete unity of historical materialism has nothing to fear from such specification and differentiation and does not lose its unity of concrete principles because of them.

The fear of eclecticism and substitution is explained by the naive notion that the specificity and individuality of a given domain is only able to be preserved through its absolute isolation, by ignoring everything outside of it. In real fact, however, every ideological domain and every separate ideological phenomenon acquires its true individuality and specificity precisely in living interaction with other phenomena.

When literature is studied in living interaction with other domains and in the concrete unity of socioeconomic life, it does not lose its individuality. In fact, its individuality can only be completely discovered and defined in this process of interaction.

The literary historian should not forget for a minute that the literary work is doubly connected to the ideological environment through the reflection of the latter in its content and through direct participation in it as one of its individual parts.

It cannot, and, of course, should not disturb the Marxist literary historian that the literary work is primarily and most directly determined by literature itself. Marxism fully grants the determining influence of other ideologies on literature. What is more, it assumes the return influence of ideologies on the base itself. Consequently, there is all the more reason why it can and should grant the effect of literature on literature.

But this effect of literature on literature is still a sociological effect. Literature, like every other ideology, is social through and through. If the individual work of art does not reflect the base, it does not do so at its own risk, in isolation and detachment from all the rest of literature. And the base does not determine the literary work by "calling it off to one side," as it were, "in secret" from the rest of literature. Instead, it acts on all of literature and on the whole ideological environment. It acts on the individual work precisely as a literary work, i.e., as an element of the whole ideological environment which is inseparably joined to the total situation provided by literature.

The socioeconomic laws of development know the language of literature, just as they know the language of all other ideologies. Confusion and gaps arise because of poor theoreticians and historians, who imagine that the sociological factor must inevitably be an "alien" factor, that it must be an "extraliterary factor," or, in science, an "extrascientific factor," and so on.

In real fact the socioeconomic laws of development work on all the elements of social and ideological life from both within and without. Science need not cease being science to become a social phenomenon. To do so would be to become bad science. But, incidently, even when science is bad, it still does not cease being a social phenomenon.

But the literary historian must be careful not to turn the literary environment into an absolutely closed-off, self-sufficient world. The notion of closed and independent cultural systems is completely inadmissible. As we have seen, the individuality of a system (more precisely, an environment) is based exclusively on the interaction of the system as a whole and in each of its elements with all the other systems in the unity of social life.

To repeat: every literary phenomenon, like every other ideological phenomenon, is simultaneously determined from without (extrinsically) and from within (intrinsically). From within it is determined by literature itself, and from without by other spheres of social life. But, in being determined from within, the literary work is thereby determined externally also, for the literature which determines it is itself determined from without. And being determined from without, it thereby is determined from within, for internal factors determine it precisely as a literary work in its specificity and in connection with the whole literary situation, and not outside that situation. Thus intrinsic turns out to be extrinsic, and the reverse.

This is a simple dialectic. Only crude mechanistic vestiges can account for the truly clumsy, inert, motionless, and irreversible division between "intrinsic and extrinsic factors" in the development of ideological phenomena which is rather often encountered in Marxist works on literature and other ideologies. And it is the "intrinsic factor" which is usually suspected of being insufficiently loyal from the sociological point of view!

Any external factor which acts on literature evokes a purely literary effect, and this effect becomes a determining intrinsic factor for the subsequent literary development. And this internal factor itself becomes an external factor for other ideological domains, which will bring their own internal languages to bear on it; this reaction, in turn, will become an extrinsic factor for literature.

But, of course, this whole dialectical opposition of factors takes place within the bounds of the unified sociological laws of development. Nothing in ideological creation goes beyond these laws; they are active in every nook and cranny of the ideological construction. Everything in this process of constant dialiectical interaction preserves its individuality. Art does not stop being art, science is always science. And, at the same time, the sociological laws of development do not lose their unity and comprehensive determining force.

The truly scholarly study of literary history can only be built on the basis of this dialectical conception of the individuality and interaction of the various ideological phenomena.

The Object, Tasks, and Methods of Sociological Poetics

However, literary scholarship has other aims besides those of literary history. What is more, literary history itself presupposes scholarship which would reveal the individuality of poetic structures as *sui generis* social structures; that is, the history of literature presupposes sociological poetics.

What is the literary work? What is its structure? What are the elements of this structure and what are their artistic functions? What is genre, style, plot, theme, motif, hero, meter, rhythm, melody, etc.? All these questions and, in particular, the question of the reflection of the ideological horizon in the content of the work and of the functions of this reflection in the whole structure are within the sphere of sociological poetics.

This poetics should first of all accomplish the tasks we surveyed in the first chapter on the basis of concrete literary material.

Literary history essentially presupposes the answers sociological poetics provides to the problems which have been set. It should begin from definite knowledge of the essence of the ideological structures whose concrete history it traces.

But, at the same time, sociological poetics itself, lest it become dogmatic, must be oriented toward literary history. There should be constant interaction between these two fields. Poetics provides literary history with direction in the specification of the research material and the basic definitions of its forms and types. Literary history amends the definitions of poetics, making them more flexible, dynamic, and adequate to the diversity of the historical material.

In this connection, one can speak of the necessity for a historical poetics to be the intermediate link between theoretical sociological poetics and literary history.

However, the distinction between theoretical and historical poetics is more technical than methodological in nature. And theoretical poetics must be historical.

Each definition formulated by historical poetics must be adequate to the total evolution of the form being defined. Thus the definition of the novel formulated by sociological poetics must be dynamic and dialectical. It must relate to the novel as to a system of changing varieties of the genre and must be adequate to this generating system. A definition of the novel which is unable to include all the previous forms of its historical development is not a scientific definition but the artistic declaration of some particular literary movement, i.e., reflects the values and views of this movement concerning the novel.

Sociological poetics must be historically oriented lest it turn into the program of some literary school (the fate of most poetics) or, at best, turn into the program of all literature contemporaneous with it. The dialectical method provides it with an indispensable instrument for the formulation of dynamic definitions, i.e., definitions adequate to the generating system of the development of a given genre, form, etc. Only dialectics can avoid both normativism and dogmatism in definitions and their positivistic atomization into a multiplicity of disconnected facts only conditionally connected.

Therefore, the role of historical poetics is to prepare the historical perspective for the generalizing and synthesizing definitions of sociological poetics. This would involve a series of monographs on the history of a certain genre, or even the history of some structural element, such as A. N. Veselovskii's *From the History of the Epithet.*[8]

The Marxist method has already been applied to literary history, but there has not yet appeared a Marxist sociological poetics. What is more, there has not even been any thought of one.

This situation has forced the Marxist literary historian to borrow specifying definitions for literary phenomena from nonsociological poetics. These definitions were, of course, either naturalistic, or positivistic, or idealist—in any case, altogether nonsociological. These specifying definitions were, of course, unyieldingly opposed to the Marxist method. They were a "foreign body" in Marxist research.

For this reason there arose the sorry tendency to declare war on anything "immanently" literary in the explanation of literary phenomena, and to reduce the Marxist method to a search for exclusively extrinsic factors which define literary phenomena independently of one another.

Instead of revealing the sociological nature of literary phenomena from within, the attempt was made to make literary phenomena appear externally and to prove at any cost that they were determined by exclusively extraliterary factors (or even by other ideologies). As if art only becomes a social factor if it is interpreted as nonart and were not social in its very nature! As if art only adapts to social reality unwillingly and in spite of its own essence and laws!

It happened that some Marxists, together with principles borrowed from non-Marxist poetics, appropriated vestiges of crude naturalism or positivism, false conceptions according to which artistic phenomena were some sort of natural, nonsocial phenomena, or some self-sufficient ideational essences estranged from social reality—as if ideas could arise outside of social intercourse!

All non-Marxist specifiers persistently emphasize and promote the intrinsic ("immanent") nonsocial nature of artistic structures. On this basis they demand that limitations be placed on the sociological method.

Actually, if the artistic structure as such were really intrinsically nonsocial, then the Marxist method should be limited. If, for example, the artistic structure were analogous to the chemical structure, which is, of course, nonsocial as such, then literature would have nonsocial laws of development which would be as inaccessible to sociological methods as chemical laws are. Then literary history would present the pathetic spectacle of a constant struggle between the intrinsic nature of literature and social demands alien to that nature. The fundamental theme of such a history would not be the class struggle, but the struggle of classes with literature.

The views of P. N. Sakulin are highly typical in this regard.[9] He contrasts an "immanent essence" of literature, which is inaccessible to the sociological method, and its immanent and likewise extrasociological "natural" evolution, to the effect of extrinsic social factors on literature. He limits the sociological method to the study of the causal effect of extraliterary factors on literature. Sakulin writes:

> If one pictures to himself the whole course of the literary historian's work, it naturally begins with the immanent study of individual works and writers....The elements of poetic form (sound, word, image, rhythm, composition, genre), thematics, and stylistics are all first studied immanently, using the methods theoretical poetics has worked out with the help of psychology, esthetics, and linguistics, the methods which, in particular, are now being used in the so-called formal method. In essence, this is the most valuable part of our work. Without it, it would be senseless to go further in our research....
>
> Because we consider literature a social phenomenon, we inevitably come to the question of its causality. For us this is social causality. Only at this point does the literary historian have the right to assume the role of a sociologist and propose his "explanation," in order that the literary facts be included in the general process of the social life of a given period, and in order that their place in the whole development of literature then might be defined. This is where the sociological method comes into force and becomes, in application to literature, sociohistorical.[10]

This view is indicative. It is not the result of Sakulin's subjective conjectures. It is, rather, a successful and intelligibly formulated expression of the actual *usus* which dominates Marxist literary scholarship at present, that methodological dualism which was formed by the course of events. And those who polemicize with Professor Sakulin and do not accept his frank and intelligible formulations, nevertheless subordinate themselves to this dogmatic *usus* in their practical work by reducing the Marxist method to the study of the effect of extraliterary factors on literature. And they borrow everything concerned with literature in its specificity (terminology, definitions, descriptions of the structural peculiarities of literary phenomena, genres, styles, and their elements) from theoretical poetics, which worked out all of these basic concepts, as Sakulin correctly states, with the help of psychology (subjective, of course), esthetics (idealist), linguistics (mainly positivist, partly idealist), but with no help of any kind from the Marxist sociological method. Professor Sakulin is also quite right that no research in literary history is conceivable without these basic concepts.

Thus, Professor Sakulin has correctly expressed the dominant *usus* of "sociological" research. But he is completely incorrect in thinking that the formulation of a sociological poetics is impossible. He is wrong when he attempts to interpret a poor *usus* as an inevitable and methodologically legitimate fact, and wrong when he attempts to legalize the limitations that have mistakenly been put on the sociological method.

The aims of sociological poetics are primarily specification, description, and analysis. That is: to isolate the literary work as such, to reveal its structure, to determine the possible forms and variations of this structure, and to define its elements and their functions. It cannot, of course, formulate laws for the development of poetic forms. Before searching for the laws of poetic forms, it is necessary to know what these forms are. These laws can only be found as the result of a large-scale literary history. Thus the finding and formulation of the laws of literary development presupposes both sociological poetics and literary history.

Therefore, we cannot agree with the conception of the aims of sociological poetics proposed by V. M. Friche in his article "Problems of Sociological Poetics."[11] Professor Friche understands poetics as the nomothetic, legislative study of the development of poetic forms. He writes:

> If the dogmatic poetics of the distant past established certain rules which poets were obliged to follow, and if the purpose of nineteenth-century historical poetics was to reveal the historic genesis of poetic forms, then sociological poetics has the task of revealing the laws of development of these forms.[12]

One wonders who will reveal and describe the forms. Who will determine their individuality and how they differ from other ideological forms?

A bit later Professor Friche says: "The first task of sociological poetics in relation to the cardinal problem of poetics [style] is to establish laws of correspondence between certain poetic styles and definite economic styles."[13]

But before establishing the laws of correspondence between poetic styles and extrapoetic styles it is surely necessary to elucidate the (social) nature of poetic style as such, as distinguished from extrapoetic styles! It is necessary to study the specific language of poetry in order to establish its correspondence to the specific language of other ideologies.

Having compared the classical poetic style to the styles of other spheres of social life, Professor Friche reaches this conclusion: "Thus the classical literary style is merely a particular manifestation, in a particular sphere, of those rationalistic energies which were active simultaneously in the spheres of philosophical and scientific thought and the spheres of economic and political construction."[14]

The above "particulars" are what sociological poetics has first of all to define. The study of ideologies must likewise define beforehand the "particular sphere" of scientific thought. When Professor Friche establishes his laws, he assumes that all of this is already known.

On subsequent pages of his article, Friche uses the concepts of the "adventure novel," "family-psychological novel," "family-everyday-life novel," "gothic novel," and so on. He establishes connections between these generic varieties of the novel and corresponding socioeconomic and ideological (extraliterary) phenomena. But he provides neither definitions nor analyses of these generic variations and their elements, assuming that they are already known. Further on he also dwells on such a formal and technical problem as the style of poetic technique and tries to find nonliterary correspondences to "free verse," assuming that the concepts of poetic technique, rhythm, free verse—that is, the whole sphere of metrics, rhythmics, and melody—are already known and studied.

In a word, our author constantly relies upon the specifying, expository, and analytic work of nonsociological poetics and tries to find extraliterary correspondences and equivalents for concepts borrowed from this poetics.

We are not taking exception to the substance and importance of Professor Friche's problems *per se*. But these are not the aims and problems of sociological poetics. It would be more accurate to call the research area he outlines in his article "the sociology of literary development." This sphere of the sociology of literature, which claims to formulate the laws of its development, already presupposes both sociological poetics, literary history, and, in addition, all the specifying activity of ideological study (scientific studies, the study of religion, etc.). The study Friche proposes is, in any event, the last in a series of literary studies. It presupposes a high degree of development in both poetics and literary history. Otherwise it could go no further than simple, semiartistic analogies.

Sociological poetics is the first in a series of literary studies. While it depends on literary history for its further development, it is the direct initiator of the latter, isolating and defining its material and indicating the basic directions its investigators should take.

Until we have a sociological poetics, albeit of a basic, exceedingly simple variety, the productive elaboration of literary history on the monistic basis of the Marxist sociological method is impossible.

But there is another sphere vitally interested in the foundation of a sociological poetics. This is literary criticism.

At the present time literary criticism is dominated by complete division between ideological (extraliterary) and artistic demands and approaches. Even now it is still unable to cope with the concept of content. While literary criticism usualy makes correct and proper social demands of literature, setting it necessary and timely social tasks, it is usually completely helpless to formulate them, i.e., it is unable to express them in the language of literature itself. It makes its assignments in an undeveloped, unspecified form. For this reason the impression sometimes is that the artist is required to realize his social tasks, not as an artist, but as a politician, philosopher, social scientist, and so on. In a word, it sometimes seems that he is required to do work "not in his line."

In order to carry out his social assignment the poet must translate it into the language of poetry itself, formulate it as a purely poetic problem to be solved by the forces of poetry itself. The assignment must be oriented and understood in the context of the means and possibilities available to poetic art, must be correlated with preceding literary phenomena, in a word, must be in all respects expressed in the real language of poetry itself. It must appear as a poetic assignment.

Competent and serious literary criticism must give the artist his "social assignment" in his own language, as a poetic assignment. In an artistically developed culture, society itself, the reading public, will naturally and easily translate its social demands and needs into the immanent language of poetic craftsmanship. It is true that this is only possible under the comparatively rare conditions of complete class uniformity and harmony between the poet and his readers. But criticism, in any case, must be a competent translating medium between them.

From the point of view of the formalists, and all other defenders of the extrasocial nature of literature, there can be no such translation of social assignment into the language of poetic art. From their point of view social life and poetic art are two different worlds, intrinsically foreign to each other and lacking a common language. All that is possible between them is external mechanistic interaction, which brings no new social possibilities into poetry and, at best, merely foregrounds the presence of the immanent possibilities of poetry.

We submit that the social assignment can and does penetrate the depths of art as into its native element, and that the language of art is only a dialect of a single social language. Therefore the translation from this dialect to the dialects of other ideologies is perfectly adequate.

It is true that there are epochs when the artist and the ruling class do not understand one another. The customer is organically unable to translate his social order into the language of art, so he demands nonart of art. The artist does not understand the social assignments of life and tries to fill them with formalistic experimentation or school exercises. But this happens only in epochs of sharp and deep social disintegration.

It is necessary to learn that poetic language is social through and through. Sociological poetics should accomplish this. The two basic functions of literary criticism—placing the social order and evaluating the order when it is filled—assume the complete mastery of this language.

The Problem of
the "Formal Method"
in Literary Scholarship

A critical clean-up of the field of research must precede a positive elaboration of the most difficult and important tasks of sociological poetics.

It can be said that poetics in the Soviet Union at present is monopolized by the so-called "formal" or "morphological" method. In their short history, the formalists have managed to cover a wide range of problems in theoretical poetics. There is hardly a single problem in this area that they have not touched upon somehow in their work. Marxism cannot leave the work of the formalists without exhaustive critical analysis.

Marxism can even less afford to ignore the formal method because the formalists have emerged precisely as specifiers, perhaps the first in Russian literary scholarship. They have succeeded in giving great sharpness and principle to problems of literary specification, which makes them stand out sharply and to advantage against the background of flabby eclecticism and unprincipled academic scholarship.

Specification, as we have seen, is an immediate task of Marxist ideological study and, in particular, of Marxist literary scholarship.

However the specifying techniques of our formalism are diametrically opposed to those of Marxism. The formalists consider specification to be the isolation of a given ideological domain, the sealing off of this domain from all other forces and energies of ideological and social life. They see specificity, individuality, as a force that is sluggish and hostile to all other forces; that is, they do not think of individuality dialectically and therefore are not capable of combining it with the living interactions of concrete social and historical life.

The fact that the formalists consistently and totally defend the nonsocial nature of the artistic structure as such makes the meeting of Marxism and formalism particularly productive and important in terms of principle.

Formalist poetics is consistently nonsociological. If this is a correct stance, if the literary structure is really nonsocial, then the role of the sociological method in literary scholarship is extremely limited and really does not involve developmental factors, but the obstacles to literary development instead, those sticks which history thrusts into the spokes of literary evolution.

If the formalists are wrong, then their theory, which is developed so consistently and fully, turns out to be a magnificent *reductio ad absurdum* of principled nonsociological poetics. And this absurdity should first of all be revealed as it pertains to literature and poetry.

For if literature is a social phenomenon, then the formal method, which ignores and denies this, is first of all inadequate to literature itself and provides false interpretations and definitions of its specific characteristics and features.

For this reason Marxist criticism of the formal method cannot and must not be disengaged or disinterested.

To repeat: Marxist literary scholarship meets and clashes with the formal method on the problem that is most important and pressing for both, the problem of specification. For this reason a criticism of formalism can and must be "immanent" in the best sense of the word. Each of the formalists' arguments must be tested and found wanting on its own grounds, on the grounds of the individuality of the literary fact. The object itself, literature in its originality, must cancel and eliminate the inadequate definitions of formalism.

We intend such a criticism of the formal method.

PART TWO

A Contribution to the History of the Formal Method

CHAPTER THREE
The Formal
Method in European
Art Scholarship [*Kunstwissenschaft*]

West European Formalism and Russian Formalism

In a wider historical perspective, Russian formalism is just one of the branches of the general European formal movement in art scholarship [*Kunstwissenschaft*].

It is true that there is no evidence that our formalists directly depended on their West European predecessors. To all appearances there was no direct genetic connection betwen them. Our formalists generally rely on no one and cite no one other than one another.

The formalists' scholarly horizons were exceptionally narrow in the first period of their development; the movement was like an exclusive circle. Their terminology, lacking any wide scholarly orientation, was suggestive of circle jargon. The subsequent development of formalism took place under the conditions of an intellectual blockade, which did not favor a wide and distinct orientation with respect to other movements and currents of West European art scholarship and literary thought [*Literaturwissenschaft*].

It must be said that all the formalist terms and definitions have yet to be oriented in the wide context of scholarship. And the formalists have not as yet made any serious and comprehensive effort to clarify their historical position or define their relationship to even the most basic phenomena of contemporary West European art and literary scholarship.[1]

The rather home-grown nature of our formalism obscures its actual participation in the general European formalist and specifying movement.

Our formalism was formed in the same atmosphere and appeared as an expression of the same changes in art and the ideological horizon that caused West European formalism to develop.

41

It is nevertheless true, as we shall see, that our formalism significantly differs from West European formalism on a number of important theoretical points.

Our task does not include a detailed historical review or critical analysis of the West European formal method. We only intend to sketch the constellation of problems from which the movement originated and to trace only the most basic lines of its development. This description of Western formalism will merely be a background against which the features of Russian formalism will stand out more distinctly.

The Historical Preconditions
for the Development of West European Formalism

The formal movement in Western art scholarship arose on the basis of the visual arts, and partly of music (Hanslick). Only recently did it begin to penetrate literary scholarship, without, however, assuming any finished form.

The formal movement in art scholarship, like all other theories of art, was grounded in the development of art itself. It was primarily the expression of the tendencies and problems which were most immediate in the work of artists themselves and in the consciousness of experts and connoisseurs of art.

The naturalistic tendencies which had dominated the previous epoch had been fully developed and exhausted by this time. Against the background of this already traveled path, which belonged to epigones, the constructive aims of art stood out particularly sharply.

These constructive aims, in reaction to the previous dominance of figurative and expressive aims, sometimes took on forms which were hostile to every reflection of content. The doctrine of nonobjective art and the attempts to create such art were reactions of this sort.

Regardless of how more or less radical these tendencies were, the development of art itself in any case favored awareness of the constructive aspects of the work of art. Theoretical research was certain to turn in the direction of this new and unstudied sphere of problems and aims.

Simultaneous with these changes there occurred within the newest European art a widening of both the artistic horizon of the expert and connoisseur and the horizon of the scholar. Whole worlds of the new forms of Eastern art were opened to the European artistic consciousness.

This extraordinary expansion of the concrete world of art was certain to reveal the extremely narrow and one-sided nature of the concepts and definitions developed by art scholarship on the basis of European art, which was primarily realistic. In the process of assimilating these new and extremely varied forms of "alien art," it was precisely the constructive aims of art that grew more and more clear. For the difficulty was not in the assimilation of new content, but in the very principles and methods of representation. It was not what was seen that was new, but the forms of seeing themselves.

Furthermore, it was clear that what was involved was not another degree of artistic ability, not another degree of technical perfection, which had been the previous naive conception of ancient art. Rather this "alien art" involved a new conception of the artistic means of expression themselves, and new artistic aims subordinate to these means. What was involved was the assimilation of what the new art scholarship had termed "artistic volition" [*Kunstwollen*].

A number of new and different "artistic volitions" were revealed to the connoisseur and art scholar. And these "artistic volitions" in their individuality and divergencies were primarily manifested in the constructive methods of the artistic object itself, i.e., in artistic reality itself.

Against the background of these "alien artistic volitions," the European "artistic volition," with its particular relationship to the reality being represented, appeared to be only one of the possible constructive modes of a work of art, and its realistic dominant (the reflection of extraliterary reality as it is) appeared as only one of the possible constructive dominants.

"Alien art" opened ways toward a new understanding of such familiar phenomena as gothic. For instance Worringer, in his book *Formprobleme der Gotik*, discovers the individuality of the gothic volition in a completely new way. "Alien art" led to a reexamination of previous opinions of ancient art.

Such were the preconditions of the formalist movement, which were prepared by the development of European art itself and strengthened and deepened as the European consciousness grew accustomed to the forms of "alien art."

The General Ideological
Horizon of West European Formalism

As we know, the crisis of both idealism and positivism occurred at this time within the general ideological horizon. This was accompanied by increased interest in and sharpening of sensitivity to all concrete expressions of world view, whether expressed in paints, spatial forms, or sounds. In short, interest was focused on the forms of concrete seeing and apprehending the things of the world, not on the forms of thinking about them.

European formalism arose and was formed in the struggle with both positivism and idealism. This position between two hostile camps was very important, completely determining the spiritual make-up of European formalism.

Both opponents posed a serious threat to formalism. Both idealism and positivism possessed formed, methodologically distinct, elaborated and detailed doctrines. Both had schools and traditions. Frivolous, half-hearted, or incompletely planned advances, sudden attacks, or tactics of disregard were all impossible. The vaudeville radicalism of some déclassé innovator not only had no chance for leadership, but did not even have a chance for any significant influence on art criticism and research. The idealist "philosophy of culture" [*Kulturphilosophie*], with its extremely complicated methodology and subtle semantic nuances, on the one hand, and positivism with its school discipline and punctilious caution on the other, created an atmosphere that hardly favored wide and frivolous generalizations and premature conclusions.

This situation could not help but have a beneficial influence on the development of European formalism by encouraging a high level of scholarship and saving it from hasty and restrictive ties with some definite artistic movement. It is true that European formalism was not without some programmatic elements—but these are an inevitability that no movement in artistic theory can avoid.

But European formalism nevertheless kept a proper distance from the ballyhoo of contending programs and the manifestoes and declarations of various groups.

The Main Line
of European Formalism

A group centered around the artist Hans von Marees (d. 1887) was the cradle of the European formalist movement.[2] From this group came the theoreticians of the movement, the art scholar Konrad Fiedler and the sculptor Adolph Hildebrand.[3] As the movement progressed, the elements of personal artistic creed present in the early and ground-breaking works of these authors, particularly strong in Hildebrand, were easily separated from what was historically important in them, namely, a new sphere of problems and a new way to solve them. The objective nucleus of their work continued to develop productively in the works of Schmarzow, Worringer, Meier-Graeffe, Wölfflin, and Hausenstein, completely independent of the various artistic tastes and preferences of these scholars.

We will try to isolate the basic and essential nucleus of European formalism, separating it as much as possible from the individualized wrappings in which it appears in the works of various scholars.

This nucleus includes the following elements: (1) the constructive aims of art; (2) the ideological nature of form itself; (3) means of representation and technique; (4) the problem of seeing; (5) "the history of art without names."

We will briefly analyze each of these points.

The Constructive Aims of Art

The work of art is a closed-off unity, each element of which receives its meaning, not in interaction with something outside the work (nature, reality, idea), but only within the structure of the whole, which has meaning in itself. This means that each element of the artistic work has primarily a purely constructive significance for the work as a closed-off, self-sufficient construction. If it reproduces, reflects, expresses, or imitates something, these are "transgradient functions"[4] which are subordinated to its basic constructive aim—to build a whole and closed work.

The task of the scholar is first of all to reveal the constructive unity of the work and the purely constructive functions of each of its elements.

In the preface to the third edition of his work Adolph Hildebrand formulates that task thus:

> We note that in the artistic activity of earlier times the architectonic construction of the work always took precedence, and the imitative side developed only slowly. This is in the nature of the activity, for the artistic sense, the instinctive requirement that we make our fragmented experiences into a certain imaginable whole, creates and directs relationships directly from itself, like music. It was only little by little that the artistic observation of nature began to provide increasingly richer material.
>
> It is characteristic of our time as a time of science that artistic practice does not exceed the bounds of imitation. The architectonic sense is either completely lacking, or is satisfied by a purely external and more or less beautiful order. In this book I strive to move the architectonic structure of the artistic work to the center of attention and to develop the problems presented by form as an essential need factually grounded in our relationship to nature.[5]

That which Hildebrand calls "architectonic" is the constructive unity of the work. The term "architectonic" was not retained because of its irrelevant associations.

How is this constructive, "architectonic" approach to a work of visual art manifested?

The work of art is a closed spatial body. It is a part of real space and is organized in this space. It is proper to begin with this real organization of the work as a constructed whole meaningful in itself. This real location of the work, the subsequent organization of its parts, and the way each of them and the whole body function in real space determines the type, means, and functions of the objective content brought into the construction. No matter what imitative, representational, or other meaning one or another element of the spatial unity may acquire, the element's place in the real and organized body of the work must be first defined, i.e., the place of its constructive meaning within the bounds of real space must be determined first of all.

For example, the flat surface of a picture remains a flat surface and is developed as such, no matter how the artist treats it. The illusory or ideal space of the picture is oriented with respect to this surface, is defined as a constructive element of it, and is only joined to real space with its help. It is necessary to proceed from this flat surface and its real organization and to consider ideal space, with all the objective values which fill it out (imitative, reproductive, expressive), to be only an aspect of this organization. It would be completely absurd to proceed from the illusory, three-dimensional space of the picture as if it were a self-contained and independent whole, having either been distracted from the flat surface, or having evaluated it as merely the technical basis of illusory space.

It is completely inadmissible to bypass the primary, real organization of the representing body and proceed from what is represented. It is a particular feature of art that no matter how significant and important the represented is, the representing body is never just a technical auxiliary or conditional vehicle for the representation. The work of art is first of all a self-valuable part of reality, and is not only oriented in it through its content but also directly, as an individual thing, a definite artistic object.

The Means
of Representation and Technique

This declaration of the primacy of the constructive function over the imitative and reproductive functions, without, however, the negation or even limitation of the latter, necessarily leads to a new understanding and reevaluation of the means of representation or expression and of artistic technique.

According to the naive notion that the visual arts reflect or reproduce nature, the means of representation have a merely technical (in the bad sense) and purely auxiliary character. They are subordinated to the object being represented and are evaluated according to how they suit it.

Thus the means of art are only evaluated as they relate to the extraartistic values of nature or the historical reality which they reproduce.

The primacy of the constructive function radically revolutionizes this notion. The object of representation—the natural or historical phenomenon—is now evaluated in terms of the means of representation, i.e., in terms of its constructive role in the closed unity of the work, in terms of its constructive expediency.

The means of representation, the "devices," do not represent some extraartistic value for its own sake. Instead, they make the work a self-contained whole and make the phenomenon being represented into a constructive element of this whole.

This revolutionary way of looking at the means of representation is particularly marked in the works of Konrad Fiedler—i.e., at the very beginning of the new movement.[6]

As long as the phenomenon of nature is perceived merely as such, i.e., in the unity of nature itself, it is not yet perceived artistically, in a painterly manner. To be so perceived it must be brought into relation with the conventions of the flat surface and the technical possibilities of a creative hand. Only in this correlation with the means of artistic representation does the perception itself become artistic. The object of the visible world of experience as it actually exists, independent of the possibilities and means of its representation, must be transferred into the system of the means of representation, the system of surface, line, shaping hand, and so forth. The object perceived from the point of view of this representational system, as a possible constructive aspect of it, for the first time becomes an object of artistic perception.

Such a conception of the means of representation allows no suggestion of a contrast between the technique of representation taken as something inferior, as an auxiliary, and creative intention as something higher, as a superior goal.

Artistic intention itself, being artistic, is from the very beginning given in technical terms, so to speak. And the object of this intention, its content, is not thought of outside the system of the means of its representation. From this point of view there is no need to draw a line between technique and creativity. Everything here has a constructive meaning. Anything incapable of such meaning has nothing to do with art.

The Ideological Dimension of Form

The basic positions of the formal movement in Western art scholarship that we have summarized give no grounds whatsoever for the denial of content in art. No matter how content is understood, i.e., no matter what elements of the artistic construction we conditionally attach to the concept, all that follows from these basic formalist principles is that content necessarily has a constructive function within the closed unity of the work, the same function as all the other elements conditionally united in the concept of form.

There are no grounds here for conclusions about the primary nonobjective nature of art, or even about the greater artistic purity of nonobjective arts. Constructivist theory and the various doctrines of nonobjectivity as the highest ideal of art are merely programmatic declarations of definite (and at times rather indefinite) artistic trends.

Behind these declarations is this one fact: in contrast to the realism which preceded it, contemporary art transfers the dominant of the artistic construction to other aspects of the work. This transfer of dominant takes place within the construction and does not change its essence.

Realistic art is just as constructivist as constructivist art. The formal movement in Western art scholarship is wider than any artistic program, and if it is not without certain artistic preferences, which vary among the various scholars, in its basic form it is impartial to all art. It establishes the specific features of art which are constitutive to all art and any artistic movement.

European formalism is least of all inclined to undervalue the semantic meaning of all the elements of the artistic construction.

The struggle against positivism and naturalism, trends which took meaning away from art, was of great importance to the European formal movement. While formalism advanced the idea of the closed unity of the work mainly in opposition to abstract, and particularly to idealist, notions of art, it was in opposition to positivism that it steadfastly insisted upon the profound meaningfulness of every element of the artistic construction.

The European formalists had no fear of the semantic meaning or content of the artistic construction. They were not afraid that meaning would unlock the closed construction and destroy its material integrity. They understood that an artistic construction deprived of profound ideological meaning inevitably finds itself in an auxiliary role or serves hedonistic or utilitarian ends. This would be to deprive the artistic work of its special place in the ideological and cultural world by making it into an instrument of production or a consumer product.

Deprived of its own grounds, the work of art would either have to assert itself on alien grounds or become a meaningless and unnecessary thing.

These words of Fiedler's perfectly express the formalists' feeling for the ideologically meaningful construction:

> We should not seek for art aims contrary to the serious aim of cognition; we should instead impartially scrutinize what the artist really does in order that

we might understand that he takes hold of an aspect of life that he alone can grasp and penetrates to a cognition of reality inaccessible to all thinking.[7]

Thus, European formalism not only did not deny content, did not make content a conditional and detachable element of the work, but, on the contrary, strove to attribute deep ideological meaning to form itself. It contrasted this conception of form to the simplistic realist view of it as some sort of embellishment of the content, a decorative accessory lacking any ideological meaning of its own.

The formalists therefore reduced form and content to one common denominator, although one with two aspects: (1) form and content were both constructive elements in the closed unity of the work, and (2) form and content were ideological elements. The principle of contrast between form and content was thus eliminated.

We shall see that Russian formalism sharply differs from West European formalism on this point. The Russian formalists began from the false assumption that an element acquires constructive significance at the cost of losing its ideological meaning.

European formalism never suggested that an element must be weakened or deprived of its semantic meaning in order to become a constructive element of the work. And the constructive significance itself, in their opinion, has a purely semantic character. The artistic construction is a system of meanings—visible meanings, to be sure.

The Problem of Seeing

The problem of seeing occupies a very important place in European formalism.

The work does not exist for thought, or for feelings or emotions, but for the sight. The concept of seeing itself underwent extensive differentiation. The perception of form, the perception of the quality of form (*Gestaltqualität*), became one of the most important problems of not only art scholarship, but of theoretical esthetics and psychology.

Here too the basic tendency was to assert the inseparability of significance and meaning from the sensually perceptible quality.

The old naive notion that quality was located in the external world and significance and meaning in the soul, and that a mechanical associative connection arises between them, was completely rejected. For this reason European formalism developed the problem of seeing as the problem of meaningful vision, as the problem of the sensual perception of meaning, or, in other words, as the problem of the sensual quality burdened with meaning.

Here too the determining factor was the struggle with positivism, which distorted the problem and reduced the sensual quality to a physical and physiological element, juxtaposing the eye, like an abstract physiological camera, to the phenomenon as an abstract physical quantity.

We will see that Russian formalism differs from West European formalism on this point too. Like positivism, it avoids the problem by simplifying the concept of "sound" in poetic phonetics to an exceptional degree.

The major aim of art, according to the European formalists, is to comprehend visual, audial, and tactile qualities, as opposed to the tendency of science toward the quantitative comprehension of reality. They contrast art's concrete orientation of the eye and the whole organism in the world of visible forms to the cognitive orientation of thought in the abstract laws of events.

"The History
of Art without Names"
[*Kunstgeschichte ohne Namen*]

Let us now move to the idea of "the history of art without names." The completely proper demand for an objective history of the arts and the history of artistic works is behind this slogan.

It is essential to discover the specific laws of the change of forms and styles. These changes have their own inner logic. They should not illustrate something happening external to themselves, but should be understood in themselves. For this reason the art historian should not study the extraartistic changes in the meaning of elements entering the construction, but the changes in the principle of the artistic construction itself, i.e., the changes in "artistic volition." Thus, according to Wölfflin, the classical and baroque alternate; according to Worringer, the alternation involves naturalism (the principle of empathy) and abstraction.

These two forms do not alternate according to the principle of simple contrast or cancellation, but under the influence of the whole system of ideological connections. The ideological dimension of the artistic construction in European formalist theory stands out with particular sharpness in this alternation of forms.

In order to become convinced of this it is sufficient to look only briefly at Worringer's two principles.

In Worringer's opinion the basis of the naturalistic [i.e., realistic] style, which follows the principle of empathy with respect to the represented object, is a positive attitude toward the world, deep trust in it and in the regularity of its laws, which govern both the world and man. Man does not fear the world, does not fear its movement, generation, and development. For this reason the organic form most fully expresses his understanding of the world as a living thing, eternally changing and close to him.

The geometric style, based on the principle of abstraction, according to Worringer expresses a purely negative relationship to the world.

When the world is frightening, when it appears to man as a hostile, arbitrary chaos, man has only one means of overcoming it: to lock it into a motionless system of invariable geometric laws. If the concrete fullness of the movement and development of the world is considered illusory and insignificant, as it is, for instance, in Eastern philosophy, then the only conceivable and possible form of the absolute will be geometric abstraction. Man strives to approximate every object to the ideal of abstraction. With the help of abstraction he hopes to save the object from the chaos of becoming, raising it to the absolute peace of motionless and ideal geometric regularity.[8]

According to Worringer gothic is characterized by a unique combination of the abstract geometric style with the movement proper to naturalism. Gothic is the endless movement of inorganic forms.

Man's basic relationship to the world thus defines his "artistic volition" and, consequently, the constructive principle of the work-object. According to Worringer:

> The Greek architect approaches his material, stone, with a certain sensuousness and therefore allows the material to express itself as such. The gothic architect, on the other hand, approaches stone with a purely spiritual desire for expression and with constructive goals which were formed independently of stone. Stone for him is only an external and dependent means of realization. The result is an abstract constructive system in which stone has only a practical, nonartistic meaning.[9]

The alternation of classical and baroque, according to Wölfflin, is likewise connected with the alternation of world views, although he does not give his opinions the ideological completeness that is found in Worringer.

Thus the "history of art without names" in European formalism does not at all lead to the denial of the ideological essence of art, and does not lead to the exclusion of art from the general ideological horizon, whether this horizon is understood idealistically or from the point of view of the fashionable "philosophy of life" [*Lebensphilosophie*].

These are the basic points of European formalism. We have seen that its assertion of the primacy of constructive aims in art did not lead it to lower the ideological significance of the artistic work. The ideological center was merely transferred from the object of representation and expression taken independently from the work to the work's artistic construction itself.

In our opinion, therefore, Boris Eikhenbaum's interpretation of Western formalism in his article "The Theory of the Formal Method" is incorrect and inspired with the spirit of Russian formalism.[10] He writes:

> The representatives of the formal method have repeatedly been reproached for lack of clarity or inadequacy in their principle positions, for indifference to general problems of esthetics, psychology, philosophy, and so on. These reproaches, in spite of their qualitative differences, are all correct in the sense that they properly grasp formalism's characteristic and intentional isolation from both "esthetics from above" and all general theories, whether finished or considered to be so. This isolation (particularly from esthetics) is more or less typical of all contemprary art scholarship. Leaving aside a whole series of general problems (such as that of beauty, the goals of art, etc.), contemporary scholarship concentrates on the concrete problems of the study of art (*Kunstwissenschaft*). The question of the meaning of "artistic form" and its evolution has, without general esthetic preconditions, again come to the fore, bringing with it a whole series of specific theoretical and historical questions. Indicative slogans have appeared following Wölfflin's "history of art without names" (*Kunstgeschichte ohne Namen*), as well as indicative experiments in the concrete analysis of styles and devices like K. Voll's "experiment in the comparative study of pictures." In Germany it was the theory and history of the visual arts, being the most experienced and richest in tradition, that occupied the central position in art scholarship and began to exert influence on both general esthetic theory and on its separate branches, in particular on literary scholarship.[11]

Eikhenbaum did not take into account the special position of European formalism between the idealist "esthetics from above" and positivist and naturalist "esthetics from below."[12] The European formalists struggled with the latter as much as with the former. Therefore the reproaches directed at our formalists are unfair if directed at European formalism. The latter is not at all indifferent to general ideological questions, which does not prevent it from striving for greater concreteness in the study of the artistic construction.

The Formal Orientation in Poetics

At present, European art scholarship has a great influence on literary criticism. A particularly avid proponent of the application of the methods of art criticism to literary scholarship is Oskar Walzel.

He develops this idea in a number of works[13] and expands his systematic views of poetics in *Gehalt und Gestalt im Kunstwerk des Dichters* (1923). The dominant idea of his work is to combine constructive aims with the fullness of ideological meaning.

From another quarter, from the standpoint of the study of the concrete phonetic construction of the poetic work, the school of Sievers and Saran formulated the same constructive problems.[14]

This school also exerted a significant influence on our formalists. However the latter significantly narrowed the aims of the study of poetic phonetics. Sievers does not tear the sound from the richness and complexity of meaningful and active speech.[15] Therefore the study of expressive intonation with its most complex semantic and emotional nuances occupies a large place in his research.

However the formal method, strictly defined, did not become the leading movement in German literary scholarship. Various trends in the application of "philosophy of life" [*Lebensphilosophie*] to the aims of scholarship are the most influential at the present time. The place of the constructive unity of the external work, the artistic object, is occupied by the unity of concrete life experience in its indissoluble individuality.[16] In this experience, according to the dominant German theory, ideal meaning is fused with material concreteness.

One should also cite the great importance in contemporary German poetics of the concept of "inner form" [*innere Form*], granted not so much in the Humboldt tradition as in that of Goethe. As it was conceived, "inner form" was to accomplish the same basic task of organically uniting material concreteness with the fullness of ideal meaning and the fluctuations of individual experience.[17]

The real motherland of the formal method is, of course, France. Here the formal method, in its general sense, has a long tradition reaching back to the seventeenth century, i.e., to classical poetics. No modern historian or theoretician of French literature avoids the formal analysis of artistic works, neither Brunetière, nor Lanson, nor Thibaudet, nor others.

The influence of French literary theory on our formalism was considerable, particularly that of the linguists of the Geneva school.[18] But it did not have a determining effect on the basic principles of formalist poetics.

Such are the basic features of West European formalism. The problems it set and even the basic tendencies toward their solution seem generally acceptable to us. What is not acceptable is the philosophical base upon which these solutions are proposed. We attempted to outline the real grounds for the productive elaboration of these problems in the first part of this book. In subsequent critical sections we will try to concretely specify the methods for solving these problems.

CHAPTER FOUR
The Formal Method in Russia

The First Positions of Russian Formalists

The Russian formal method is already fourteen years old.

The first historical document of the movement was V. B. Shklovskii's brochure *The Resurrection of the Word*,[1] which appeared in 1914. It was followed in 1916 and 1917 by two collections of works on the theory of poetic language and, finally, by the collection *Poetics* in 1919. These three collections, the last of which included some repetitions from the first two, determined the subsequent fate of the whole movement.

A look through Shklovskii's brochure gives the impression that it is the manifesto of a definite literary school rather than the beginning of a new movement in literary scholarship.

Here is the brochure's program as set out by the author on its title page:

> The word-image and its petrification. The epithet as a means of renewing the word. The history of the epithet is the history of poetic style. The fate of the works of past artists of the word is the same as the fate of the word itself—to complete the journey from poetry to prose. The death of things. The task of futurism—to resurrect things, to return the experiencing of the world to man. The link between the devices of futurist poetry and the devices of general language thinking. The half-understood language of ancient poetry. The language of the futurists.

This program is a curious historical document of the spiritual atmosphere in which the Russian formal movement took shape.

Here we have an original combination of A. N. Veselovskii ("From the History of the Epithet")[2] with futurist declarations and some intellectual talk about the "crisis of art and culture."[3] At the same time, here, in embryo, the basic positions of the future formal method are outlined.

These positions were somewhat modified in the first OPOIAZ collection.[4]

Here, next to literary declarations like Shklovskii's "Transrational Language and Poetry," are dry, specifying articles of pure scholarship:

Polivanov's "On the 'Sound Gestures' of Japanese,"[5] a translation of Nyrop,[6] and the like. The mixing of sportive futurist declarations and systematic scholarly research creates the specific atmosphere of these collections.

These publications mark the first and basic period of formalism, when its defenders and apologists came forth in an orderly phalanx, in closed ranks.

What was formalism in its first period, and what were its historical roots?

The Historical Situation
in Which Russian Formalism Arose and Developed

The historical situation in which our formalism arose and was formed was somewhat different from that of Western formalism. In Russia there was no formed and consolidated idealist school and method. Its place was taken by ideological journalism and religious-philosophical criticism. This free, Russian type of abstract thinking could not, of course, play the beneficial role of restraining and intensifying its opponent, the role idealism played in relation to Western formalism. It was too easy to toss out as irrelevant the esthetic formulations and critical experiments of our self-styled thinkers.

The situation with regard to positivism was no better. In Russia the place of positivism was taken by a trivial and flaccid eclecticism which lacked scholarly substance and rigor. The positive tasks accomplished by positivism for West European humanistic scholarship—teaching it restraint, discipline, and the weight of the empirical, concrete fact—were unaccomplished in Russia at the time when the formalists appeared.

Russian positivism had only one major figure, the solitary A. N. Veselovskii.

His work, while incomplete in many ways, has not yet been assimilated and, in our opinion, has not yet played its rightful role. The formalists scarcely debated with him. Rather, they learned from him, but they did not continue his work.

And so, in neither esthetics nor literary scholarship did our formalists find genuinely strong opponents, the kind with whom it would be beneficial nourishment for a new scholarly movement to struggle.

Eikhenbaum's description of the situation in his article "The Theory of the Formal Method" is completely correct:

'Academic' scholarship, having completely ignored theoretical problems and sluggishly made use of outmoded esthetic, psychological, and historical 'axioms,' had by the time of the formalists' debut so completely lost contact with the actual object of research that its very existence had become phantasmal. It was hardly necessary to struggle with it. There was no reason to force the gate—there was no gate; in place of a fortress we found a courtyard. The theoretical legacy of Potebnia[7] and Veselovskii, having passed to their students, lay as dead capital, a treasure they were afraid to touch and which therefore depreciated. Authority and influence gradually passed from academic scholarship to a, shall we say, journalistic variety of scholarship, to the work of critics and the theoreticians of symbolism. It is a fact that in the years 1907-12 the books and articles of Viacheslav Ivanov, Briusov, A. Belyi, Merezhkovskii, and Chukovskii[8] were much more influential than the scholarly research and dissertations of university professors.[9]

Given this situation, our formalists were not able to be highly deliberate and precise in the formulation of methodological problems. They understood and defined their own methodological position, as well as their enemies', extremely indefinitely and summarily.

They did not do battle with positivism. They opposed eclecticism in general, but not positivism as such. Therefore it was with complete inevitability that they fell into positivist and naturalist deviations.

In the West the positivist school preceded the appearance of the formalists by a good half-century. It was as if our formalists had to make up for belated development.[10]

The circle of formalists was most directly shaped by the Pushkin seminar of Professor S. A. Vengerov.[11]

However, this seminar was hardly the historical basis of formalism. Its role was rather to bring together future formalists to study specific problems of literary scholarship, a role favored by the benevolent eclecticism of the seminar director.

As for the Potebnia tradition, it only influenced formalism in the sense that formalism reacted against it. For instance, in criticizing the Humboldt-Potebnia theory of the image, the formalists appropriated from it the contrast between poetic language and other language systems and made this contrast one of their own basic concepts.

It is possible that the works and lectures of academician V. N. Peretts[12] on the methodology of Russian literary history had a certain significance for the development of the formal method.[13] Still, their only influence could have been to stimulate interest in methodological problems. The works themselves were examples of academic eclecticism and did not include any positive or productive points of view.[14]

In fact, that covers the scholarly context in which the Russian formal method had to orient itself and develop its methodological consciousness.

The Formalist Orientation toward Futurism

But the environment which actually nourished formalism in its first period was contemporary poetry, the changes which took place within it, and the theoretical battle of opinions which accompanied these changes. These theoretical opinions, expressed in artistic programs, declarations, and declarative articles, were not a part of scholarship, but of literature itself, directly serving the artistic interests of the various struggling schools and movements.

The most radical currents of literary art and the most radical aspirations associated with this art determined formalism. Here the major role belonged to futurism and then to Velimir Khlebnikov first of all.[15]

The influence of futurism on formalism was so great that had the latter ended with the OPOIAZ collections the formal method would only have become a subject of literary scholarship as a theoretical program of one of the branches of futurism.

This is the most important difference between our formalism and West European formalism. In order to comprehend the importance of this difference it is enough to imagine what would have resulted if the Western formalists, Hildebrand, Wölfflin, and others, had been directly oriented toward constructivism and suprematism!

Victor Shklovskii's expression "the resurrection of the word" best defines the spirit of early formalism. The formalists led the captive word out of prison.

However they were not the first to resurrect it. We know that the symbolists already spoke of a cult of the word. And the direct predecessors of the formalists, the acmeists or Adamists, also were resurrectors of the word.[16]

It was symbolism that propounded the self-valuableness [*samotsennost'*] and constructive nature of the poetic word. The symbolists strove to combine the constructive nature of the word with a most intense ideological nature. This is the reason that in symbolism the self-valuable word figures in the context of such elevated concepts as myth and the ideoglyph (V. Ivanov), magic (K. Balmont), mystery (the early Briusov), magianism (F. Sologub), the language of the gods, and so on.[17]

The word for them is a symbol. The concept of the symbol was to satisfy the aim of combining the constructive self-value of the word with the full weight of its semantic ideological significance.

The symbolist word neither represents nor expresses. It signifies. Unlike representation and expression, which turn the word into a conventional signal for something external to itself, this "signification" [*znamenovanie*] preserves the concrete material fullness of the word, at the same time raising its semantic meaning to the highest degree.

Although this aim was correctly formulated, symbolism lacked the grounds necessary to methodologically substantiate and attain it. The aim was too tightly interwoven with the narrowly ideological passing interests of a definite literary movement. Nevertheless, the statement of the aim and its generally correct formulation (the synthesis of constructive significance and semantic fullness) could not help but have a beneficial influence on poetics.

Symbolism was the basis for the first scholarly works which treated the substance of poetry, even if they were distorted by false ideological views. There is no doubt that A. Belyi's *Symbolism,* some articles by V. Ivanov, and Briusov's theoretical works occupy a significant place in the history of Russian literary scholarship.

Acmeism was even more distinctly and acutely aware of the constructive aims of the poetic word.

This meant a much greater materialization [*oveshchestvlenie*] of the word. Here constructive aims combined with a tendency to at least conventionalize, if not lower, the ideological semantic significance of the word.

The acmeist word—not in their declarations, but in their actual practice—is not selected from the generation of ideological life, but directly and exclusively from a literary context. The acmeists' exoticism and primitivism are pure stylization, which further emphasizes the fundamental conventionality of poetic theme.

The acmeists perceive literature as detached from the other spheres of ideology. The ideological refraction of reality in a lyric theme or in the plot of a ballad becomes something like a three-fold refraction: already refracted, it passes through the literary environment, where it is saturated with purely literary associations and reminiscences.

However, what is involved here does not concern the superficial and trite "poetic nature" of plot and motif, or trite poetic associations, but rather much more subtle and profound "structural" associations of a given plot and motif with a definite literary context, a definite school and style, and so on. Reminiscences concern the structural place and constructive functions of the motif or plot in a definite style and genre, matters ordinarily accessible only to experts and master poets. This gives acmeist poetry its refined nature.

The acmeists were even more aware than the symbolists of the guild interests and professional craftsmanship of the poet. In symbolism, particularly early symbolism, these were obscured by priestly and prophetic pretensions.

In acmeism the basic aim of poetics was distorted by the interests of the movement and its partisan ideology.

The constructive significance of the word does not necessarily entail the ideological conventionality of its meaning. This conventionality is merely a specific constructive feature of certain artistic movements, and relative even as such. Nevertheless, behind this conventionality is an unconditional ideological position.

Artistic convention is generally a highly ambiguous and unsuccessful term, one which has brought much confusion to the study of the concrete meaning of the artistic word.[18]

The acmeist cult of the word, being less elevated than that of symbolism, is therefore closer to that of formalism. It was no accident that two representatives of the new movement, B. M. Eikhenbaum and V. V. Vinogradov, wrote books on the poetry of Anna Akhmatova.[19] But the acmeist materialization of the word was insufficiently radical for the formalists.

To the formalists the resurrection of the word did not merely mean freeing it from all elevated accents and hierarchical significance. Particularly in their early period it specifically meant the elimination of the ideological meaning of the word.

To the formalists a word is just a word and, first and foremost, its phonetic empirical material and concrete nature. They wanted to save this sensual minimum of the word from being overburdened and completely absorbed by lofty meaning, as it was under symbolism.

For the formalists the resurrection of the word amounted to the full materialization of the word, and in this it is difficult to miss the deep, organic connection with futurism.

It was quite natural that formalism's first task was to battle with symbolism.

Eikhenbaum writes: "The basic slogan uniting the initial group of formalists was the emancipation of the word from the shackles of the philosophical and religious tendencies with which the symbolists were possessed to an ever increasing degree."[20]

In addition to this negative aspect of "the resurrection of the word," which was polemically directed against symbolist poetics and also partly against the "thematics" and "moralizing" of journalistic and philosophical criticism, there was another, positive aspect, which formalism also shared with futurism.

This was the tendency to find new artistic effects in those elements of the word which seemed vulgar, second-class, and almost artistically indifferent to the symbolists, namely, its phonetic, morphological, and syntactic structures taken independently of meaning. It was discovered that one could play an aloof esthetic game with words taken as grammatical units and transrational sound images and create new artistic combinations from them.

The futurists, particularly Velimir Khlebnikov, provided practical examples of such grammatical games, and the formalists were their theoreticians.

The Nihilistic Slant of Formalism

The first, negative aspect of the formalists' "resurrection of the word," which had brought the word down from its symbolist heights, had great significance. It was particularly important during the first period of Russian formalism. It was precisely here that the nihilistic tone of all formalist statements finds its origin.

The formalists do not so much find something new in the word as expose and do away with the old.

The basic formalist concepts of this period—transrational language [*zaum*], "making it strange" [*ostranenie*], device, material—are completely infused with this tendency.

Indeed, transrational language was not proposed by those possessed with the "spirit of music,"[21] or those intoxicated with the rhythms and sounds of poetry, as were Balmont, Blok, and the early Briusov. The formalists learned to value the sound in the phonetic laboratories of Jan Baudovin de Courtenay[22] and L. V. Shcherba.[23] They made the sober sound of experimental phonetics the transrational language of poetry and contrasted it to the meaningful word.

The formalists only needed references to the glossalalia of the early Christian prophets and the transrational language of possessed sectarians as scholarly background information. They were extremely distant from the meaning and spirit of this transrational language. The formalists were not so much inspired by the discovery of new worlds and new meaning in the sound of the word as they were by the subtraction of meaning from the word's meaningful sound.

The negative aspect of "making it strange" [*ostranenie*] is just as strong as that of transrational language. Its original definition, far from emphasizing the enrichment of the word with new and positive constructive meaning, simply emphasizes the negation of the old meaning. The novelty and strangeness of the word and the object it designates originates here, in the loss of its previous meaning.

It is typical that Shklovskii views Tolstoi's *Kholstomer* this way, and only this way. He writes: "The story is told by a horse, and things are made strange by a horse's perception, not by ours."[24] And he says this without any irony!

Shklovskii's understanding and interpretation of the device Tolstoi uses in this story and other works is utterly incorrect, but this distortion of the device is quite characteristic of the new movement. Tolstoi does not admire a thing that is made strange. On the contrary, he only makes it strange in order to move away from it, push it away in order to put forth the more sharply what is positive: a definite moral value.

Thus, an object is not made strange for its own sake, in order that it be felt, in order to "make a stone stony," but for the sake of something else, a moral value, which against this background stands out all the more sharply and vividly precisely as a moral value.

At other times in Tolstoi this device serves another purpose, actually revealing the value of the thing made strange. But in such a case too the object is not made strange for the sake of the device. Making it strange creates neither positive nor negative ideological values, but only reveals them.

Shklovskii therefore radically distorts the meaning of the device, interpreting it as an abstraction from semantic ideological significance. But, in fact, the whole meaning of the device is in the latter.

In Tolstoi this device has a distinctly ideological function. It is not meaning that makes perception of the object automatic, but, on the contrary, the object that screens and automatizes the moral meaning. It is not the thing that Tolstoi wants to deautomatize by means of the device, but this moral meaning.

It is quite obvious that Tolstoi's device of "making it strange" is based on certain displacements [*sdvigi*] and recombinations of semantic values. A transfer of ideological values occurs. The device itself would not exist if divorced from these values.

Shklovskii did violence to the meaning of this Tolstoian device because it was absolutely necessary that "making it strange" be a purely negative concept.

In early formalism the concept of "deautomatization of the word" was closely connected with "making it strange."

The negative tone is also dominant in this concept: deautomatization is primarily understood as abstraction from semantic context.

The same is true of the formalist definition of the device.

Shklovskii's "Art as Device" is probably the most typical article of early formalism.

It is a truism that art is a device or system of devices. But the idea of Shklovskii's article is that art is *only* a device.

The device is constantly contrasted to meaning, thought, artistic truth, social content, etc.[25] All of these do not exist for Shklovskii; there is only the naked device. A polemical and even mocking tone penetrates the very nucleus of this basic formalist concept.

The Distortion of
the Poetic Construction
by the Negative Approach

Thus the formalists attained their "discoveries" in a rather unique way: by subtracting various essential aspects from the word and other elements of the artistic work. The new constructive meaning appears as the result of these purely negative acts of subtraction and elimination.

It goes without saying that the word without meaning looks new, looks different than the meaningful word. Certainly the idea with no pretensions to truth looks different than the normal idea which strives toward cognition.

But, of course, such subtraction cannot gain anything positive, new, or profitable.

This negative, nihilistic slant of formalism shows the tendency common to all nihilism to add nothing to reality, but, on the contrary, to diminish, impoverish, and emasculate it, and by doing so attain a new and original impression of reality.

The exclusively polemical emphasis of all these positions and definitions played a sorry and fatal role in the history of formalism.

It is inevitable that every new scholarly movement engage in polemics with preceding trends in order to defend its positive program. This is natural and proper.

But it is bad if polemic changes from a secondary concern to what is practically the main and only concern, if polemic penetrates every term, definition, and formulation of the new movement. In such a case the new doctrine is too tightly and inseparably tied to that which it negates and rejects, with the result that it finally turns into the simple opposite of the doctrine it has negated, into a purely reactive formation.

This was the case with formalism.

The polemical negation that penetrated their definitions caused the artistic construction itself to become, in their theory, a thoroughly polemical construction, every element of which only realizes its constructive purpose by being polemically directed at and negating something.

The basic aim of poetics—to reveal the constructive significance of the literary work and each of its elements—was therefore radically distorted. Constructive unity was purchased at the high price of the distortion of the whole intrinsic meaning of the poetic fact.

The essence of poetics directly depends upon mastering the concrete and material unity of the poetic construction without losing its full semantic meaning and ideological significance. All of this meaning should be included in the concrete construction, materialized in it, so that the whole construction in all its concreteness can be understood as meaningful. In this is the essence and the difficulty of the task before poetics.

By way of the subtraction of meaning the formalists attained, not the poetic structure, but rather some chimerical production, something midway between a physical phenomenon and a consumer good. Subsequently, their theory had to strike a balance between pure naturalism and hedonism.

This statement from the preface to Shklovskii's book *The Theory of Prose* is typical: "The word is a thing. And the word changes according to its own philological laws, which are connected with the physiology of speech, etc."

Thus philological laws turn out to be completely natural, physiological laws. Here the materialization of the word is attained at the price of a naturalistic subtraction of meaning.

Shklovskii's article "Transrational Language and Poetry" shows that it is possible to hedonistically sample and savor transrational words. The same is true of L. Iakubinskii's "On the Sounds of Poetic Language," which amounts to a collection of examples drawn mainly from literary works for the purpose of such hedonistic sampling. Here materialization results from the hedonistic subtraction of a word's meaning, thus turning it into a consumer good.

The formalist negation of the ideological meaning of the poetic construction inevitably caused the latter to vacillate between the poles of naturalism and hedonism.

The Positive Content
of the First Formalist Studies

The positive side of the formalists' "resurrection of the word" was mainly their sharpened interest in the poet as craftsman and in craftsmanship in poetry.

It is true that the nihilistic tone gets in the way here too. In their first period, the formalists would never have said "A poet is a craftsman," but rather "A poet is *only* a craftsman."

Nevertheless, the research into the phonetic (mainly qualitative) structure of poetry, which had begun with the symbolists (A. Belyi, V. Briusov), was carried to a higher scholarly level by the formalists.

The external design of the artistic work (composition, plot formation) had hardly been studied in Russian literary scholarship. The formalists were almost the first to make it the subject of serious research. But it is significant that in this research too the accent was on negation and depreciation.

The artistic work is not only created, but also made. But for the formalists it is only made.

It is necessary to note, however, that in the first period of its development formalism was primarily concerned with the qualitative analysis of the phonetic composition of the artistic work. In its first collection on the theory of poetic language, all the articles, original and translated, were without exception devoted to this problem. In the second collection, there is only one article devoted to other problems, Shklovskii's "Art as Device." Only in the collection entitled *Poetics* do we find articles on plot formation (Shklovskii) and prose composition (B. Eikhenbaum's "How Gogol's *The Overcoat* Is Made").

It is characteristic that even where problems of plot and prose composition are treated for the first time, this is done by analogy with the
qualitative phenomena of poetic phonetics.

For instance, in Eikhenbaum's article on Gogol's *The Overcoat*
research centers on the phonetic aspect of Gogolian *skaz*.[26]

Shklovskii perceives plot formation by analogy with the sound
repetitions and rhymes of poetry.[27] This is typical of Russian formalism.

Results of the First
Period of Russian Formalism

What were the results of the First Period of Russian Formalism?

1) Russian formalism was tightly interlaced with the artistic program
and partisan interests of Russian futurism.

Scholarly poetics should be adequate to the whole generating series
of literary development. The union with futurism could do nothing but
narrow the scholarly purview of formalism in the highest degree by
providing it with a system of biases for the selection of only certain of the
phenomena of literary life.

2) The formalists did not polemicize with other scholarly movements
in literature as much as with other artistic programs (realism, symbolism),
or even simply with the bourgeois view of art.

3) Having been carried to extremes, formalist polemic passed from
their research into the subject of their research, making it also polemic in
tone. The poetic construction, as such, became a polemical construction.

4) The formalists lacked a clear and distinct methodological position.
Methodological precision and awareness can only develop and grow
strong in the process of the new movement's interaction and struggle
with organized, methodologically combative and defined scholarly movements. These were lacking in Russia.

5) Formalism did not struggle with positivism. Formalist specification
slid over into positivist specification, in which the object of research is
isolated and torn away from the unity of ideological and historical life.
Simple reaction against and negation of anything "different" was sub-
stituted for real interaction with other ideological phenomena.

6) Their struggle against idealist detachment of meaning from
material led the formalists to negate ideological meaning itself. As a
result the problem of the concrete materialized meaning, the meaning-
object [*smysl-veshch*], was not raised, and in its place we find the mere
object, which is not quite a natural body, and not quite a product for
individual consumption.

7) The problem of constructive meaning was simplified in the
extreme and distorted by the fact that the constructive significance of

any poetic element depended on its losing ideological meaning.

It is interesting to compare our points with Eikhenbaum's summary of the first period of formalism. He writes:

> It was natural in the years of struggle and polemic with such a tradition that the formalists directed all their efforts toward showing the meaning of constructive devices and put everything else to the side as motivation. In speaking of the formal method and its evolution, it is constantly necessary to keep in mind that many principles from those years of tense struggle with the opponents of formalism were not only scholarly principles, but were also slogans, with emphasis on paradox for the purposes of propaganda and contrast. To ignore this fact and treat the 1916-21 works of OPOIAZ as academic works is to ignore history.[28]

It is possible to agree with almost everything Eikhenbaum says here. His summary is generally correct. But one cannot agree with the conclusions he is inclined to draw from the situation.

It seems to us necessary to conclude that the fundamental formalist principles and slogans which Eikhenbaum characterizes as being "not only scholarly" (we would say: "not so much scholarly") need radical and merciless revision. If their "emphasis on paradox for purposes of propaganda and contrast" were removed, then, as we shall see later, little would be left of them. Their specifically "formalist" spirit would be gone.

Another conclusion is also necessary: if the years of struggle and polemic caused the formalists to show the significance of constructive devices by putting "everything else to the side as motivation," then it is now absolutely necessary to return all this "everything else," i.e., all the richness and depth of ideological meaning, to the foreground of research.

If this is done, the constructive meaning of the devices becomes radically different. It is then their task to construct ideologically rich material, without losing an iota of meaning. Only here is the real difficulty, but at the same time the profound productivity, of constructive problems revealed.

To fail to make the deductions required by the situation of formalism as we have described it would mean to ignore history and its present demands. History demands of formalism a radical reexamination and decisive revision of its past.

The Second Period
in the Development of Russian Formalism

In the second period of Russian formalism, 1920-21, a certain discord within its membership became apparent, and elements and tendencies which had been fused in the first period began to settle apart.

This discord was intensified by the fact that a number of new supporters and fellow travelers joined the original OPOIAZ group.

In connection with the necessity of passing from general declarations of a semibelletristic, semischolarly type to specialized research work, interests of scholarly specification began to stand out. The scholar's study was separated from the stage. The right flank of formalism hostilely opposed the pugnacious and provocative manners borrowed from the futurists.

It is true that the futuristic Khlebnikov flavor which became basic to the movement in its first period is still present in formalism even now. Without it formalism would not be itself. But formalism began to acquire a more and more presentable and scholarly appearance in its second period. What had been the "resurrection of the word" and "transrational language" became the orientation of poetics toward linguistics.

This tendency is most completely typified by the monographs of V. V. Vinogradov and, in part, V. M. Zhirmunskii.[29]

Shklovskii, on the other hand, was not inclined to change his original manner and became somewhat isolated, no longer setting the tone for the whole movement.

In the works of all the formalists except Shklovskii, the journalistic, semiartistic style gave way to the usual forms of scholarly research.

Zhirmunskii's position, as defined in his article "On the Question of the Formal Method," is characteristic of the whole second period.[30]

Although certain premises of his scholarship were extremely close to formalism, in this article Zhirmunskii decisively distinguishes between formalism as a method of scholarship and the "formalist world view," which was unacceptable to him but characteristic of the formalist movement in Russia. It is curious that this sensible distinction was interpreted, polemically, it is true, as a betrayal of the formal method.

The various tendencies which appeared within formalism included such "events" of formalist history as its link with LEF [Left Front of Art] and attempts to join formalism with Marxism (B. Arvatov and the "Forsotsy").[31]

In the process of polemics with the representatives of Marxist thought it became rather common practice to transfer the center of gravity to specification, evidently to escape from general problems of world view and public opinion.

In this period formalism was subjected to sharp polemical attacks from other movements of Russian ideological thought.

It is a sad necessity to state that these polemics were generally of little benefit to either side.

Academic literary scholarship, such as it was, reacted feebly and reluctantly to formalism. Formalism found it completely unprepared for any distinct formulation of methodological problems. In the majority of cases academic objections amounted to saying that other methods were also satisfactory, and there was no need to sharpen methodological problems. In short, academic scholarship stubbornly adhered to non-principled methodological eclecticism.

The criticism of philosophers (Sezeman and Askol'dov)[32] and younger literary scholars (A. A. Smirnov, B. M. Engel'gardt, and others)[33] was more substantial and active. But here too there was no successful working out of grounds for mutually beneficial ideological struggle.

It is unfortunate to have to add that Marxist criticism, which was called upon to battle formalism on the essential issues and enrich itself in this battle, refused to meet formalism on the real territory of the problems of specification and constructive meaning.

Most often the Marxists enlisted in the defense of content. In doing so they improperly contrasted what they were defending to the poetic construction as such. They simply evaded the problem of the constructive function of content in the structure of the work. It was as if they did not see it. Of course, this problem was the crux of the whole matter.

The Marxists stubbornly tried to convince the formalists that social factors affect literature.

In fact, the formalists never denied the effect of these factors, or if they did so it was only in the heat of argument.

All kinds of external factors intrude into the development of literature. It would be absurd to deny that D'Anthes's bullet cut short Pushkin's literary career. It would be naive not to consider the significance of Nicholas I and the Third Section in the development of our literature.[34] Nor did anyone deny the effect of external economic conditions on the development of literature.

The essence of formalism in no way denies the influence of external factors on the factual development of literature. But formalism does and must deny the importance of these factors for literature, their ability to directly affect the intrinsic nature of literature. From the point of view of a consistent formalist, external social factors could completely destroy literature, wipe it from the face of the earth, but they are not able to change the intrinsic nature of the literary fact, which is, as such, non-social.

In a word, formalism is not able to admit that an external social factor acting on literature could become an intrinsic factor of literature itself, a factor of its immanent development.

Formalism stands opposed to Marxism on this point. But this point did not become the center of polemics.[35]

For this reason the whole argument was essentially fruitless. And one cannot deny the "Forsotsy" a certain consistency in trying to reconcile

Marxism and formalism by way of an amicable division of the historical and literary material that amounted to saying: "You take the extrinsic, I'll take the intrinsic," or "I'll take the content, you get the form."

Thus the polemics that took place in the second period of the formal method did not play the significant historical role that they might have played. They became neither an internal nor an external factor in the history of formalism.

In the works of the second period of formalism problems of poetic phonetics began to be supplanted by problems of style in the wider sense of the term, and by problems concerning the composition of the work of art. In addition, metrics and rhythmics came to occupy an important place in formalist research, and perhaps represent their most solid contribution to scholarship.

There were also attempts at this time to develop research in literary history following formalist methods.[36]

The formalists' research in literary history exhibits the same sharply polemical tendency as their work in poetics, a tendency which here too passes from the research to its object and infects it.

The historical life of a literary work thus becomes a polemic and a negation.

Eikhenbaum acknowledges that polemic was the dominant tendency of formalist research in literary history:

> Thus the basic spirit of our works in literary history had to be the same spirit of destruction and negation as that of our first theoretical statements, which only later took on a more peaceful nature in the elaboration of separate problems.
>
> That is why our first statements in literary history took the form of almost reflex theses which were advanced in connection with some concrete material. An individual question unexpectedly grew into a general problem— theory merged with history.[37]

All this simply goes to prove that the formalists too often reduced literary history to a simple illustration of their theoretical problems.

In general, it is necessary to say that nothing essentially new in the way of basic theoretical principles was introduced in the second period of formalism. Principles developed in the first period were differentiated and applied to new material. The resistance of this new, wider material caused tears and unraveled threads to appear in formalist theory. But this did not lead to any productive reevaluation.

Thus the basic feature of the second period of formalism was the differentiation of its elements and the individual interests of its various representatives. Formalism was no longer the unified movement it had been in its first period, although its basic premises and habits of thinking were still completely intact.

The Present Situation of Formalism

The process of the dissolution of formalist theory and the disagreement among its practitioners is reaching its climax at the present time.

Strictly speaking, formalism should now be considered a thing of the past.

The movement has no unity. The militant slogans have faded. There have become as many formalisms as formalists.

It is now possible to distinguish at least four basic tendencies within formalism. Since they are only now in the process of formation, we shall speak about them provisionally.

The first tendency is academic formalism, characterized by the desire to smooth out contradictions and avoid principle in the formulation of problems.

A typical representative of academic formalism, which is at times even difficult to call formalism, is Zhirmunskii.[38] Works of his, like *Byron and Pushkin* (1924), painstakingly avoid all extremes of methodology and principle and, in striving to treat the material as fully as possible, make use of the most varied methodological orientations.

The second tendency amounts to a partial return to the psychological and philosophical interpretation of literary problems.

In his latest works Eikhenbaum is the most typical representative of this tendency.

It is true that his book on Akhmatova (1923) and his book on Lermontov (1924) contain elements which do not fit into the formalist scheme. In the former, for example, the author has much to say about the "concrete life of the soul," about the "tension of emotions" and "the image of a vital person." In the second book, he postulates the "historical individuality" of Lermontov, is inclined to analyze some of Lermontov's works, "not as literary works, but as psychological documents" (the poems of 1833-34), and, finally, poses the purely sociological problem of the reader.[39] In Eikhenbaum's most recent works on literary life, in his address on Gor'kii and his book on Tolstoi, one can hear ethical, philosophical, and even publicistic tones which are completely alien to formalism. In these works, Eikhenbaum almost returns to the old traditions of Russian literary criticism, to ethical and social instruction. Of course, we know that formalism originated as a reaction against these very traditions, granted, in their late and degenerate form.

The third tendency is characterized by a move in the direction of the sociological method and is evident in the latest works of Tomashevskii and Iakubinskii.[40] What concrete forms the views of these authors will take in the future remains to be seen.

Finally, the fourth tendency is the preserved ["canned"] formalism of Shklovskii.[41]

In the preface to his *The Theory of Prose* Shklovskii does not deny that "language is under the influence of social relations," and defines his methodological position in the following way:

> My research in literary theory is concerned with the intrinsic laws of language. To draw an industrial parallel, I am not interested in the state of the world cotton market, nor in the politics of trusts, but only in the thread count and the methods of weaving.

It is hardly necessary to prove that the intrinsic laws of this or that phenomenon cannot be explained without being related to the general laws of social development. The methods for the preparation of thread are conditioned by the level of technical development and the laws of the market.

The Reasons
for the Dissolution of Formalism

How can the disorganization and dissolution of formalism in such a comparatively short time be explained? First of all, there was a change in the orientation of formalism because what connected it to the real life of literature and public opinion changed. There was a sharp change in the socioliterary environment and the general ideological horizon.

Formalism was born in the epoch of the dissolution of symbolism. It was the ideology of those literary movements which emerged from disintegrating symbolism—futurism and, in part, acmeism. These movements did not or could not provide anything positive, solid, or new, because, lacking a firm and creative social base, they carried on the purely negative work of the corruption of the forms established in the symbolist epoch. Typical singers and ideologists of the déclassé, it was only in connection with the October Revolution that the representatives of these movements found their social foundations—whether in a positive or in a negative sense.

In contemporary post-Revolution prose, which gravitates toward socially realistic prose, the historical novel, and the social epic and is deeply interested in general problems of world view, there is nothing to nourish formalism. Formed under the influence of futurism, formalism gravitates toward transrational language and experimentation in the small genres, and toward the adventure story in the large prose genres.

Thus formalism's tie with contemporary literature was broken. The elements of the artistic program which formalism had borrowed from futurism were no longer relevant to the real literary situation. Therefore, the artistic principles of formalism were no longer relevant either. Their ties with the stage show were broken. The study and the university remained.

But matters were no better there. As it passed from the general declarations backed by randomly collected examples of the OPOIAZ collections, the scholarly research of formalism, particularly in literary history, revealed the methodological sterility and narrowness of the basic formalist premises and their inadequacy to the facts being studied.

A futuristic poetics makes it impossible to productively approach and deal with the mainstream of Russian literature—the novel. The constructive principle that still might help interpret some superficial aspects of *Tristram Shandy* or help make a more or less substantial analysis of an adventure novella nevertheless cannot provide an organic approach to the basic phenomena of the Russian novel.

It is obvious that an awareness of this fact caused the more responsible and living part of formalism to seek new philosophical and methodological bases for future scholarship. According to Eikhenbaum:

> The principle of evolution is extremely important to the history of formalism. Our opponents, and many of our followers, lose sight of this. We are surrounded by eclectics and epigones who would turn the formal method into some fixed system of "formalism," that would work out terms, schemes, and classifications for them. This system is quite convenient for criticism, but not at all characteristic of the formal method. We do not have, nor did we ever have, such a finished system or doctrine. In our scholarship we only value theory as a working hypothesis which might help to reveal and comprehend facts, i.e., help comprehend their laws and make them material for research. Therefore, we do not occupy ourselves with the definitions epigones so desire, nor do we construct the general theories eclectics find so pleasing. We establish concrete principles and retain them, to the extent that they are verified in the material. If the material demands that they be elaborated or changed, we elaborate or change them. In this sense we are sufficiently free from our own theories, as scholarship should be, in as much as there is a difference between theory and conviction. There is no finished scholarship—scholarship does not live by establishing truths, but by overcoming mistakes.[42]

If these assertions are incorrect when applied to the formal method as such, they are extremely valuable as the personal convictions of one of the leaders of formalism.

When all formalists look at the matter as Eikhenbaum does in the above instance, formalism is ended. Only the problems it has raised will remain—the problem of specification, constructive meaning, etc.—but the formalist principles and methods for solving these problems will be viewed as mistakes, and overcome.

Formalism is confronted with the necessity of liquidating its nihilistic tendencies and ending its positivistic isolation of the literary series. It is confronted with the necessity of breaking with the OPOIAZ past, something which will not deprive the latter of any of its historical significance. To do so the formalists need to acquire solid philosophical principles. This is the historical task of each of them.

Sometimes the formalists think it to their credit that they brought no philosophical world view to scholarship. This could only be a credit to a naive positivist, who would think that the best examination of details demands that one be near-sighted.

It is not necessary to renounce normal vision, to renounce a wide ideological horizon, in order to examine the total specificity of art. The wider the horizon, the brighter and more distinct is the individuality of each concrete phenomenon.

PART THREE
The Formal Method in Poetics

CHAPTER FIVE
Poetic Language as the Object of Poetics

The Formal Method as a Unified System

The Russian formal method is a consistent and sustained method for the conception of literature and the methods by which it is studied, a system permeated by one spirit which inculcates definite and persistent ways of thinking in its adherents. It is possible to recognize a formalist in the first words of a paper or the first pages of an article.

The formalists are not eclectics and in their basic modes of thought are not at all empiricists or positivists, whom one can neither see nor recognize behind a mass of facts and observations that are both too narrow and too random.

Russian formalism is not only a unified system of views but also a special way of thinking, even a particular style of scholarly exposition.

It is true that formalism as an organic unity, a single way of thinking and writing, is to a certain extent a fact of the past.

However, formalism is not a fact of the past in the sense that it simply ceased to exist. In fact, the opposite is true. The number of its adherents has perhaps even increased, and in the hands of epigones it has become even more systematic, undeviating, and precise.

Formalism has ceased to exist in the sense that it no longer leads to the further development of the system, and the system no longer pushes its creators forward. On the contrary, it is necessary to react against it in order to move forward again. And this reaction must be against formalism as a whole and consistent system, the form in which it continues to exist as a breaking factor in the personal development of the formalists themselves.

The creators of this system, their talents and their temperaments, remain. And to a significant degree their modes of thought are still with us. But the majority of them already feel this system to be a burden and are striving to overcome it; each, however, in his own way, as we have seen.

75

In vain do the formalists say that their method is evolving. That is not so. Each of the individual formalists is evolving, but their system is not. In fact, the evolution of the formalists themselves is taking place at the expense of the system, at the expense of its dissolution, and is only productive to that extent.

The actual, complete evolution of the formalists will be the death of formalism.

It is at the formal method as a unified and consistent system that criticism must be directed.

To do this it is first necessary to distinguish its basic principles and concepts. Each of these concepts and principles must be taken in connection with the whole formalist system rather than in isolation. Moreover, criticism of one or another concept must be constructed on the basis of the actual role of the given concept in the whole system and its methodological role in concrete formalist research, rather than on the basis of formalist declarations of its role.

Only criticism that is so oriented will be a systematic criticism of the essential issues.

The Basic Elements of Formalist Doctrine

The very name "formal method," it must be admitted, is completely unsuccessful, and falsely characterizes the very essence of the formalist system.

Eikhenbaum is completely right that

> The so-called "formal method" was not the result of the creation of a special "methodological" system, but was formed in the process of struggle for the independence and concreteness of literary scholarship. The concept of "method" was in general incommensurately widened and came to mean too much. The problem of the methods of literary study is not principle for the formalists, but rather the problem of literature as the object of study. In essence, we do not speak and argue about methodology. We speak, and can only speak, about certain theoretical principles—and these have not been prompted by some finished methodological or esthetic system, but result from the study of the concrete material in its specificity.[1]

In actual fact, the formalists are not methodologists like the neo-Kantians, for whom the method of cognition is something sufficient in itself and independent of the object.

From the neo-Kantian point of view it is not the method which adapts to the real existence of the object, but the object which obtains the whole individuality of its existence from the method: it becomes definite reality only in those categories which help the methods of cognition fill it out. In the object itself there is no definitiveness which would not be definitive of cognition itself.

Here the formalist position is generally correct. For them method is a dependent and secondary value. Method must be adapted to the distinctive features of the object being studied. Method is not good in itself, but only in so far as it is adequate to those features and able to master them. The main thing is the object of study and its specific organization.[2]

However, one must not go too far to the other extreme and neglect method.

This is the formalists' mistake. In the majority of cases their methodology is very naive.

Method must of course be adapted to the object. On the other hand, without a definite method there can certainly be no approach to the object. It is necessary to be able to isolate the object of study and correctly make note of its important features. These distinctive features are not labeled. Other movements see other aspects of the object as distinctive features.

It is not so easy to reach the concrete material of the humanities and its essence. Pathetic references to "the facts themselves" and to the "concrete material" do not say or prove anything. Even extreme representatives of, say, the biographical method find a concrete basis in facts and concrete material. Every eclectic is particularly "factual" and "concrete."

The crux of the matter is the extent to which these facts and this concrete material relate to the real essence of the object being studied. Consequently, the question is how, in what way, i.e., by what method are these distinctive features and this essence to be approached.

We may repeat that this question is particularly difficult and crucial for the study of ideologies.

It is necessary to be able to isolate the object of study and correctly establish its boundaries in such a way that these boundaries do not sever the object from vital connections with other objects, connections without which it becomes unintelligible. The setting of boundaries must be dialectical and flexible. It cannot be based on the crude external data of the isolated object. Of course, every ideological object is at the same time a physical object, and every creative act is a physiological act.

If, when we isolate the ideological object, we lose sight of the social connections which penetrate it (of which it is the most subtle manifestation), if we detach it from the system of social interaction, then nothing of the ideological object will remain. Only a naked object will be left, with perhaps a slight ideological tinge.

Therefore, the approaches to the work, the first methodological orientations, the first simple explorations of the object, are of extreme importance. They have a decisive significance.

These primary ideological orientations cannot be created *ad hoc,* following subjective "instinct." In the case of the formalists, for instance, this "instinct" was simply their futurist taste.

Primary approaches and orientations must be set in the broad methodological context. Literary scholarship enters the sphere of other disciplines. It must be oriented in this sphere, must be in harmony with the methods and objects of allied disciplines. The interrelationships of disciplines must reflect the interrelationships of their objects.

In all of these basic methodological questions the formalists displayed extreme carelessness and acted blindly. It was here that they took the first fatal steps that predetermined their whole future development and all their mistakes and deviations.

Therefore, it is necessary to analyze critically the formalists' isolation of the object of study, the devices of this isolation, and, finally, the devices for the more precise definition of specific aspects of the isolated object.

The formalists did not isolate the construction of the poetic work as the primary object of study. They made "poetic language" the specific object of their research. It was no accident that the formalists formed the "Society for the Study of Poetic Language" ["Obshchestvo izucheniia poeticheskogo iazyka," OPOIAZ].

In place of the study of poetic constructions and the constructive functions of their various elements, the formalists studied poetic language and its elements. Poetic language is here an object of research *sui generis;* it cannot be likened to the work or its construction.

Such was the primary object of formalist study.

They then developed and applied special devices to the definition of the specific characteristics of this object (poetic language). Here the methods of specification that subsequently became typical of formalism were assembled and defined for the first time. Here the formalists constructed the basic concepts of their system and acquired their characteristic modes of thought.

When the formalists made the transition to the study of the closed poetic construction, they brought along the features of poetic language and the devices they had used to study it. Their conception of the constructive functions of the elements of the poetic work was predetermined by their characterization of the elements of poetic language. The poetic construction had to illustrate the theory of poetic language they had already developed.

The basic elements of the artistic construction and their constructive meanings were thus defined as elements of a unique system of poetic language.

Thus, the poetic phoneme and its functions were first defined, and then motif and plot were defined as elements of poetic language.

It was with the problem of plot [*siuzhet*] that the formalists completed the transition from poetic language to the poetic construction of the work.[3] This transition was gradual and extremely vague methodologically.

The basic definitions of the two components of the poetic construction—"material" and "device"—were developed in the process of this vacillating transition from the language system to the study of the construction of the work. These concepts were to replace "content" and "form." The hidden logic behind the further development and detailing of "material" and "device" was completely determined by their polemical juxtaposition to "content" and "form," to such an extent, in fact, that they became the converse of the concepts they had banished from poetics.

Under the aegis of this hidden polemic and juxtaposition the constructive significance of the material and device was differentiated into the theories of theme, plot, and composition.

These concluded the system of the basic concepts and devices of formalist poetics.

The basic formalist approaches to literary history were also defined at this time. They defined the work as a "datum external to consciousness." However this formula does not tear the work away from the subjective psychological consciousness, but from the ideological horizon.

The problem and methods of literary history are consistently determined by the formalist theory of the literary construction. However, it is also evident that the revision of formalism itself begins here too. The new concepts of "the literary fact" (Tynianov, Tomashevskii) and "literary life" [*byt*] (Eikhenbaum) were based on problems of literary history.[4] If carried to their logical conclusions, these concepts do not fit within the framework of the formalist system.

The theory of perception and the associated theory of artistic criticism occupy a special place in the formalist system. These theories were not worked out in detail, but they must be explained if that system is to be understood.

Thus, criticism of formalism must deal with the following six points: (1) poetic language (and poetic phonetics) as the object of poetics; (2) material and device as the two components of the poetic construction; (3) genre and composition, theme, story, and plot as the detailing of the constructive functions of material and device; (4) the concept of the work as a datum external to consciousness; (5) the problem of literary history; (6) the problem of artistic perception and criticism.

The first three points comprise the content of formalist poetics. The other three belong to formalist literary history (or are allied to it).

The present chapter is devoted to a critical analysis of poetic language as the primary object of formalist poetics.

Poetic Language
as a Special Language System

The foundation of the whole formalist method is its theory of poetic language.

What is this theory and what devices are used to define its distinctive features?

The first question that arises concerns the possibility and permissibility of the task itself—the definition of poetic language and its laws.

The very concept of a special system of poetic language is methodologically extremely complex, confused, and controversial.

It is certainly immediately obvious that the term "language" is being used in a special way here, that we do not speak of poetic language in the same way that we speak of French, German, dialects of the Russian language, etc.

This is not a dialectological concept of language, one which might be obtained by the methods of dialectology. For instance, if we determined the dialectological features of the Russian literary language (the Moscow dialect, Church Slavonicisms, etc.), the linguistic reality we would obtain, the Russian literary language, would have nothing to do with the system of poetic language and would not bring us one step closer to the concept.

This becomes particularly clear when the literary language of a people is a foreign tongue, Latin in medieval Europe, for example. Latin was the special language of poetry, but was not poetic language. The difference between these two concepts, their absolute methodological divergence, is obvious. Another language of poetry, for example, the Latin of medieval Germany, is not different in the sense of poetic language, but different as Latin. But in formulating the problem of poetic language the formalists played extremely naively with the ambiguity of the concept of "another language." We will take an example from Shklovskii. He says:

> According to Aristotle, poetic language must have an alien, surprising nature; in practice this means it is often foreign: Sumerian among the Assyrians, Latin in medieval Europe, Arabic among the Persians, Old Bulgarian as the basis for the Russian literary language; or it is heightened language, such as that of folk songs, which is close to literary language. The widespread archaisms of poetic language are relevant here, and the "made-difficult" language of the *dolce stil nuovo* (XII), the language of Arnaut Daniel,[5] with its obscure style and made-difficult [*harte*] forms which cause difficulties

in pronunciation (Diez, *Leben und Werke der Troubadour,* p. 213). In his article L. Iakubinskii proved the rule according to which the phonetics of pure language are made difficult by the repetition of identical sounds....

At present an even more characteristic phenomenon is taking place. The Russian literary language, which is of non-Russian origin, has so penetrated the people that it has brought to its level much in the way of popular speech, and literature, in return, has begun to exhibit a liking for dialects..., and barbarisms....Thus popular speech and literary language have changed places (Viacheslav Ivanov and many others). Finally, there appeared a strong tendency toward the creation of a new, special poetic language; this school, as we know, was led by Velimir Khlebnikov.[6]

Here we find a continual naive confusion of the linguistic definition of language (Sumerian, Latin) with its poetic significance ("heightened language"), confusion of dialectological characteristics (Church Slavonicisms, popular dialects) with the poetic functions of language. The author consistently tight-ropes from one concept to the other, led on by vague and naive confidence that linguistic definitions and poetic qualities can coincide, that poetic properties can be posited in language itself as well as in the linguistic datum.

In the final analysis, the author is led by the futurist belief in the possibility of the creation of a new, special poetic language, which would be another language linguistically and, thereby, according to the same indices [*priznaki*], also a poetic language. That is, in it the linguistic indices of a particular language (phonetic, morphological, lexical, etc. indices) would coincide with the poetic indices. This is no less naive than the idea that the artistic characteristics of a painting could be determined by chemical analysis.

If the futurists had succeeded in creating a linguistically new language, it would only have become poetic to the extent that it became a basis for the creation of poetic constructions. Only the constructive function would make it poetic language. Outside the artistic structure, as a special language, it would be as external to poetry as French, German, and other languages.

What is more, Shklovskii raises considerations which overturn his own views. If popular speech and literary language have changed places, it directly follows that the matter does not concern the dialectological characteristics of popular speech and literary language. In themselves, these characteristics are completely indifferent and only acquire significance depending on a definite artistic assignment or the definite demands of the poetic construction. These demands have changed, and other linguistic characteristics have become preferable. One can *a priori* admit that the artistic demands of some literary movement might prefer a language other than its own. The very "foreignness" of this language acquires its functional significance in the artistic construction. Nevertheless, this foreign language will not be poetic language, and no analysis of its linguistic characteristics as language will bring us one step closer to an understanding of the characteristics of the poetic structure.

Shklovskii's methodological confusion over the concept of poetic language is typical of all the members of OPOIAZ. They did not see the methodological difficulty and profound ambiguity of this concept.

Iakubinskii's "The Accumulation of Identical Liquids in Practical and Poetic Language" is extremely instructive in this connection.

This article is no less than an attempt to provide the almost dialectological index of poetic language as such. Of course, methodological clarity and precision are completely lacking. The author's idea is that the accumulation of liquids in poetic language can only be the result of a law of difficulty. Clarity here would have revealed the unreliability and methodological fallaciousness of the article's purpose. Instead, the article accomplishes its paradoxical task. Iakubinskii approaches poetic language as if it were a dialect. As a result, he was to have obtained the strictly linguistic index of poetic language as such. Shklovskii evaluates Iakubinskii's work this way:

> L. P. Iakubinskii's article about the lack in poetic language of a law for the assimilation of liquids and his explanation of the fact that that language permits the confluence of difficult-to-pronounce similar sounds is one of the first scientifically sound, factual indications of the opposition (although, we will add for the time being, only in this case) between the laws of poetic language and the laws of practical language.[7]

In a subsequent OPOIAZ work, it was revealed that dissimilation of liquids also takes place in poetic language.[8] Thus there is no linguistic difference between the two languages. Roman Jakobson reaches the following conclusion on this point:

> It would be correct to say that dissimilation of liquids is possible in both practical and poetic language, but in the former it is conditional, while in the latter it is, so to speak, aimed [*otselena*], i.e., these are essentially two different phenomena.[9]

Thus, the concern here is not with the linguistic index, but with the functions of this index, indifferent in itself, within the poetic teleological whole.

The question then arises: without these purely linguistic indices, what is left of the language system? The proposed phonetic difference between practical and poetic language was not found. Nor, or course, will other purely linguistic indices be found.

Poetic Language
and the Construction of the Literary Work

As a matter of fact, dissimilation and all other linguistic phenomena within the construction of the poetic work are "aimed." If this construction and its demands are not known, there is no way to judge the possible poetic significance of the literary phenomenon. As long as the phenomenon remains in the language system without entering into the system of the work or without being considered from the point of view of a definite poetic assignment, it is only poetic in potential. But in this sense every linguistic phenomenon, every element of language possesses a completely identical artistic potential and only specific artistic movements, i.e., definite methods of poetic construction, provide criteria which give preference to some phenomena as poetic and reject others as nonpoetic. Language itself lacks these criteria.

When language bears the artistic functions in a poetic work, or when a dialect of a given language ("literary language") primarily bears these functions, then the primary fulfillment of artistic tasks leaves a trace in the language or dialect, a linguistically certified trace [*sled*]. What this trace will be like, i.e., in what linguistic features it appears, will depend on the nature of the ruling poetic movement. Thus, if the ruling artistic school is linguistically conservative, the development of the literary language might regress in some respects; the lexicon of "literary language" might grow in a certain direction, certain changes in phonetic composition are possible, and so on.

But all of these traces, taken as linguistic features of language itself — lexical, morphological, phonetic — cannot be called features of poetic language as such. Other ruling movements will leave completely different traces in language. New constructive principles will make demands on other aspects of language and force it to develop in another direction.

It is necessary to see language as a closed poetic construction in order to speak of it as a single system of poetic language. According to this understanding, the conditions and elements of language turn out to be poetic elements having definite constructive functions.

Of course, the notion that language is a closed artistic construction is absolutely inadmissible. However, it is this very notion that is tacitly and unconsciously proposed in the formalist theory of poetic language.

It goes without saying that the formalists were not the first to think of the concept of poetic language. It was current earlier, particularly in the work of Potebnia, who in this connection continued the traditions of Humboldt.

However, Potebnia's concept of poetic language was completely different from the formalists'. Potebnia's teachings did not concern the system of poetic language, but the poetic nature of language as such. In this connection he was quite consistent in asserting that the word is an artistic work, i.e., a poetic construction. Every meaningful element of language was for him a little artistic work, and every elementary philological act (a name, a definition, etc.) an artistic creation.

Potebnia's point of view can scarcely be accepted. But its mistakes lead in another direction than the mistakes of the formalists. It is necessary to note that the ideas of poetic language developed by the symbolists Andrei Belyi and Viacheslav Ivanov were the development of the views of Potebnia and therefore different in principle from formalist ideas.

Language acquires poetic characteristics only in the concrete poetic construction. These characteristics do not belong to language in its linguistic capacity, but to the construction, whatever its form may be. The most elementary everyday utterance or apt expression may be perceived artistically in certain circumstances. Even an individual word may be perceived as a poetic utterance—only, of course, under certain circumstances in which it is related to a definite background and supplied with a theme or other elements.

But one cannot disengage oneself from the forms and the concrete organization of the utterance without losing the indices of poetry. These indices belong to the organizational forms of language within the bounds of the concrete utterance or the poetic work. Only the utterance can be beautiful, just as only the utterance can be true or false, bold or timid, etc. All of these definitions only pertain to the organization of the utterance and work in connection with the functions they fulfill in the unity of social life and, in particular, in the concrete unity of the ideological horizon.

Linguistics, while building the concepts of language and its syntactic, morphological, lexical, etc. elements, digresses from the organizational forms of concrete utterances and their socioideological functions. Therefore, the language of linguistics and linguistic elements are indifferent to cognitive truth, poetic beauty, political correctness, and so on.

Such an abstraction is completely permissible and necessary, and is dictated by the cognitive and practical goals of linguistics itself. Without it the concept of language as a system could not be developed. Therefore, it is possible and necessary to study the functions of language and its elements within the poetic construction, as well as its functions in the various types of everyday utterances, oratorical addresses, scholarly formulations, and so on. It is true that this study must be guided by linguistics, but it will not be linguistic. Only the forms and goals of corresponding ideological formations are able to provide guiding principles for the selection and evaluation of linguistic elements. But such a study of the functions of language in poetry is radically different from the study of "poetic language" as a special language system.

Poetics and Linguistics

The formalists uncritically projected the constructive features of the poetic work into the system of language and transferred the linguistic elements of language directly into the poetic construction. This led to the incorrect orientation of poetics toward linguistics—in a veiled or overt form, to a greater or lesser degree.

Iakubinskii's article "On the Poetic Combination of Glossemes" is quite typical in this respect.[10] Iakubinskii begins from the breakdown of speech into phonemes, morphemes, syntagmas, and sememes, and proposes that this breakdown is essential to the poetic construction as well. He supposes that the poetic work is purposely oriented toward phonemes, morphemes, and so on. Therefore, he ascribes an independent poetic meaning to the creative combinations of these elements, i.e., to combinations of pure grammatical forms.

The breakdown of language into phonetic, morphological, etc. elements is important and essential from the point of view of linguistics. As a system, language is really made of these elements. But it does not follow from this that morphemes, phonemes, and other linguistic categories are independent constructive elements of the poetic work, that poetic works are also made of grammatical forms.

Of course, Iakubinskii is wrong. It is necessary to disengage oneself from the actual constructive forms of the poetic work and from its ideological significance and to look at it with the eyes of a linguist to detect glosseme combinations in it. The linguistic analysis of a poetic work has no criteria for separating what is poetically significant from what is not. Within the bounds of such an analysis there is absolutely no way to judge the extent to which the linguistic elements isolated are elements of the poetic construction itself.

For the same reason, Zhirmunskii's attempt to formulate poetics as poetic linguistics was completely unfounded.

"In as much as the word is the material of poetry," says Zhirmunskii, "the foundation of the systematic development of poetics should be the classification of the facts of the language which linguistics provides. Each of these facts, being subordinated to the artistic assignment, becomes a poetic device. Thus each chapter of theoretical poetics should have a corresponding chapter in the study of language."[11] According to Zhirmunskii the divisions of poetics are poetic phonetics, poetic syntax, poetic semantics, etc.

Zhirmunskii's attempt is based on the totally unproven proposition that the linguistic element of language and the constructive element of the work necessarily coincide. We submit that they do not and cannot coincide because they are phenomena from different levels.

Results of the Methodological
Analysis of the Problem of Poetic Language

Our analysis of the problem of poetic language may now be summed up:

1) There is no such thing as a system of poetic language. The indices of the poetic do not belong to language and its elements, but only to poetic constructions.

2) One can only speak of the poetic functions of language and its elements in the construction of the poetic work or in the construction of more elementary poetic formulations (utterances). The nature of these functions and the extent to which elements of language can become independent bearers of constructive functions (not as language elements, but as elements of constructions) completely depends upon the features of the given poetic construction.

3) The formalists, taking the possibility of poetic language as something self-evident, did not notice any of the methodological difficulties and ambiguities of the concept. Therefore, without any precautions, they constructed a theory in which poetic language was a special language system and then attempted to find purely linguistic laws and indices for the poetic.

4) Their initial vague conception was to a significant extent determined by naive futurist visions of a special poetic language, of the possibility that poetic and linguistic indices could directly coincide. As a result the formalists' theory of poetic language was an uncritical transference of the narrowly partisan conception of poetic structure they had borrowed from the futurists to language and its forms.

The Apophatic Method
of Determining the Characteristics of Poetic Language

Without considering whether the very concept of poetic language was correct, the formalists immediately set to work establishing its distinctive features. In the course of this work, all the basic concepts of the formal method were developed, to be later applied to the poetic construction.

Let us, like the formalists, assume that this work is proper and follow it to its conclusion; that is, let us see how the formalists determined the distinctive features of poetic language.

The formalists began with the juxtaposition of two language systems—poetic and practical (communicative) language. Their major task was to prove this juxtaposition. This naked juxtaposition determined once and for all not only the bases of their method but also their habits of thought and observation, by inculcating in them the ineradicable tendency to seek and to find everywhere only dissimilarity, only unlikeness.

"The creation of scholarly poetics must begin with the recognition, supported by massive factual material, of the fact that there exist 'prosaic' and 'poetic' languages, the laws of which are different, and with the analysis of these differences," writes Shklovskii.[12] This definition of the distinctive features of poetic language was developed in such a way that each of the basic indices of communicative language would have an opposite sign in poetic language.

The basic concepts of formalism—"transrational language," "deautomatization," "deformation," "deliberately difficult form" [*zatrudnennaia forma*], and others—are merely negations corresponding to various indices of practical, communicative language.

In practical, communicative language the meaning of the communication (content) is the most essential element. Everything else is a means to this end.

According to formalism, on the contrary, in poetic language the expression itself, i.e., the verbal shell of meaning, becomes the end, and meaning is either eliminated altogether (transrational language), or becomes only a means, the indifferent material of a philological game.

"Poetry," says Roman Jakobson, "is nothing other than utterance oriented toward expression....Poetry is indifferent to the object of the utterance."[13]

Whatever formalist term we choose, we will become convinced that it was obtained by the same way of thinking. All that it will provide is the negation of some positive aspect of practical language. Thus, the formalists did not define poetic language by what it is, but by what it is not.

This method of studying poetic language by "making it strange" is absolutely unjustified methodologically.

This "method" does not help us find out what poetic language is in itself, but rather what it differs from, how it is unlike practical language. All that results from the formalist analysis is a thorough selection of the differences between the two language systems. This analysis excludes likenesses between the two systems, as well as those aspects of poetic language neutral or indifferent to the juxtaposition.

This listing of chance differences between poetic and practical language is based on the tacit premise that it is precisely these differences that are important. But such a premise can hardly be deemed obvious. There is just as much justification to assert the opposite, that only the similarities are important, and the differences are completely unimportant.

And both assertions are equally arbitrary.

We cannot judge the importance of any given similarity or difference until the positive essence of the content of poetic language, which is completely independent of all similarities and differences, is revealed. Only when the essence of the poetic word is revealed will it be possible to establish which differences and similarities between this and other language systems are essential and important and which are not.

But it is precisely this positive definition of poetic language that the formalists do not give.

Eikhenbaum notices the primary significance of the contrast between poetic and practical language. He writes:

> In order to put into practice and strengthen this specifying principle without recourse to speculative esthetics, it was necessary to contrast the literary fact to another series of facts, this series having been selected from the limitless number of series because, while contiguous to literature, it at the same time differed in function. The contrast of "poetic language" to "practical language" was such a methodological device. It was worked out in the first collections of OPOIAZ (the articles of L. Iakubinskii) and served as a point of departure for the formalists' works on the basic problems of poetics.[14]

Unfortunately, the author does not even try to substantiate this strange apophatic method of characterizing by means of bare negation and difference. What is more, the basis for these negations and differences was the vague, undefined, and, as we shall see later, fabricated practical language, which was selected by chance from "the limitless number of series."

In theology the apophatic method is understandable: god is unknowable, and it is therefore necessary to characterize him by what he is not. But we do not understand why a positive characterization cannot be made of poetic language.

Poetic Language
as the Converse of Practical Language

The application of this methodologically impermissible method inevitably transforms the phenomenon being described into the actual converse of the basis of the difference. Difference is, so to speak, ontologized, and the whole content of the phenomenon being described is reduced to the striving to be unlike the basis and negate it at any cost.

And this is what happened. Poetic language became the converse and parasite of practical language.

Indeed, let us look closely at the distinctive features of poetic language as defined by the formalists.

If one scrutinizes the series of negative descriptions developed by the formalists, a certain system becomes apparent. All descriptions are reducible to one center, are subordinate to one purpose, which is best defined in the words of Shklovskii: "to make the construction of language perceptible" [sdelat' oshchutimym postroenie iazyka]. This theory is still the cornerstone of formalism, although it subsequently grew more complicated and acquired new terminological aspects.

Here is Shklovskii's definition of poetic speech:

> In our studies of the lexical and phonetic composition of poetic speech, of word order, and of the semantic structures of poetic speech, we everywhere came upon the same index of the artistic: that it is purposely created to deautomatize the perception, that the goal of its creation is that it be seen, that the artistic is artificially created so that perception is arrested in it and attains the greatest possible force and duration, so that the thing is perceived, not spatially, but, so to speak, in its continuity. These conditions are met by "poetic language."...Thus we arrive at the definition of poetry as speech that is braked [zatormozhennyi], distorted. Poetic speech is a speech construction. And prose is usual speech: economical, easy, correct (dea prosae is the goddess of normal, easy births, of the nondistorted position of the infant).[15]

An important stage in the development of this position was Tynianov's theory of the dynamic construction of poetic language,[16] which he conceived of as the continuous disruption of automatization by means of the domination of one factor of the language construction and the associated deformation of the other factors. For example, the domination of the metrical factor deforms the syntactic and semantic factors.

According to Tynianov, poetic language is the constant struggle of its various factors—sound, rhythm, syntax, semantics. Each factor puts obstacles and hindrances in the way of others, thereby creating the perceptibility of the speech structure.

This is the basic definition of poetic language. All the other negative characteristics serve this supreme aim, the perceptibility of the construction, its deautomatization. They do so, of course, in a purely negative way, by subtracting meaning, by "making it difficult," by piling up obstacles, by intrusive repetitions.

All of the preceding led the formalists to an important and fatal conclusion: if the only difference between poetic and practical language is that the construction of the former is perceptible owing to the negative devices enumerated above, then poetic language is absolutely unproductive and uncreative.

Indeed, according to the formalists, poetic language is only able to "make strange" and deautomatize that which has been created in other language systems. It does not create new constructions itself. Poetic language only forces the perception of the already created, but imperceptible and automatized, construction. Poetic language must wait while practical language, governed by its own goals and intentions, deigns to create some new speech construction and then wait until it becomes ordinary, automatized. Only then is it allowed to appear on the scene and triumphantly lead the construction out of automatization. This is the parasitic existence to which formalist theory condemns poetic language.

In this connection, for the sake of contrast, it is useful to recall Potebnia and that the formalists began with a criticism of his theory of the image.

We know that for Potebnia, as for Humboldt, the inner form of the word and the image were themselves creative aspects of language, were the very element which caused language to grow and develop. According to Potebnia, the same creative character, albeit in another direction, belonged to the concept.

All aspects of poetic creativity, according to the formalists, essentially create nothing. Poetry uses the creations of other ideological areas as material which it makes perceptible with the help of negative devices, all sorts of disrupting and braking devices.

In this regard, Shklovskii's statement about rhythm is quite characteristic. Rhythm, it turns out, is not created by poetry. He supposes the existence of two rhythms, prosaic and poetic:

> The rhythm of prose is, on the one hand, the rhythm of the work song, the "dubinushka," and replaces the order to "heave-ho"; but, on the other hand, it makes work easier, automatizes it. And it actually is easier to walk to music than without it, but it is also easier to walk during animated conversation, when the act of walking becomes unconscious. Thus, prosaic rhythm is important as an automatizing factor. But the rhythm of poetry is different. There is "order" in art, but no column of a Greek temple precisely fits the requirements of a particular order; artistic rhythm is prosaic rhythm disrupted. Attempts have already been made to systematize these disruptions. This is the present purpose of rhythmic theory. One may assume that this systematization will not be successful. Indeed, what is involved is not the complication of rhythm, but its disruption, and, moreover, disruption that cannot be predicted. If the disruption is canonized, the device loses its power to "make it difficult."[17]

Everything in this quotation is typical to the highest degree.

The basic tendency of formalism is vividly exposed here. It turns out that artistic rhythm is prosaic rhythm disrupted. The only plus of art is disruption. The aim of poetics is to systematize disruption. This includes a profound indifference to all meaningfulness, not only of the content, but of the form itself: it is all the same, what is disrupted, and how, because the disruption cannot even be predicted. Art is reduced to empty combinations of forms whose purpose is purely psychotechnical: to make something perceptible, no matter what it is or how.

This basic tendency of formalism continues to live even now, although it no longer appears in such a vivid, naked form.

Scientific Abstraction
and Dogmatic Negation

The literature about formalism includes an attempt to treat the formalists' negative descriptions of poetic language as proper scientific abstractions, i.e., to declare a conventional scientific abstraction that which the formalists themselves proclaimed to be the essence of poetry (for instance, transrational language), that which the formalists themselves did not consider the conventional device of the scholar, but the device of the poet himself, that which first makes the word poetic.

This was the attempt of B. M. Engel'gardt,[18] who even tried to justify transrational language as a productive scientific abstraction by comparing it to the abstractions from meaning performed by all linguists.

We think this attempt is absolutely incorrect.

There is not a single scientific abstraction which exists by means of bare negation. An abstraction is a limitation, a conditional renunciation of the fullness of the object in favor of some definite, isolated, and positively characterized aspect of it. The study of this abstracted aspect must always be conducted against the background of the whole.

What is more, in the final analysis, the goal of scientific abstraction is the mastery of this whole in all its concrete fullness. Only if this condition is satisfied is scientific abstraction alive, productive, and justified in its progressive movement, continuously penetrating newer and newer areas of the object under study.

In every scientific abstraction, negation is dialectically joined with assertion; only this can stop it from congealing and ossifying. So, although the linguist may move away from the word's full meaning, he does not negate it. Quite the contrary: only against the background of this fullness of meaning is the linguistic abstraction of scientific value.

But the formalists went astray and became hardened in their negations.

The formalists could not make forward progress because they categorically cut off the only aspect of the object—its "integral meaning" [*edinotselostnyi smysl*][19]—which could be the avenue of progressive movement.

The formalists' negative definitions of poetic language are not abstractions, but dogmatic negations. They are not conditional deductions from certain aspects of the object being studied, but unconditional negations of the presence of these aspects in the object.

Engel'gardt's work, incorrect methodologically, is also wrong from a historical standpoint. His assertion contradicts the letter and spirit of the formal method, particularly as it took shape in its first period. For this reason, Engel'gardt undervalues the vital historical link between formalism and futurism.

But even if one should grant that the basic formalist concepts are merely abstractions, it is nevertheless necessary to ask whether they respond to the essence of the poetic construction. If not, we fall into methodologism, into pragmatic methodologism. This is the point of view that any method is good if it is productive. But this is to sever the method from all correspondence to the actual reality of the object, and consequently from truth.

The study of the poetic work as the "orientation toward expression" (as the formalists understand the term) is only permissible if the work is really oriented toward expression, as the formalists assert. If it is not, then no discussion of "productivity" can justify this methodological device. It will not help us in the study of the poetic construction, the poetic construction as such.

The Apophatic Method in Literary History

The apophatic method of formalism carries over into literary history. Only here, in the study of separate works, literary styles, and schools, the role of practical language is assigned to historically earlier phenomena and forms of poetic language itself.

Each phenomenon of literary history is studied primarily, or even exclusively, as the negation of what preceded it, in a sort of pseudo-dialectic. Style is always described exclusively against the canon it destroys. In this area too, negative description dominates.

Shklovskii formulates the situation with his usual decisiveness:

> As a general rule, I will add that the work of art is perceived on the background of and by means of association with other works of art. The form of a work of art is determined by its relationship to the forms which existed before it. The material of the artistic work is pedaled, i.e., accentuated, singled out. Not just parody, but every work of art is created as a parallel and contrast to some model.[20]

The Problem of Practical Language

Given the method the formalists use to define the specific features of poetic language, the selection of a base for the negative description is exceptionally important and decisive.

Indeed, another base means another system of differences. If the base of the formalist theory were not their understanding of practical language, but something else instead, then the whole theory of poetic language they formulated by means of the negative method would have been completely different.

But what is this practical language, the negation and deformation of which account for the parasitical existence of poetic language? How did the formalists arrive at it?

The formalists saw none of the difficulties of the concept of practical language. They immediately took it as self-evident.

Meanwhile, the problem with practical language is the same as with poetic language; the same difficulties and equivocations appear here.

There is no need to consider practical language a special language system. What is more, while one can and should speak of the functions of language in the poetic construction, the analogous aim with respect to the practical construction is exceptionally complicated.

We know that no practical construction exists, and that the utterances of life, the reality that underlies the nature of language's communicative functions, are formed in various ways, depending on the different spheres and goals of social intercourse. The formal differences between individual practical communicative constructions can be even more profound and important than those between a scientific and a poetic work.

The painstaking and arduous analysis of the various types of speech performance and the corresponding forms of utterance from all spheres of practical interchange and practice is absolutely necessary if one is to be able to speak of the functions of language in any of the types of communicative construction. Moreover, it is constantly necessary to keep in mind all the social characteristics of the communicating groups and all the concrete complexity of the ideological horizon—concepts, beliefs, customs, etc.—within which each practical utterance is formed. Contemporary linguistics is only beginning to approach this most difficult problem of speech communication in the schools of Vossler and the philosopher Benedetto Croce.

Linguistics formed its concept of language and its elements for its own theoretical and practical purposes, in complete abstraction from the characteristics of diverse practical constructions and from the characteristics of the poetic construction as well.

Such features of language as precision, economy, deceit, tact, caution, etc. cannot, of course, be attributed to language itself, just as poetic indices cannot be attributed to it. All these definitions do not pertain to language, but to definite constructions and are completely determined by the conditions and goals of intercourse.

If we take the word "communicative" in its widest and most general sense, then every language and utterance is communicative. Every utterance is oriented on intercourse, on the hearer, on the reader, in a word, on another person, on social intercourse of any kind whatever. Every word, as such, is involved in intercourse and cannot be torn away from it without ceasing to be a word of language. The formalists' "orientation toward expression" (Jakobson), "transrational language," and the "self-valuable word" are all communicative in this general sense, because all these forms presuppose a hearer and are all elements of social intercourse (granted, of a special type) to the same extent as telling someone what time it is. The various differences between these two types of intercourse, constructive and otherwise, are completely within the sphere of general linguistic communication.

Understood in this wide sense, communication is a constitutive element of language as such. For this reason linguistics does not and cannot disengage itself from communication. But it does not follow from this that linguistics is primarily oriented toward practical language. Linguistics is disengaged from all forms of practical language to precisely the same extent as it is from the forms of poetic utterance.

One can, incidentally, put the question this way: what material was linguistics studying when it acquired its basic concepts and elements, i.e., what spheres of language creativity provided it with most of its material?

That question must be answered in the following way: the material linguistics used to elaborate its basic concepts and elements is least of all the utterance of practical language. This material was mainly composed of literary monuments in the broad sense, which includes the vast field of rhetoric. This is the source of the one-sided monologism of linguistics. The whole series of language phenomena connected with the forms of direct dialogue have until very recently remained outside its field of vision.

Practical Language and the Formalists

The whole problem, as we said, did not arise for the formalists. So what is their conception of practical language and its features: "automatization of the means of speech," "speech economy," "disregard for sound," etc.?

Practical language and its features were a completely arbitrary construction of the formalists themselves.

It is true that there is some sort of language reality at the bottom of this construction. Certain types of the practical utterances of business and everyday speech interchange of the contemporary city bourgeoisie correspond to the formalists' descriptions to a certain, admittedly small, degree. But, even in this melieu, as soon as intercourse becomes more substantial and the philological performance becomes more responsible (even if only within the bounds of family life and salon communication), the formalists' descriptions seem extremely simplified, one-sided, and schematic.

In addition, the formalists' descriptions in part correspond to another type of speech intercourse which is, however, not practical, everyday language in the true sense of the word. We have in mind interchange in the narrowly technical, industrial, and business sense. Here, under certain definite conditions, forms of expression are worked out that to a certain extent correspond to the formalists' descriptions: a word is a command, a symbol, information. Here the word is a completely inseparable element of the productive process or of some other business, and its functions cannot be understood without an understanding of the characteristics of the given process. Here the word may be immediately replaced by a signal or symbol of another type.

In general, it is possible to state that where speech communication is completely formed and has a fixed, frozen character, and where the content being communicated is also ready so that all that is involved is its transmission from one person to another within the bounds of set, generated intercourse, then the utterance to a certain extent corresponds to the formalist description. But such cases are far from typical for practical speech interchange.

In reality, practical intercourse is constantly generating, although slowly and in a narrow sphere. The interrelationships between speakers are always changing, even if the degree of change is hardly noticeable. In the process of this generation, the content being generated also generates. Practical interchange carries the nature of an event, and the most insignificant philological exchange participates in this incessant generation of the event. The word lives its most intense life in this generation, although one different from its life in artistic creation.

Speech tact has a practical importance for practical language communication. The formative and organizing force of speech tact is very great. It gives form to everyday utterances, determining the genre and style of speech performances. Here tact [*taktichnost'*] should be understood in a broad sense, with politeness as only one of its aspects. Tact may have various directions, moving between the two poles of compliment and curse. Speech tact is determined by the aggregate of all the social relationships of the speakers, their ideological horizons, and, finally, the concrete situation of the conversation. Tact, whatever its form under the given conditions, determines all of our utterances. No word lacks tact.

Under certain circumstances, in certain social groups, speech tact creates grounds favoring the formation of utterances having characteristics the formalists consider typical of poetic language: brakings, evasions, ambiguities, crooked speech paths. It is from this source that these phenomena sometimes penetrate the poetic structure, granted, only to its periphery.

In themselves these phenomena are extremely diverse and are due to various social causes. But it is typical that wherever they appear in literature, the peripheral construction of the work is markedly that of dialogue. The form is that of a concealed or overt dialogue with the reader, a game with him. This applies to *Tristram Shandy* and other works, and to the parts of Gogol and Dostoevskii that the formalists enlist to prove or, more precisely, to illustrate their theoretical positions.

In general, the formalists are predominately oriented toward works which apprehend the more direct (albeit external) forms of direct speech intercourse: the *skaz* and the dialogue (authorial, first-person). Something of the specific logic of practical speech penetrates such works. It is precisely this logic that creates the phenomena which the formalists consider typical of poetic language. Of course, when the unique logic of practical utterances, with its characteristic immediacy and the acute perceptibility of the listener-interlocutor, penetrates the artistic construction, it is reworked and subordinated to the laws of the construction and becomes, to a certain extent, conventional.

The formalists' preference for certain reflected forms of practical utterance in the poetic structure is explained by their close connection with futurism. Futurist poetics is characterized by the extremely direct and acute perceptibility of the listener, which is polemically embellished and to some extent vaudevillized.

Therefore, the formalists' practical language is an arbitrary construction with no definite language reality behind it, except the phenomena we have indicated, which are the least characteristic phenomena which could still be included in the practical language construction by stretching the point.

The Formalist Conception of Creativity

It is now necessary to take note of yet another aspect of the matter. As we have seen, poetic language, as the formalists understand it, is just a parasite of practical language and merely forces the perception of constructions already created by the latter. But it turns out that the formalists' conception of practical language also deprives that language of all creative potential.

A language which transmits prepared communications within the bounds of fixed, generated intercourse cannot, of course, be creative. The vocabulary, grammar, and even the basic themes are already prepared. All that remains is to combine them, adapting them to circumstances, and to economize the means of expression. Given such presuppositions, there can be no impulses or bases for the creation of anything new. Thus the formalists' poetic language is the parasite of a parasite.

The question arises: where, in this scheme, does the creative enrichment of language take place? Where are its new forms and new content created?

The formalists provide no answers to these questions. The creation of the really new is at a dead end here. There is no place for it in any of the formalists' conceptions.

Even in literary history, as we shall see, the new only appears as the result of the canonization of the younger line, i.e., is already assumed present. Nowhere is it shown how something new initially appears.

The basic premises of formalist thinking are such that they only provide the basis for an explanation of regroupings, transferences, and recombinations of material that is already present and completely finished. Not one qualitatively new feature is added to the world of language and literature as given. All that changes are the systems by which the material at hand is combined, and these periodically return, since the number of combinations is limited.

"Deautomatization," "making-it-strange," "deformation," etc.— whatever basic concept of formalism one selects—it is obvious that all it has to do with is external arrangement and localized transference, and everything substantial with respect to content, everything qualitative, is assumed to be already at hand. As a result of this, its basic characteristic, formalist thinking is profoundly nonhistorical. The qualitative development of existence and the ideological world that is history is completely inaccessible to formalism.

The Current State
of the Problem of Poetic Language in Formalism

In their further development, even the formalists themselves partially realized the accidental nature of their contrast between practical and poetic language. But they did not even try to draw any real conclusions from this.

Roman Jakobson was the first to draw attention to the vague and summary nature of the definitions of practical language. He introduced the concept of emotional language, which also was contrasted to poetic language. Then Iakubinskii, in his article "On Speech Dialogue," distinguished between conversational, scientific, oratorical, and emotional language.[21] But no methodological clarification of the problem was forthcoming.

In his article "Lenin's Oratorical Style" (1924) Eikhenbaum states:

In our works devoted to the study of poetic language, we usually began by contrasting it to "practical language." This was important and fruitful for our initial formulations of the features of poetic speech. But, as was later indicated (L. Iakubinskii), the area of so-called "practical language" is extremely wide and diverse. It is doubtful that there exists an area of speech in which the word could be exclusively a signal.[22] And, as far as such forms as oratorical speech are concerned, in spite of their "practical" nature they are close to poetic speech in many ways. All that is characteristic of poetic speech is a special orientation toward the separate elements of speech and their specific use (particularly in poetic language).[23]

If one takes all of Eikhenbaum's assertions seriously, then it is hardly possible to prove the "fruitfulness and importance" of the initial contrast between poetic and practical language. As we have seen, this contrast completely defined the content of poetic language as the converse of practical language. This contrast, which determined all the formulations of the formalists, was a fatal one. Anything fruitful could only appear in spite of it.

If the poetic construction had been placed in a complex, many-sided relationship with science, with rhetoric, with the fields of real practical life, instead of being declared the bare converse of a fabricated practical language, then formalism as we know it would not have existed.

The revision suggested in Eikhenbaum's remarks was never really implemented in his practice. On the contrary, he steadfastly continued to defend the old positions in their totality, even though it was obvious that he felt they had no real solid bases.

Such was the formalists' theory of poetic language.

The Problem of Sound in Poetry

It now remains for us to examine the problem of sound in poetry, which the formalists based directly upon their theory of poetic language.

The problem of sound in poetry is the problem of the constructive meaning of sound in the whole poetic work.

It is immediately clear that the constructive significance of sound is different in the various forms of literary creation: in some forms it plays an independent constructive role; in others it does not enter the artistic construction at all and is only a technical auxiliary, an indicator, like a grapheme. All the other possible constructive meanings of sound are situated between these two extremes.

The formalists made a muddle of this already difficult and complex problem by raising it in connection with the construction of the work.

They improperly changed the problem.

If we consult Shklovskii's article "On Poetry and Transrational Language" and Iakubinskii's "On the Poetic Combination of Glossemes," we will see that the ultimate aim of these authors is to show that sounds pronounced or heard, even those lacking meaning, are able to give pleasure, and that people need words, even if they are meaningless. A great number of examples from newspapers, novels, and memoirs are brought to prove this. The examples are without exception restricted to various instances of the savoring of language in life, the enjoyment of language. But the conclusion drawn from these examples is that sounds may have an independent significance in poetry as well, even apart from meaning, as in "transrational language."

All of Shklovskii's and Iakubinskii's examples have nothing to do with the poetic construction. In the overwhelming majority of examples, the sounds of practical utterances are savored and enjoyed. In the other examples, purely meaningless sounds give pleasure.[24] It is absolutely impossible to draw any conclusions about the significance of sound under the specific conditions of the poetic construction on the basis of this material.

Further, in proving that the sounds of language in general give pleasure, the formalists emphasize that this pleasure is at the expense of meaning, either annulling it completely ("transrational language") or, in any event, weakening it, pushing it into the background. Here, too, the controlling factor is the contrast between practical and poetic language,[25] although "transrational language" is mainly proved on the basis of practical utterances.

In practical language, sound only serves to designate meaning, i.e., has only an auxiliary function. This makes it necessary to lower meaning, in order to make the sound self-valuable. It follows that the transrational word is the highest limit in the self-value of sound. Such is formalist logic.

This leads them even further away from the correct formulation of the problem of the constructive significance of sound in poetry. For the reverse proportionality of sound and sense has no place in poetry or, even if one considers the transrational experiments of the futurists, is not typical of poetry.

The classical situation in poetry is the combination of fullness of sound with fullness of meaning, i.e., a direct proportionality between these two values. It is necessary to begin with this classic situation in order to understand the constructive significance of sound. It is necessary to show how meaning and sound combine in the constructive unity of the artistic whole.

Of course, when meaning enters the artistic construction it becomes something other than it was in the practical utterance or the scientific proposition. Sound does the same. Sound and meaning meet on the same plane—the plane of the artistic construction. Here they enter into a new interrelationship, one different from their interrelationships in practical or scientific expressions.

It is necessary to define and understand this new interrelationship of sound and meaning within the poetic construction. It cannot be interpreted as a simple battle, with one taking ascendancy at the other's expense. And if the latter does sometimes take place in poetry, it does so as only one of the possible instances of the constructive interrelationship between sound and meaning, and this is hardly typical.

It would seem that Iakubinskii came somewhat closer to the correct statement of the problem in his article "On the Sounds of Poetic Language." Here are his conclusions:

> In concluding my brief notes on sounds in poetic language, I will repeat my main conclusions: in poetic-language thinking [*stikhotvorno-iazykovoe mysh-lenie*] sounds come to light in a shining field of consciousness; in connection with this an emotional relationship to the poem arises, which in its turn entails the establishment of a certain dependence between the "content" of a poem and its sounds; the expressive movements of the speech organs also contribute to the latter.[26]

The author bases this conclusion on a series of random examples from novellas, novels, and poetic confessions, and supports it with fortuitous citations from linguistic works.

What is most striking here is the purely psychological orientation of the author—"poetic-language thinking," "emotional relationship," etc. However, we need not dwell on this: the formalists almost completely overcame this kind of psychologism in their later works.

What is important to us is another side of Iakubinskii's methodological approach: he takes the interrelationship between sound and meaning on the plane of language and not on the plane of the artistic work. Therefore, according to Iakubinskii, the interrelationship between sound and sense must be realized within the bounds of the elements of language itself: within the bounds of the separate word, within the phrase as a purely linguistic unit, etc. This leads to the conclusion that sound and meaning correspond within language and that a stable and even constant correspondence between them is possible, that, for example, the emotional coloration of vowels is a possible constant.

If such a constant emotional coloration is possible, then a constant correspondence between sound and meaning is possible in language itself. In a word, for Iakubinskii and the other members of OPOIAZ the matter concerns sound in language itself: sound in the word, in the phrase, and so on.

But all that such a statement of the problem makes possible are the most fantastic hypotheses about the correspondences between meaning and sound—hypotheses which greatly hinder the correct solution of the problem and which it has long been time to abandon. Any correspondence between sound and meaning is out of the question.[27]

However, the above does not even touch our problem of the constructive meaning of sounds in poetry. Sound enters into a constructive interrelationship with meaning, not in the word, not in the phrase or in any other element taken independently of the work, i.e., taken as a phenomenon of language, but in the poetic work taken as a whole. There can be no question here of constant correspondence because the poetic work as such is unique and nonrepeatable, and its integral individual poetic image is also unique. It is only possible to speak of correspondences between these individual unities. Consequently, the correspondence itself is individual and nonrepeatable.

Sound in the poetic construction is not only an element of the word, phrase, or period—of language in general—but also an element of the nonrepeatable phonetic unity of the whole work, and it is precisely as such that it enters into a constructive interrelationship with other elements.

Every concrete utterance is a compact and singular phonetic unity. In scientific statements and in certain literary works, in some varieties of the novel genre, for instance, the material, phonetic body of the utterance does not undergo artistic elaboration and does not enter the poetic construction. Here each sound is only interpreted as the sound of a word, phrase, etc., i.e., has only the auxiliary functions of "a sign of language" for the conceptualization of meaning.[28]

In other, poetic works, for instance lyric poems, the phonetic body of the whole undergoes independent artistic elaboration and acquires constructive significance. Rhythm, stanzaic forms, rhyme, and sound repetitions are expressions of this elaboration of the phonetic whole. Their constructive meaning can only be understood within the whole, for they break down and in various ways regulate the whole phonetic body as such.

Their purpose is to create the impression of the material unity and organized nature of the phonetic body of the whole. This whole is organized in real time and real space, particularly if it is a poetic genre performed on a large scale. Meaning, with its organization, gravitates toward this material whole, is built and develops in unbroken connection with it. For this reason one cannot be understood without the other. Only in the unity of the construction does sound, as one of its elements, become poetic sound, does meaning become poetic meaning, and their interrelationship becomes not an accidental, but a constructive interrelationship. There is none of this in language itself, taken apart from the organization of the utterance as a whole.

That is how the problem of poetic sound must be stated.

However, the positive contributions of the formal method to this problem must also be stated here. Although they were on the wrong track, the formalists nevertheless widened and deepened the concrete study of the phonetic organization of the work. Their information on sound repetitions,[29] which occur with a far greater regularity than was previously supposed, is an uncontestable achievement. It is true that this amounted to a registration of purely extrinsic phenomena, which were sometimes dubious. There was no real attempt to make sense of them. Nevertheless, the phenomena and the problems connected with them were raised and put into order for scholarly study.

In order to correctly formulate the problem of the constructive meaning of sound it is necessary to take account of one other extremely important aspect of the problem.

The phonetic body of the work, as we have seen, is organized in real time and space. It must now be emphasized that this time and space are social. This time and this space are events of social intercourse.

The work is a part of social reality, not of nature. There is no need to speak of its physical nature. It is not the physical sound or the psycho-physiological act of its pronunciation and perception that is artistically organized. What is organized is the socially meaningful sound, the ideological body of social intercourse. The sound cannot be understood within the bounds of the individual organism or of nature.

Therefore, the problem of the meaningful sound and its organization is connected with the problem of the social audience, with the problem of the mutual organization of the speaker and the listener, and the hierarchical distance between them. The sound of the meaningful sound is different, depending on the character of the social interaction of people, of which the given sound is an element. The social audience is constitutive to the meaningful sound and its organization.

The formalists simply did not see this whole constellation of problems presented by the sociology of the meaningful sound. Their contrast between the communicative word, i.e., the word as an "instrument of production," and the poetic "self-valuable word" [*samovitoe slovo*] reduced the latter to an object of individual consumption. In the majority of their examples, the phoneme is simply savored and enjoyed in its individuality. The phoneme is lifted out of intercourse and locked into the sensations of the organs of articulation or hearing, i.e., is reduced to a hedonistically embellished process within the individual organism.

Shklovskii's following statement is typical:

The articulatory aspect of speech is undoubtedly important to the enjoyment of the meaningless "transrational word." Perhaps it is even true in general that the greater part of the enjoyment poetry brings is found in the articulatory aspect, in the distinctive dance of the speech organs.[30]

This is a profession of the most naive artistic hedonism. Shklovskii radically distorts the true nature of the poetic sound. Sound is not in the organism and not in nature, but is between people, between socially organized people. It cannot be understood outside the concrete conditions of this organization.[31]

Therefore, the study of the organization of the phonetic body of the work cannot be torn away from the study of the organized social intercourse which implements it.

Summary

1) Artistic works or more elementary poetic utterances are the actual reality which corresponds to the concept of "literature," not poetic language, which only leads the formalists away from this reality. The object of poetics must be the construction of the artistic work.

2) In the process of literary study, literature can and should be compared with nonliterature, but this comparison should not be turned into a contrast and should at all times be accompanied by the demonstration of the positive content of literature.

3) The literary work can only be compared with other products of ideological creation—with scientific, ethical, and other formulations. There is nothing to justify the exclusive comparison—not to mention contrast—of the literary work with practical language. Literature is found in real and active interaction with other spheres of ideology, but least of all with practical utterances. Interaction between literature and practical utterances is only dominant in rare and decadent literary movements.

4) As a literary movement, futurism was characterized by the extreme narrowness and poverty of its spiritual horizon. It was alien to the formulation of problems of ethics and epistemology and to the formulation of the essential and serious aspects of the ideological horizon in general. Unlike literary movements with genuine content, futurism stood aside from the profound ideological conflicts of the day. A vaudeville movement (at least in its prerevolution period), futurism was oriented on philistine views and practical utterances and, before all else, strove to astound the bourgeoisie with its paradoxes by turning their petty merchant's logic inside out. Formalism's one-sided orientation toward futurism was evident in its contrast between practical and poetic language. The one-sided and extreme nature of this marked contrast was due to the influence of futurist poetics.

CHAPTER SIX
Material and Device
as Components of the Poetic Construction

"The Transrational Word"
as the Ideal Limit of the Poetic Construction

We have shown that the three collections of OPOIAZ were dominated by problems of poetic phonetics; the first two collections were almost exclusively devoted to this problem. The battle cry of these collections was "the transrational word."

The "transrational word" was the most complete expression of both the artistic (futuristic) and theoretical aspirations of the formalists. And it remained for them the expression of that ideal limit to which every artistic construction aspires.

The "transrational word" became the blueprint for the understanding of all the basic phenomena of poetic creation. For instance, it became the blueprint for the understanding of Gogolian *skaz*.[1] The following is Eikhenbaum's definition of Gogol's *skaz* in his formalist classic "How Gogol's *The Overcoat* Is Made."[2]

> The foundation of the Gogolian text is *skaz*....His text is composed of living speech performances and verbalized emotions. What is more, his *skaz* does not simply narrate, does not simply speak, but tends to reproduce words in mimic and articulation, while sentences are not only selected and linked according to the principle of logical speech, but even more according to the principle of expressive speech, in which articulation, mimic, sound gestures, etc. play a special role. This is the source of the phonetic semantics of his language: the phonetic membrane of the word, its acoustic characteristics, become meaningful in Gogol's speech, independently of logical or material meaning. Articulation and its acoustic effect move into the foreground as an expressive device.[3]

Shklovskii terms Gogol's landscapes "phonetic," since they are only the motivation for phonetic constructions.[4]

The transrational word is also the blueprint for understanding the construction of the novel, as in Shklovskii's definition of *Tristram Shandy,* the "most typical novel of world literature":

Sterne was an extreme revolutionary of form. It is typical for him to lay bare the device. Artistic form is given without any motivation whatsoever, given simply as such. The difference between Sterne's novel and the novel of the usual type is exactly the same as that between an ordinary poem with usual orchestration and a futurist poem written in transrational language.[5]

Thus, according to the formalists, transrational language is always the ideal limit of the artistic construction. It is only rarely that art attains this limit, for example, in the transrational poems of the futurists, but it is the intrinsic essence of all art to strive toward this ideal. Therefore, the formalists consistently study every constructive phenomenon as directed toward this limit.

In one of his latest articles, "Literature and Cinema," Eikhenbaum distinctly expressed this striving of all art toward the ultimate, "transrational" limit:

The primal nature of art is the need to utilize those energies of the human organism which are in disuse or are used only partially or unevenly. This is the biological principle of art, which imparts to it the force of a physical need which searches for satisfaction. This principle, which is essentially playful and is not connected with any distinct expression of "meaning," is embodied in those "transrational," "self-directed" tendencies that are visible in all art and which are its organic ferment. Art is organized as a social phenomenon and a special kind of "language" by turning this ferment into expression. These "self-directed" tendencies are sometimes revealed and become the slogan of revolutionary artists—then one hears of "transrational poetry," about "absolute music," and so on. The constant nonconvergence of "transrationalism" and "language" is the inner dialectic of art that directs its evolution.[6]

How can the all-determining importance of transrational language in formalist theory be explained?

The ordinary meaningful word does not gravitate toward or completely converge with its material, physical presence. It has significance and is consequently directed at an object, at meaning, which is located extrinsic to the word. But the transrational word completely coincides with itself. It leads nowhere beyond its boundaries; it is simply present here and now, as an organized material body.

The fear of meaning, which, with its "not here" and "not now" is able to destroy the material nature of the work and the fullness of its presence in the here and now, is the fear which determines the poetic phonetics of the formalists. This fear motivated the formalists' attempts to establish a reverse proportionality between meaning, with its general, extratemporal "othertimeness," and the material presence of the integral "work-object" [*proizvedenie-veshch'*]. The notion of the "transrational word" satisfies this formula.

This reverse proportionality became the guiding idea in the study of plot as well. As we know, the formalists made their vague transition from the study of problems of poetic language to the study of the artistic construction with this problem. The problem of plot also led to the first, ground-breaking division of the poetic construction into material and device.

The Unfolding of Plot

In their first period, the formalists had already identified two methods for the constructive development of the prose work: unfolding of plot and *skaz*.

Let us first examine the unfolding of plot. It is necessary to distinguish plot [*siuzhet*] from story [*fabula*]. This distinction is essential in formalist theory and reveals its basic tendencies particularly clearly.

Story is the event which underlies plot, an event from life, ethics, politics, history, and so on. This event took place in real time, had a duration of days or years, and had a definite ideological and practical significance. All of this becomes material for the unfolding of plot. Plot unfolds in the real time of performance or perception: listening or reading. The line of plot is a crooked path of digressions, brakings, retardations, evasions, and so on. As Shklovskii puts it:

> The concept of *siuzhet* is too often confused with the description of events, with what I tentatively suggest be called "story". Story is really only the material for the filling-out of plot. Thus, the plot of *Eugene Onegin* is not the love story of the hero and Tat'iana, but the elaboration of this story in plot, which is accomplished by the introduction of interrupting digressions. One clever artist (Vladimir Miklashevskii) suggests that most of the illustrations for the novel should be taken from the digressions (the digression on "little feet," for instance), and from the compositional point of view this would be quite correct.[7]

Thus plot is completely contained within the framework of the work-object. It is completely present here and now, in no way going beyond the boundaries of the work. The brakings, deliberately difficult places, and repetitions are not brakings and repetitions of the event being conveyed by the narrative, but are the brakings and repetitions of the narrative itself, are not of the event being shaped by the word, but of the shaping word itself. Therefore, the repetitions of plot are completely analogous to sound repetitions such as rhyme.

What, then, is the event being depicted, i.e., the story? For the formalists story is merely material for the motivation of the devices of plot. Thus, if the event being narrated includes various difficulties and obstacles which the hero must overcome, these obstacles from life merely serve to motivate the brakings of plot, i.e., the retardations of the actual process of narration. If the narrative is about the travels of a hero, as in *Don Quixote,* these travels only serve to motivate the device of "stringing together" [*nanizyvanie*]. Thus every element of the story, i.e., of the event being related, is only significant to the extent that it motivates some constructive device, some object of the tale itself, which is taken as a self-valuable whole independent of the event being narrated.

From here we arrive at an important basic principle of formalism: the material is the motivation of the constructive device. And this device is an end in itself.

If we look closely at this position, we see that it is the converse of the assertion which the formalists began by criticizing. According to the usual, naive point of view, which was formed on a realistic basis, the content of the work, i.e., the object of the narration, was an end in itself and the narrative devices were only technical, auxiliary means to that end. The formalists turned this position upside down by reversing its elements.

But they retained *in toto* the completely inadmissible division of the work into technical, auxiliary elements and self-directed elements.

Inside out is always worse than right side out. In the view of the previous criticism, the means of representation had at least played a substantial role. They had to be adequate to the represented and in this respect were indispensable and irreplaceable. Not just any means of representation, but only one definite means satisfied the given end of representation.

But, as the motivation of the device, material becomes something totally unimportant and replaceable. One and the same device can be motivated by the most varied material.

Essentially, every motivation is equally good. In order to motivate a digression, it is possible to put the hero in prison or lay him down to sleep, to make him eat breakfast or simply blow his nose. The formalists insistently emphasize the equal value of all motivations. What is more, it is possible to do without motivation altogether, to "lay bare the device" [*obnazhit' priem*]. This makes it more pure, more artistically finished, as a symphony is musically more pure and finished than an opera. This, for example, is what Sterne does in *Tristram Shandy.* According to Shklovskii:

> The forms of art are explained by their artistic laws of development, and not by real life [*bytovoi*] motivation. When he brakes the action of a love affair by a simple rearrangement of its parts rather than by the introduction of a third character to separate the lovers, the artist thereby shows us the esthetic laws which lie behind both compositional devices.
>
> It is commonly stated that *Tristram Shandy* is not a novel. For those who make this statement only an opera is music and a symphony is disorder. *Tristram Shandy* is the most typical novel of world literature.[8]

Thus, from a formalist point of view, motivation in art tends toward zero. Every element of material is replaceable and, within limits, quite dispensable. Death may be replaced by a character who separates lovers, and this character may be replaced by simply rearranging chapters.

The meaning of a word is only motivation for its sound. If we do without this motivation, we obtain the self-valuable transrational word, the ideal limit of poetry. Similarly, in prose the transrational device, the device without motivation, is the highest goal.

Such an understanding of material inevitably follows from the formalist concept that material must be absolutely indifferent. If death were to enter the construction of the work precisely as death, and not as an essentially indifferent motivation for a digression, the whole construction would have to be completely different. Death could not be replaced by the rearrangement of chapters. Story would have to change from an indifferent support for the development of plot to an independent and irreplaceable element of the artistic construction.

Material as the Ideologically Indifferent Motivation of the Device

The doctrine of the indifference of material occupies an important place in formalist theory.

Shklovskii's work "The Connection of the Devices of Plot Formation with General Stylistic Devices" begins with a criticism of the ethnographic school.

The ethnographic school holds that fairy tale motifs are the reflection of situations that actually existed. Thus, the struggle of the father with the son reflects a matriarchy, the motif of incest reflects a system of communal marriage, the helpful animals in fairy tales recall totemism, and so on. The coincidence of fairy tale motifs, when not the result of borrowing, is explained by similar conditions of everyday life and religion.

Shklovskii opposes these teachings of the ethnographic school with his theory of plot formation.

According to Shklovskii plot is formed according to special laws. These laws also explain the selection of motifs. The source of the motif and its relation to past or present reality is absolutely unimportant. All that is important is its function in the plot. The coincidence of complex linkages of motifs among various peoples is not explained by borrowing, but by the common character of the laws of plot formation. According to Shklovskii the basic laws of plot formation are stair-step structure, parallelism, frame structure, and linking structure.

The material (i.e., motifs) which serves to motivate these devices is of no importance *per se*. The device is not only indifferent to the relationship of the motifs to reality, but to their ideological meaning as well. The devices of plot formation are only a particular instance of the general devices of art. Thus, stair-step structure has to do with repetition and its particular instances of rhyme, tautology, tautological parallelism, psychological parallelism, retardation, epic repetitions, fairy tale imagery, peripeties, and so on.

In itself, the semantic meaning of the repeated element of a tautology, of the harmonized element of a repetition, or an element of a parellelism is completely unimportant. The repeated element can be completely meaningless. For example: "He finds six seeds,/ He picks up seven grains." Or, in the Finnish *Kalevala:* "She passed away on the seventh day/ And on the eighth she died."

Synonyms have an analogous significance; they are not justified by sense, but by the demand for a device indifferent to meaning.

Shklovskii says:

This phenomenon shows the general rule: form creates its own content. When language cannot provide a word with a corresponding twin, the place of the synonym is taken by a fanciful or derived word. For example: *kudy-mudy, pliushki-mliushki* (Saratov district), *pikniki-mikniki* (Teffi),[9] *shalosti-malosti* (Odessa), etc.[10]

All plot situations are of this nature. They are only chosen to realize the device. Their semantic meaning is unimportant. Thus, only the formal contrast of the father with the son is important to the plot.

Shklovskii sums up his analysis of plot formation in these words:

The methods and devices of plot formation are similar to and in principle identical with the devices of any phonetic orchestration [*instrumentovka*]. Works of art produce a weaving of sounds, of articulatory actions and thoughts.

A thought in a work of literature is either the same material as the articulatory and phonetic aspect of the morpheme, or it is an alien body . . . .

A fairy tale, a novella, or a novel is a combination of stylistic motifs. For this reason plot and its nature [*siuzhetnost'*] are the same form as rhyme. Analysis of a work of art from the point of view of its plot has no need for the notion of content.[11]

The Construction of *Skaz*

The other method for the constructive development of the work is *skaz.* Eikhenbaum's definitive article "How Gogol's *The Overcoat* Is Made" is devoted to *skaz.*

Like plot, *skaz* organizes the work at hand, its "here" and "now," using all the semantic material only to motivate the self-directed play of devices. Here the center of attraction shifts from plot to the personal tone of the author and the style of the *skaz*.

According to Eikhenbaum, Gogol's novella is a grotesque, in which the mimicry of laughter alternates with the mimicry of sorrow, and both are only a game with the relative alternation of language gestures and intonations. Eikhenbaum interprets the famous "humane passages" in this way: the sentimental, melodramatic declamation unexpectedly intrudes into the general punning style and creates a sharply grotesque effect.[12] According to Eikhenbaum:

> The melodramatic episode is used as a contrast to the comic *skaz*. The more involved the puns are, the more pathetic and stylized in terms of sentimental primitivism the device that destroys the comic play will be. A form of serious reflection would not produce the contrast and would not be capable of giving the whole composition a grotesque character.[13]

Thus the subject of *skaz*, i.e., the whole complex of semantic meanings which are being discussed, is only the motivation of the *skaz* as the total of speech devices. In principle, *skaz* can be freed from this motivation. In fact, according to Eikhenbaum, Gogol's *skaz* at times becomes transrational.[14]

"Material and Device" as the Converse of "Content and Form"

That is the formalist concept of material. The governing tendency in its formulation is as follows. Material is everything which has an immediate ideological significance and was previously considered the essence of literature, its content. Here content is just material, merely the motivation of the device, completely replaceable and, within limits, quite dispensable.

Thus, the basic tendency of the formalist concept of material is the abolition of content.

Behind "material" and "device" there is no difficulty in seeing the old dyad of form and content, moreover, in its most primitive form. The formalists merely turn it inside out.

The formalists fearlessly reduce all ideological meaning to the motivation of the device. They have no fear of paradoxes. Even Dostoevskii's ideology is only motivation of the device. Shklovskii says:

> Many plots are based on oxymoron; for instance, the taylor kills the giant, David kills Goliath, the frogs kill an elephant, etc. Here the plot plays the role of justification, of motivation, and, at the same time, of developing

the oxymoron. Dostoevskii's "justification of life" is also an oxymoron in Marmeladov's prophecy about the drunkards at the Last Judgment.[15]

Shklovskii also interprets Rozanov in this manner.[16] Eikhenbaum applies essentially the same concept, although more conservatively, in his interpretation of Tolstoi. Here confession, ethical pathos, and auto-biographical material incorporated into the novel are the motivations of the devices.

The Constructive Significance of the Elements of the Material

Therefore, according to formalist theory, the poetic construction turns out to be the aggregate of its artistic devices. In Shklovskii's words: "The content (the very soul) of the literary work is equal to the sum of its artistic devices."[17] The purpose of all devices is the same: to make the construction perceptible. Every device accomplishes this same task in its own way. The formalists know no other purposes.

The question now arises: just what in the work is perceptible? For the formalists it is, of course, not the material. We know that this is a quantity tending toward zero. The construction itself must be what is perceptible. But, we know that it is the purpose of the construction to create its perceptibility. Thus we arrive at a paradoxical conclusion: we arrive at a perceptible device, the sole meaning of which is to create perceptibility!

This absurd conclusion is completely unavoidable.

If ideologically significant material were made perceptible, it would cease to be indifferent motivation and would bring all of its meaning into the construction. For example, if the devices of the plot were to make the story perceptible, i.e., the event of life being narrated, then the event would cease being replaceable motivation and would be turned right side out. Consequently, a braking device can only make the braking itself perceptible, and not the event to which the braking is applied. Repetition can only make the repetition perceptible, and not the objective content being repeated. And so on. In fact, it turns out that there is nothing perceptible to perceive.

There is no way out of this dead end for the formalists. They are not able to admit the perceptibility of the material, i.e., of the ethical, cognitive, and other values in it. This would mean admitting what their whole system denies. Therefore, they stop at a system of formally empty devices.

By being applied to neutral material the device itself is neutralized and deprived of all positive meaning. The only quality possessed by the formalist device is its innovation. And this innovation is only relative in that it is theoretically based and "perceptible" only against the background of either practical language or another literary work, school, or style.

Thus the device is deprived of all positive content and reduced to a bare "difference from . . . ."

The formalist conception of the construction as the sum total or a "system" of devices is in fact only a "system" of the differences of a given poetic utterance from practical language or from other poetic utterances. And this system of differences is made perceptible. Perceptibility can have no other meaning for the formalists. The reduction of the material to mere motivation condemns the device to complete emptiness.

But this is not the last of the contradictions between the theory and its object. A new question arises: how can one draw a line between device and material? Where does one stop and the other begin?

The very word "material" as used here is ambiguous in the highest degree. It forces one to assume that the artist gets his material ready-made, as a product of nature, the way a sculptor gets marble, a carver gets wood, etc. Their work amounts to shaping the raw material: the artist does not make marble, he finds it in nature.

It seems to us that it is only permissible to consider artistic material to be something found by the artist. It is not permissible to speak of material as something the artist creates according to an artistic plan. Now, according to the formalists, the material is not found by the artist, but is entirely created by him in the unity of his artistic plan.

It is possible to consider language the material of literature, as Zhirmunskii does, since language in its linguistic specificity is really found by the individual artist.

But it is absolutely impermissible to treat the story (in the sense of an actual event), the hero, the idea, and everything ideologically significant in general as material, since all this does not exist ready-made outside the work. All of this is created within the work itself, reflecting in detail the laws of its plan.

We are not finding fault with the word "material" without reason. We know that the formalists called the motivation of the device "material," and considered everything ideologically significant to be "material" as well. They wanted this word to emphasize the extraartistic nature of the phenomenon, its technical, auxiliary role in the artistic construction. By doing so they purposely provide grounds for the false assumption that the material is found by the artist.

In fact, of course, this is not the case. Whatever motivation (in the formalist sense) we may choose, we will easily become convinced of its direct importance for the artistic plan.

For instance, it is not only in the process of the development of plot that story acquires its unity. We can, to a certain extent, ignore this development and the story will still not lose its inner unity and meaningfulness.

For example, if we ignore the development of the plot in *Eugene Onegin,* i.e., all the digressions, interruptions, brakings, and so on, we will, of course, destroy the work's construction, but the story, the unified events of the love affair between Tat'iana and Onegin, will continue to follow its intrinsic ethical, social, etc. laws of development.,

No matter what functions the material may bring into the construction, the work is internally governed by its own organic laws of development. But, at the same time, every atom of material is also saturated with purely artistic laws.

The material is artistic through and through. Extraartistic (ethical, cognitive, etc.) laws of development are in constant contact with purely artistic laws in whatever small element of the material we may choose. Therefore, although we can separate story from plot as the formalists understand it, the story itself is, nevertheless, artistically organized. And to separate "only material" from its artistic organization is completely impossible.

A Criticism of the Formalist
Theory of Material and Device

No boundary can be drawn between material and device. The formalists do so without any substantial principle.

As a matter of fact, if one looks deeper into the concept of "motivation," one becomes convinced that it is incapable of clarifying any aspect or element of the artistic construction. Here we are not finding fault with the word, but with the very concept of motivation, with its meaning in formalist theory.

Two kinds of objections to the concept of motivation in art may be advanced.

First, motivation is conditional and reversible.

There are no grounds which obligate us to consider a given aspect of the work to be motivation. For instance, why should a character introduced to break up a romance be considered the motivation for a braking device instead of the opposite? That is, what is to stop us from considering the braking device to be the motivation for the introduction of the character? In general, why should the device not be considered the motivation for the introduction of ever newer and more diverse material? This is exactly how every work appears to the naive artistic perception.

In the work itself, there are no indications as to what exactly is brought in as an end in itself and what serves as motivation for this introduction. Only poor works include parts which clearly have no constructive significance and only serve as the motivation for the intro- duction of other elements which do have constructive significance. Parts lacking constructive significance hardly owe their existence to the artist's plan; rather, they result from his inability to carry out his plan.

In this connection, the formalists' difficulties with the so-called "laying bare of the device" [*obnazhenie priema*] are extremely instructive. We particularly have in mind Shklovskii's interpretation of *Tristram Shandy* and Eikhenbaum's interpretation of a novella by O. Henry.

Tristram Shandy is not a parody of a good novel, not a parody of an artistically regular novel, but of a bad novel, and, at the same time, a parody of bad reality. In Shandy's house nothing is hung as it should be, in its proper place, and the same is true of the novel. The parody of a bad novel is only one of the elements of *Tristram Shandy*. Shklovskii is entirely wrong when he asserts that in this work "the achievement of form by means of its destruction is the content of this novel."

Our task does not include revealing the actual content of this novel, something which is not even touched upon in Shklovskii's work. All that is important to us here is the meaning of the element of parody. The object of the parody is poor literature, literature poor from Sterne's point of view. The literature Sterne considers bad is precisely the kind of literature which completely fills the formalist prescription. The parody is directed at the novel as Shklovskii understands it, the novel into which material is clumsily introduced, in which braking is perceptible, in which the development of the plot conceals the story. Here it is necessary to add that inept handling of the external construction is the main object of the parody.

The same is true in O. Henry. He writes parodies on the stupid and banal American commercial novel. O. Henry does not expose the real structure of the novella, but maliciously parodies the literary hackwork of American newspaper stories.

The following statement by Eikhenbaum is interesting:

The whole novella is built on this constant irony and accentuation of devices, exactly as if O. Henry had gone through the "formal method" in Russia and had often chatted with Viktor Shklovskii. But, as a matter of fact, he was a druggist, a cowboy, a clerk, and spent three years in prison, all of which might have turned him into your usual observer of life and writer of not-very-philosophical stories about how much injustice there is in the world.[18]

Actually, if O. Henry had chatted with Shklovskii, he would certainly have made him the target of parody. And Eikhenbaum's surprise is hard to understand: there are plenty of people in America who understand literature like Shklovskii does. And it is precisely this way of understanding literature that O. Henry makes the object of his mockery and irony.

We are further inclined to suggest that precisely because he was a druggist, a cowboy, a clerk, etc. he knew the real moving forces of life and, therefore, made such cruel fun of bad literary stereotypes. He knew the real value of life and, therefore, also knew what such "literature" was worth.

There is no way that Eikhenbaum's last assertion can make sense. He himself knows very well that O. Henry was in fact an observer of life and actually did write, without undue philosophizing, about how much injustice there is in the world. And Eikhenbaum knows very well that parody on bad literature occupies a small place in O. Henry's work. He himself writes at the beginning of his article that "his sympathetic stories about poor New York sales girls say more to the American reader."[19] In the same place he notes that sentimental stories of everyday life predominate in O. Henry's American anthologies. Why, then, was it so necessary for Eikhenbaum to purposely distort the real state of affairs?

The concept of "laying bare the device" is in a bad way. Nothing shows more clearly and obviously that the formalists are wrong in thinking that the device is the essential thing and the material is just motivation than a work like *Tristram Shandy*.

It is necessary to be completely blinded by one's theory not to see that the examples brought to prove one's point are in fact the best evidence against it. To see that this is the case it is sufficient to consider this one fact alone: *Tristram Shandy* is a novel of philosophical world view composed of vast ideological material, which, moreover, does not appear as motivation for "laid bare" (i.e., nonmotivated) devices. A work like *Tristram Shandy*, which is a successful and profound parody of poor literary construction, shows the abstractness of the concepts of device and motivation particularly clearly, shows that they can change places, and that they have no basis at all in the real artistic structure.

And so the first objection amounts to this: in the artistic work itself there are no criteria to differentiate between what is an end in itself and what is just motivation for the introduction of a given element.

It is possible to consider any element an end in itself. Then any other elements connected with it will turn out to be its motivation. We have just as much right to consider the formalist device to be motivation and the ideological material to be an end in itself. One has just as much right to assert that some word in a poem is selected "for the rhyme" as to assert the opposite—that the rhyme was selected to introduce a given word.

We are only provided with a real criterion for a decision when there is an obvious contradiction between the artistic plan and its fulfillment, i.e., when the work is immanently unsuccessful. Only such a work contains elements which are superfluous to the construction and only function to introduce others. Other than this, only caprice and crude subjectivism are able to make a differentiation between motivation and device a part of the interpretation of the poetic structure.

But there is a still more fundamental objection to the concept of motivation in the work of art: all motivation needs is a fact which lacks intrinsic significance.

If the device, in the formalist conception, were really an end in itself, then the notion of motivation would not even arise. To understand material as the motivation of the device would be irrelevant. The device would not need motivation.

But, obviously, the formalists themselves understood the emptiness and senselessness of the device, its lack of inner justification. It is no accident that their theory only finds the "laid-bare device" in the form of parody.

It is possible to assert the opposite, to assert that only such a phenomenon as is meaningful in itself and in no need of external validation or motivation is able to obtain constructive significance. The concept of motivation is organically foreign to the artistic construction. This concept may have a place in technology, in practical action, or in cognition. But there is no motivation in art and, therefore, nothing that is replaceable or can be eliminated. It is completely unjustified to say that something in the work of art is replaceable.

Thus, beyond the fact that the distinction between device and motivation is relative, the very concept of motivation is alien to the nature of the object of study, the artistic construction. The formalists would have avoided this contrast between device and motivation if they had not been busy with setting a contrast between poetic language and their fictional practical language, and had instead compared the poetic construction with technology, cognition, morals, etc. for the purpose of a real clarification of the differences between these ideological spheres.

Therefore, the division of the poetic construction into device and material is clearly untenable. Everything that the formalists regard as material has an unconditional constructive significance. And that which they consider device turns out to be an empty diagram devoid of content.

A Second Conception of "Material" in Tynianov

It is necessary to note that the concept of material we have examined is a basic principle of formalism. It was completely formed in the first period of OPOIAZ as an essential component the system cannot do without.

Subsequently, however, certain formalists and fellow travelers of the movement gave yet another meaning to the term "material."

We have already referred to Zhirmunskii's conception of material. We have seen that he considers the literary language, the word as a linguistic phenomenon, to be raw material.

But Zhirmunskii can only be considered a fellow traveler of formalism. However, Tynianov adheres to Zhirmunskii's concept of material, although not without some haphazard deviations in the direction of the original understanding of the term.

For Tynianov the material of literature is the word as such. He states: "There are two kinds of difficulty in the study of literary art. One has to do with the material being filled out, of which the simplest element of designation is speech, the word. Second, there is the constructive principle of this art."[20]

Subsequently, Tynianov tries to establish the constructive meaning of the material, material, however, being understood as language and not as motivation of the device. He says that

> One loses sight of the variety of types and the multiplicity of meanings the material might have, depending on its role and purpose. One loses sight of the fact that all the elements of a word are not equal and, depending on its functions, one element may be emphasized at the expense of the rest, which causes these others to be deformed, and sometimes to be brought to the level of neutral props.... The concept of "material" does not go beyond the bounds of form; it is also formal; it is a mistake to mix it with elements external to the construction.[21]

Consequently, what is involved here concerns the constructive significance of various linguistic elements of language, language being understood as the raw material of poetry, and has nothing to do with ideological meaning being understood as motivation for the device. That is, the original and basic meaning of the term "material" is not what is involved here.

Material, in its original sense of motivation, could not acquire independent constructive significance for the formalists without destroying their whole conception of art.

For then there would be no need to talk about "art as device." The core of Jakobson's famous statement would turn out to be false: "If the study of literature wants to become a science, it must recognize the device as its only hero."[22] In fact, there would be nothing left of the formalist devices. They would be completely absorbed by the ideological material entering into the construction.

Therefore, Eikhenbaum's statement about the historical evolution of the concept of "material" is completely incorrect. He considers Tynianov's book *The Problem of Poetic Language* the basic step in this evolution. He writes:

> From the concept of the plot as construction, we passed to the concept of the material as motivation, and from there to the understanding of the material as an element participating in the construction depending on the nature of the shaping dominants.[23]

This statement rests upon a *quaternio terminorum*. The ideological material which was originally understood as motivation of the device did not enter into the construction but, as before, remained outside it.

And it could not have been otherwise. Indeed, what would have remained of formalism if the idea, esthetic event, problem, etc. had become constructive factors of the literary work?

The Proper Formulation
of the Problem of the Poetic Construction

The problem the formalists raised and incorrectly solved has lost none of its force.

How, within the unity of the artistic construction, is the direct material presence of the work, its here and now, to be joined with the endless perspectives of its ideological meaning? How is the development of the story in the real time of performance or perception to be joined with the development of the narrative event in an ideal time that may stretch on over years?

We have seen that the formalists' solution cannot withstand criticism. They began from the false assumption that the fullness, generality, and breadth of meaning could not be included in the material here and now of the poetic construction. Their fear of meaning in art led the formalists to reduce the poetic construction to the peripheral, outer surface of the work. The work lost its depth, three-dimensionality, and fullness. Their concepts of material and device are expressions of this superficial view of the construction. Having established a reverse proportionality between meaning and artistic significance, the formalists inevitably arrived at the device, which, as the combination of indifferent material, was formalistically empty.

The problem must be solved in another way.

The problem would have been solved if the formalists had succeeded in finding an element in the poetic work which would simultaneously participate in both the material presence of the word and in its meaning, which would serve as a medium joining the depth and generality of meaning with the uniqueness of the articulated sound. This medium would create the possibility of a direct movement from the periphery of the work to its inner significance, from external form to intrinsic ideological meaning.

It is precisely in this sense, as the quest for such a medium, that the problem of the poetic construction has always been understood.

In West European poetics at the present time, there is a particularly acute awareness of this aim. The key to the solution is most often found in the concept of the "inner form of the word." Potebnia, who continued the Humboldt tradition of "inner form" in Russia, understood and solved the problem precisely this way in his theory of the image.

The image was the medium which united the sensual concreteness of sound with the generality of its meaning. Being graphic and practically sensual, the image had something in common with the unique material datum of sound. And, being able to generalize, typify, symbolically widen its significance, it was akin to meaning.

As we have seen, the symbolists formulated the problem of the poetic construction in this same way. For them too the symbol and symbolic signification functioned to unite the external sign with internal meaning.

All of these solutions were grounded in idealism and joined with an individualistic psychological conception of ideological creation and are unacceptable to us. But they correctly marked the way toward the true solution.

It is typical that the formalists, while criticizing the symbolists and the Potebnia theory of the image, did not understand the meaning of the problem, and did not take its true center of gravity into account. This is understandable: from the very beginning they cut off meaning and oriented themselves toward the transrational word, so it was inevitable that they would miss the whole problem.

Social Evaluation and Its Role

What, in fact, is the element which unites the material presence of the word with its meaning?

We submit that social evaluation is this element.

It is true that social evaluation is not the exclusive property of poetry. It is present in every active word to the extent that the word enters the concrete and individual utterance. The linguist does not engage in social evaluation, since he is not concerned with concrete forms of the utterance. Therefore, we do not find social evaluation in language taken as an abstract linguistic system.

What is social evaluation? What is its role in language or, more precisely, in the utterance, and what is its significance for the poetic construction?

The connection between meaning and sign [*smysl i znak*] in the word taken concretely and independently of the concrete utterance, as in a dictionary, is completely random and only of technical significance. Here the word is simply a conventional sign. There is a gap between the individuality of the word and its meaning, a gap which can only be overcome by a mechanistic linkage, by association.[24]

But the individual concrete utterance, even if it consists of only one word, is a different case. Every concrete utterance is a social act. At the same time that it is an individual material complex, a phonetic, articulatory, visual complex, the utterance is also a part of social reality. It organizes communication oriented toward reciprocal action, and itself reacts; it is also inseparably enmeshed in the communication event. Its individual reality is already not that of a physical body, but the reality of a historical phenomenon. Not only the meaning of the utterance but also the very fact of its performance is of historical and social significance, as, in general, is the fact of its realization in the here and now, in given circumstances, at a certain historical moment, under the conditions of the given social situation.

The very presence of the utterance is historically and socially significant. This presence passes from natural reality to the category of historical reality. The utterance is not a physical body and not a physical process, but a historical event, albeit an infinitesimal one. Its individuality is that of a historical achievement in a definite epoch under definite social conditions. This is the individuality of a sociohistorical act, which is fundamentally different from the individuality of a physical object or process.

But the meaning of the word-utterance is also joined to history through the unique act of its realization, becoming a historical phenomenon. For it is the given meaning which becomes the object of discussion in the here and now, and the fact that this topic is discussed in a certain way and enters the concrete purview of the speakers is completely determined by the aggregate sociohistorical conditions and the concrete situation of the given individual utterance.

Out of the enormous diversity of subjects and meanings accessible to the given social group, only a certain meaning and definite subject enter the purview of those engaged in the given type of ideological intercourse at the given time and place. An organic, historical, and actual connection is established between the meaning and act (utterance), between the act and the concrete sociohistorical situation. The material individuality of the sign and the generality and breadth of meaning merge in the concrete unity of the historical phenomenon-utterance.

This meaning is itself historical. The organic connection between the sign and meaning attained in the concrete historical act of the utterance exists only for the given utterance and only under the given conditions of its realization.

If we tear the utterance out of social intercourse and materialize it, we lose the organic unity of all its elements. The word, grammatical form, sentence, and all linguistic definiteness in general taken in abstraction from the concrete historical utterance turn into technical signs of a meaning that is as yet only possible and still not individualized historically. The organic connection of meaning and sign cannot become lexical, grammatically stable, and fixed in identical and reproducible forms, i.e., cannot in itself become a sign or a constant element of a sign, cannot become grammaticalized. This connection is created only to be destroyed, to be reformed again, but in new forms under the conditions of a new utterance.

It is this historical actuality, which unites the individual presence of the utterance with the generality and fullness of its meaning, which makes meaning concrete and individual and gives meaning to the word's phonetic presence here and now, that we call social evaluation.

Social evaluation actualizes the utterance both from the standpoint of its factual presence and the standpoint of its semantic meaning. It defines the choice of subject, word, form, and their individual combination within the bounds of the given utterance. It also defines the choice of content, the selection of form, and the connection between form and content.

The deeper and more stable social evaluations are determined by the economic existence of a class in the given epoch of its existence. One may say that the major historical aims of a whole epoch in the life of the given social group are formed in these evaluations. Other evaluations are connected with the more immediate and brief phenomena of social life and, finally, with the news of the day, hour, and minute. All these evaluations interpenetrate and are dialectically connected. The aim of the epoch unfolds in the aim of every day and even every hour. Social evaluation unites the minute of the epoch and the news of the day with the aim of history. It determines the historical physiognomy of every action and every utterance, its individual, class, and epochal physiognomy.

It is impossible to understand the concrete utterance without accustoming oneself to its values, without understanding the orientation of its evaluations in the ideological environment.

For to comprehend an utterance does not mean to grasp its general meaning, as we grasp the meaning of a "dictionary word." To understand an utterance means to understand it in its contemporary context and our own, if they do not coincide. It is necessary to understand the meaning of the utterance, the content of the act, and its historical reality, and to do so, moreover, in their concrete inner unity. Without such an understanding, meaning is dead, having become some dictionary meaning of no necessity.

Social evaluation defines all aspects of the utterance, totally permeates it, but finds its most pure and typical expression in expressive intonation.

As distinct from the more stable syntactic intonation, expressive intonation, which colors every word of the utterance, reflects its historical uniqueness. Expression is not determined by the logical scheme of meaning, but by its individual fullness and integrity and the whole concrete historical situation. Expressive intonation colors meaning and sound equally, bringing them intimately near one another in the unique unity of the utterance. Of course, expressive intonation is not obligatory, but it is the most distinct expression of social evaluation when it does occur.

In the utterance, every element of the language-material implements the demands of social evaluation. A language element is only able to enter the utterance if it is capable of satisfying these demands. It is only to express the social evaluation that a word becomes the material of an utterance. Therefore, the word does not enter the utterance from a dictionary, but from life, from utterance to utterance. The word passes from one unity to another without losing its way. It enters the utterance as a word of intercourse, permeated with the concrete immediate and historical aims of this communication.

Every utterance is subject to this condition, including the literary utterance, i.e., the poetic construction.

Social Evaluation
and the Concrete Utterance

The material of poetry is not language understood as the aggregate or system of linguistic possibilities (phonetic, grammatical, lexical). The poet does not select linguistic forms, but rather the evaluations posited in them. All the linguistic characteristics of the word that remain after the abstraction of these evaluations are not only unable to be the material of poetry, but cannot even be examples of grammar.

For instance, a linguistic example is a conditional utterance; a pure linguistic form only lends itself to symbolic designation. A linguistic form is only real in the concrete speech performance, in the social utterance.

Even the transrational word is spoken with some kind of intonation. Consequently, some value orientation can be observed in it, some evaluating gesture.

When the poet selects words, their combination, and their compositional arrangement, he selects, combines, and arranges the evaluations lodged in them as well. And the resistance of the material we feel in every poetic work is in fact the resistance of the social evaluations it contains. These existed before the poet took them, reevaluated them, renewed them, and gave them new nuances. Only a schoolboy toiling over his Latin exercise experiences linguistic resistance from material.

This deduction of Shklovskii's is typical: "The literary work is pure form. . . . It is not a thing, not material, but the relationship of materials."[25] As we know, Shklovskii thinks the material is indifferent in value:

> The scale of the work, the arithmetical value of its numerator and denominator, is unimportant; what is important is this relationship. Comical or tragical works, works of the world or parlor — the juxtaposition of world to world or cat to stone — all are equal.[26]

This statement, of course, is not a scholarly principle, but a paradox of the feuilleton variety, that is, a little work of art.

All of its effect is based on the value equilibrium between the words "cat" and "world," "stone" and "world," i.e., precisely on their "arithmetical value." Without the evaluations lodged in these words, there is no paradox.

For the poet, as for any speaker, language is a system of social evaluations; and the richer, more differentiated and complex it is, the more significant the work will be.

But, in any case, only that word or form in which the social evaluation is still living and perceptible is able to enter the artistic work.

Only through evaluation do the possibilities of language become real.

Why are two particular words next to each other? Linguistics only explains how this is possible. The real reason cannot be explained within the limitations of linguistic possibilities. Social evaluation is needed to turn a grammatical possibility into a concrete fact of speech reality.

Let us imagine that two inimical social groups have at their disposal the same linguistic material, absolutely the same lexicon, the same morphological and syntactical possibilities, etc.

Under these conditions, if the differences between our two social groups arise from important socioeconomic premises of their existences, the intonation of one and the same word will differ profoundly between groups; within the very same grammatical constructions the semantic and stylistic combinations will be profoundly different. One and the same word will occupy a completely different hierarchical place in the utterance as a concrete social act.

The combination of words in the concrete utterance or the literary performance is always determined by their value coefficients and the social conditions under which the utterance is produced.

Of course, our example is fictitious. For we assumed that the various evaluations were active within the bounds of one and the same ready-made language.

As a matter of fact, though, language is created, formed, and constantly generates within the bounds of a definite value horizon. Therefore, it is not possible for two significantly different social groups to have the very same language.

Only for the individual consciousness do evaluations develop within the sphere of readily available language possibilities. From the sociological point of view language possibilities themselves find their origin and development within the sphere of evaluations which necessarily form within a given social group. Even the formalist theory of the indifference of the material acknowledges this.

This theory arose as the theoretical expression of the perception of the material practiced by the futurists.

The futurists began their work with a disorganized system of social evaluations.

They took words lightly, as witness their "orientation toward nonsense" and on speech "as simple as a moo." Words lost their evaluational weight, the distance between them was decreased, and their hierarchy shaken. It was as if words were taken from the idle conversations of people having nothing to do with life.

This is connected with the fact that the futurists were examples of that social group which was cast into the periphery of society, which was socially and politically inactive and rootless.

The system of evaluations which found its expression in symbolist poetry decomposed, and life did not create conditions for the formation of a new system. Where the symbolist had seen meaning, activity, a theurgical act, the futurist saw only a meaningless word, its bare linguistic possibilities consequently brought into the foreground.

The material of poetry is language, language as a system of social evaluations, not as the aggregate of linguistic possibilities.

It is obvious that the study of poetry cannot be based exclusively on linguistics,[27] although it can and should use the latter.

What is more, in studying the life of the concrete speech performance, the study of poetry has much to teach contemporary formalist linguistics.

In general, the ideological studies concerned with the life of the concrete utterance and, consequently, the actualization of language as an abstract system of possibilities, must constantly take account of linguistics.

Linguistics will, of course, reach a point at which it will depart from the concrete social evaluation, as dictated by its practical and theoretical aims. But it must take the role of social evaluation into account.

Thus, the poetic work, like every concrete utterance, is an inseparable unity of meaning and reality based on the unity of the social evaluation which totally permeates it.

All the elements which an abstract analysis of a work (quite proper within its limits) can isolate—phonetic composition, grammatical structure, thematic elements, and so on—all these elements are united by and serve social evaluation.

It is social evaluation which inseparably weaves the artistic work into the general canvass of the social life of a given historical epoch and a given social group.

For the formalists, who ignore social evaluation, the work of art breaks down into abstract elements which they study in isolation, only looking at the connection between elements from a narrowly technical standpoint.

If we may conditionally use the term "device," we may say that it in fact does not operate in a neutral linguistic medium, but cuts into the system of social evaluations and thus becomes social activity.

It is precisely this positive aspect of the device, the rearrangements, renewals, and nuances it creates for values, that is important. In this is the meaning and role of the artistic device.

In disregarding this the formalists emasculate the living meaning of the device and trace its secondary and purely negative features, following, as it were, the dead trace left by the device in an abstract linguistic construct of a language deprived of meaning.

Social evaluation therefore mediates between language as an abstract system of possibilities and the concrete reality of language. Social evaluation determines the living historical phenomenon of the utterance, both from the standpoint of linguistic forms and the standpoint of meaning.

The advocates of "inner form" do not understand the mediating role of social evaluation. They try to make social evaluation into some kind of linguistic attribute of the word itself, of language itself, independent of the concrete utterance. They do not understand its historical nature.

In the final analysis, most of the advocates of inner form see it as some kind of naturalized evaluation, mostly psychological in nature. The evaluation is lifted from the process of generation and given a naturalistic substance. This is the origin of the absurd attempts to show inner form in the word itself, in the sentence, in the period, in the language construction in general, taken independently of the utterance and its historical situation.[28] But the fact is that it is only for the given utterance under its particular historical conditions that the unity of meaning, sign, and reality is realized through social evaluation. If we take the concrete utterance outside of its historical generation, in abstraction, we are turning away from precisely what we are seeking.

The notion that evaluation is an individual act is widespread in the contemporary *"Lebensphilosophie,"* and leads to conclusions no less false. Evaluation is social; it organizes intercourse. Within the bounds of the individual organism and psyche it could never have led to the creation of the sign, i.e., the ideological body. Even the inner utterance (interior speech) is social; it is oriented toward a possible audience, toward a possible answer, and it is only in the process of such an orientation that it is able to take shape and form.

Social Evaluation
and the Poetic Construction

The theory of social evaluation and its role that has been developed above applies to every utterance as a historical speech performance, not just to the poetic work.

But our aim is to clarify the specificity of the artistic construction.

Although we always had the poetic utterance in mind during our brief analysis, we have not yet tried to be specific.

Social evaluation always establishes an organic tie between the unique presence of the utterance and the generality of its meaning. But it does not always penetrate all aspects of the material, does not always make all aspects equally necessary and irreplaceable. The historical reality of the utterance may be subordinate to the reality of the act or object, and so become a mere preparatory stage for the action. Such an utterance is not complete in itself. Social evaluation leads beyond its borders to another reality. The presence of the word is only an accessory to another presence. Social evaluation is such a preparatory action in the fields of epistemology and ethics. It selects the object of the act or cognition.

Every epoch has its sphere of objects for cognition, its own sphere of epistemological interests. The object enters the epistemological purview and becomes the focus of its social energy only to the extent that the actual needs of the given epoch and the given social group dictate. Social evaluation determines the choice of objects for cognition, just as it determines the poet's choice of a theme. Social evaluation also organizes the scientific utterance on all stages of scientific work. But it does not do so for the sake of the utterance. It organizes the work of cognition itself, and the word only as a necessary but dependent aspect of this work. Here evaluation is not complete in the word.

The poetic work is a different matter.

Here the utterance is detached both from its object and from action. Here social evaluation is complete within the utterance itself. One might say its song is sung to the end. The reality of the utterance serves no other reality. Social evaluation pours out and concludes in pure expression. Therefore, all aspects of the material, meaning, and concrete act of realization without exception become equally important and necessary.

What is more, since the utterance is detached from both the real object and from action, its material presence in the here and now becomes the organizing principle of the whole construction. No matter how deep and wide the semantic perspective of the work might be, this perspective should not destroy or remove the plane of the utterance, just as the ideal space of a painting does not destroy the surface of the picture.[29]

For this reason the formation of the utterance, its development in the real time of performance and perception, is the initial and concluding point in the whole organization. Everything is compactly situated on this real plane of expression. But it does not at all follow that this plane becomes "transrational." It can accommodate any semantic perspective without losing its concreteness and nearness.

Therefore, story is not dispensable (in nonmotivated art) or mere motivation for the development of plot (brakings, digressions, etc.). The story develops together with the plot: the event being narrated and the event of narration itself merge in the single event of the artistic work. Social evaluation organizes how we see and conceptualize the event being communicated, for we only see and conceptualize what interests or affects us in one way or another. Social evaluation also organizes the forms by which the event is communicated: the arrangement of the material into digressions, returns, repetitions, etc., is permeated with the single logic of social evaluation.

In the same way, the plane of *skaz* contains the full depth of the narrative. Eikhenbaum is wrong in asserting that "humaneness toward one's inferior fellow man" and Akakii Akakievich's "insignificance" are only motivation for the device of grotesque change from punning intonation to that of sentimental melodrama.[30]

The same principle organizes the way the author sees and conceptualizes the life of someone like Akakii Akakievich and the intonation of the *skaz* about him. The fictional event in the life of Akakii Akakievich and the event of the actual *skaz* about it merge in the historical event of Gogol's story. In this way, *The Overcoat* entered the historical life of Russia and became an active factor in it.

Thus, the reality of the artistic representation, its development in the real time of social intercourse, and the ideological significance of the event being represented interpenetrate each other in the unity of the poetic construction.

But this construction cannot be completely understood at a remove from the conditions of its social realization. For the actual development of the work, of the plot or *skaz,* for example, is constantly oriented toward an audience and cannot be understood outside of the interrelationship between speaker and listener or author and reader.

Even the superficial phenomena of plot development that Shklovskii analyzes—digressions, brakings, hints, riddles, etc.—express the unique interaction between author and reader, the play of two consciousnesses, one of which knows while the other does not, one of which waits while the other destroys the expectation, and so on.

Similarly, *skaz* is constantly oriented toward a corresponding audience reaction, on its support as a chorus, or on its opposition. Every *skaz* sharply and profoundly reacts to the atmosphere of social values.

The curve of the *skaz* is the graph of the fluctuations of the value atmosphere of the social collective within which the *skaz* is oriented, or which it stylizes.

Such is the role of social evaluation in the poetic construction.

In the next chapter we will consider in more detail the constructive significance of the various separate elements of the poetic work.

CHAPTER SEVEN
The Elements
of the Artistic Construction

The Problem of Genre

The last problem the formalists encountered was that of genre. This problem was inevitably last because their first problem was poetic language rather than the construction of the work.

They arrived at the problem of genre when all the other basic elements of the construction were already studied and defined and the formalist poetics was finished.

The formalists usually define genre as a certain constant, specific grouping of devices with a defined dominant. Since the basic devices had already been defined, genre was mechanically seen as being composed of devices. Therefore, the formalists did not understand the real meaning of genre.

Poetics should really begin with genre, not end with it. For genre is the typical form of the whole work, the whole utterance. A work is only real in the form of a definite genre. Each element's constructive meaning can only be understood in connection with genre. If the problem of genre, as the problem of the artistic whole, had been formulated at the right time, it would have been impossible for the formalists to ascribe independent constructive significance to abstract elements of language.

Genre is the typical totality of the artistic utterance, and a vital totality, a finished and resolved whole. The problem of finalization [*zavershenie*] is one of the most important problems of genre theory.[1]

Suffice it to say that, except for art, no sphere of ideological creativity knows finalization in the strict sense of the word. Outside of art, all finalization, every end, is conditional, superficial, and is most often defined by external factors rather than factors intrinsic to the object itself. The end of a scientific work is an illustration of such a conditional finalization. In essence, a scientific work never ends: one work takes up where the other leaves off. Science is an endless unity. It cannot be broken down into a series of finished and self-sufficient works. The

129

same is true of other spheres of ideology. There are really no finished works there.

Furthermore, where the practical or scientific utterance does show a certain superficial finalization, this finalization is semiartistic in nature. It does not affect the object of the utterance.

To put it another way: compositional finalization is possible in all spheres of ideological creation, but real thematic finalization is impossible. Only a few philosophical systems, such as that of Hegel, pretend to thematic finalization in epistemology. In the other spheres of ideology, only religion has such pretensions.

But the essence of literature is in substantial, objective, thematic finalization, as opposed to the superficial finalization of the utterance in speech. Compositional finalization, confined to the literary periphery, can at times even be absent. The device of vagueness [*nedoskazannost'*] is possible. But this external vagueness only sets off the inner thematic finalization more strongly.

Finalization should not be confused with ending. Termination is only possible in the temporal arts.

The problem of finalization has not yet been properly appreciated, despite its importance as a specific feature of art that distinguishes it from all other spheres of ideology.

Every art has its own proper types and modes of finalization, depending upon the material and its constructive possibilities. The breakdown of the various arts into genres is, to a significant extent, determined by types of finalization. Every genre represents a special way of constructing and finalizing a whole, finalizing it essentially and thematically (we repeat), and not just conditionally or compositionally.

We will see that when the formalists formulated the problem of the whole and the problem of genre they only touched upon questions of compositional ending. The problem of genuine thematic finalization was unknown to them. In place of the problem of the three-dimensional constructive whole, they always dealt with the surface problem of composition as the distribution of literary themes and masses, or even of simply transrational masses. It is clear that there was no basis in this for the productive formulation and solution of the problems of genre finalization.

The Two-fold
Orientation of Genre in Reality

An artistic whole of any type, i.e., of any genre, has a two-fold orientation in reality, and the characteristics of this orientation determine the type of the whole, i.e., its genre.

In the first place, the work is oriented toward the listener and perceiver, and toward the definite conditions of performance and perception. In the second place, the work is oriented in life, from within, one might say, by its thematic content. Every genre has its own orientation in life, with reference to its events, problems, etc.

The first orientation is in the direction of real space and real time: the work is loud or soft, it is associated with the church, or the stage or screen. It is a part of a celebration, or simply leisure. It presupposes a particular audience, this or that type of reaction, and one or another relationship between the audience and the author. The work occupies a certain place in everyday life and is joined to or brought nearer some ideological sphere.

The ode, for instance, was part of the civil celebration, i.e., was directly connected with political life. The lyrical prayer could be part of religious worship or, in any case, could be associated with it.

Thus the work enters life and comes into contact with various aspects of its environment. It does so in the process of its actual realization as something performed, heard, read at a definite time, in a definite place, under definite conditions. Its phonetic temporal body occupies a definite place in life. It takes a position between people organized in some way. The varieties of the dramatic, lyrical, and epic genres are determined by this direct orientation of the word as fact, or, more precisely, by the word as a historic achievement in its surrounding environment.[2]

But the intrinsic, thematic determinateness of genres is no less important.

Each genre is only able to control certain definite aspects of reality. Each genre possesses definite principles of selection, definite forms for seeing and conceptualizing reality, and a definite scope and depth of penetration.

The Thematic Unity of the Work

What is the thematic unity of the work? In what plane is its unity defined?

Here is Tomashevskii's definition of the thematic unity of the work:

> The various sentences of the artistic expression combine according to meaning and result in a definite construction unified by a common idea or theme. Theme (what is talked about) is the unity of the meanings of the separate elements of the work. One may speak of the theme of the whole work and of the themes of its separate parts. Every work written in a meaningful language has a theme . . . .
>
> For a literary construction to be a unified work, it must have a unifying theme which unfolds as the work develops.[3]

This is a typical definition of thematic unity. When the formalists speak of thematic unity, this is what they mean. Zhirmunskii's definition in his "The Aims of Poetics" is analogous.

We think Tomashevskii's definition is radically wrong. The thematic unity of the work is not the combination of the meanings of its words and individual sentences. The extremely difficult problem of the relationship of word to theme is distorted by this definition. The linguistic conception of the meaning of the word and sentence is satisfactory for the word and sentence as such, but not for the theme. The theme is not composed of these meanings; it is formed with their help, but they only help to the same extent as all the other semantic elements of language. Language helps us master the theme, but we should not make theme an element of language.

Theme always transcends language. Furthermore, it is the whole utterance as speech performance that is directed at the theme, not the separate word, sentence, or period. It is the whole utterance and its forms, which cannot be reduced to any linguistic forms, which control the theme. The theme of the work is the theme of the whole utterance as a definite sociohistorical act. Consequently, it is inseparable from the total situation of the utterance to the same extent that it is inseparable from linguistic elements.

Therefore, one cannot place theme in the utterance as if locking it into a box. The aggregate of the meanings of the work's literary elements is only one of the means of controlling the theme and is not the theme itself. And it is only possible to speak of the themes of the various parts of the work by imagining these parts to be separate and finished utterances independently oriented in reality.

The fact that theme does not correspond to the aggregate of meanings of the work's literary elements and cannot be made an element of the word gives rise to a number of important methodological principles.

Theme cannot be studied on the same plane as the phoneme, poetic syntax, etc., as Zhirmunskii proposes and the formalists in fact do. This method of study is only good for the meanings of words and sentences, i.e., for semantics as one aspect of the literary material participating in the construction of the theme. The theme itself, theme being understood as the theme of the whole utterance, cannot be studied this way.

Further, it becomes clear that the forms of the whole, i.e., the genre forms, essentially determine the theme. It is not the sentence, the period, or their aggregate that implement the theme, but the novella, the novel, the lyric, the fairy tale—and these genre forms do not lend themselves to any syntactic definition. The fairy tale as such does not consist of sentences and periods. It follows that the thematic unity of the work is inseparable from its primary orientation in its environment, inseparable, that is to say, from the circumstances of place and time.

Thus, between the two-fold orientation of the work in reality, between the external, direct orientation and the internal, thematic orientation, an unbreakable connection and interdependence develops. One determines the other. The two-fold orientation turns out to be a single, two-sided orientation.

The thematic unity of the work and its real place in life organically grow together in the unity of the genre. The unity of the factual reality of the word and its meaning which we discussed in the preceding chapter is most fully realized in the genre. Reality is comprehended with the help of the real word, the word-utterance. The word's definite forms of reality are connected with the definite forms of reality the word helps comprehend. In poetry this connection is organic and comprehensive, which makes the finalization of the utterance possible. Genre is the organic unity of theme with what lies beyond it.

Genre and Reality

If we approach genre from the point of view of its intrinsic thematic relationship to reality and the generation of reality, we may say that every genre has its methods and means of seeing and conceptualizing reality, which are accessible to it alone. Just as a graph is able to deal with aspects of spatial form inaccessible to artistic painting, and vice versa, the lyric, to choose one example, has access to aspects of reality and life which are either inaccessible or accessible in a lesser degree to the novella or drama. The dramatic genres, for their part, possess means of seeing and demonstrating aspects of the human character and fate which the means of the novel can only reveal and illuminate to a lesser degree, if they can do so at all. Every significant genre is a complex system of means and methods for the conscious control and finalization of reality.

The old concept that man is conscious of and conceptualizes reality through language is basically correct. It is true that no distinct or clear consciousness of the world is possible outside of the word. Language and its forms play an essential role in the process of the consciousness's refraction of existence.

However, an important point must be added to this principle. The consciousness and cognition of reality is not achieved through language and its forms understood in the precise linguistic sense. It is the forms of the utterance, not the forms of language, that play the most important role in consciousness and the comprehension of reality. To say that we think in words, that the process of experiencing, seeing, and comprehending is carried along in a stream of inner speech, is to fail to clearly realize what this means. For we do not think in words and sentences, and the stream of inner speech which flows within us is not a string of words and sentences.

We think and conceptualize in utterances, complexes complete in themselves. As we know, the utterance cannot be understood as a linguistic whole, and its forms are not syntactic forms. These integral, materially expressed inner acts of man's orientation in reality and the forms of these acts are very important. One might say that human consciousness possesses a series of inner genres for seeing and conceptualizing reality. A given consciousness is richer or poorer in genres, depending on its ideological environment.

Literature occupies an important place in this ideological environment. As the plastic arts give width and depth to the visual realm and teach our eye to see, the genres of literature enrich our inner speech with new devices for the awareness and conceptualization of reality.

It is true here that our consciousness is not concerned with the finalizing functions of genres. It is concerned with conceptualizing, not finalizing. Only crude, unjustifiable estheticism finds finalization in reality outside of art.

The process of seeing and conceptualizing reality must not be severed from the process of embodying it in the forms of a particular genre. It would be naive to assume that the painter sees everything first and then shapes what he saw and puts it onto the surface of his painting according to a certain technique. In real fact, seeing and representation merge. New means of representation force us to see new aspects of visible reality, but these new aspects cannot clarify or significantly enter our horizon if the new means necessary to consolidate them are lacking. One is inseparable from the other.

The same is true in literature. The artist must learn to see reality with the eyes of the genre. A particular aspect of reality can only be understood in connection with the particular means of representing it. On the other hand, the means of expression are only applicable to certain aspects of reality. The artist does not squeeze pre-made material onto the surface of the work. The surface helps him to see, understand, and select his material.

The ability to find and grasp the unity of an anecdotal event of life presupposes a certain ability to construct and relate an anecdote, and to a certain extent presupposes an orientation toward the means for the anecdotal development of the material. But these means would mean nothing in themselves if there were not an anecdotal aspect to life.

In order to create a novel it is necessary to learn to see life in terms of the novelistic story [*fabula*], necessary to learn to see the wider and deeper relationships of life on a large scale. There is an abyss of difference between the ability to grasp the isolated unity of a chance situation and the ability to understand the unity and inner logic of a whole epoch. There is, therefore, an abyss between the anecdote and the novel. But the mastery of any aspect of the epoch—family life, social or psychological life, etc.—is inseparable from the means of representation, i.e., from the basic possibilities of genre construction.

The logic of the novelistic construction permits the mastery of the unique logic of new aspects of reality. The artist organically places life as he sees it into the plane of the work. The scientist sees life in a different way, from the point of view of the means and devices for mastering it. Therefore other aspects of life, other relationships, are inaccessible to him.

Thus the reality of the genre and the reality accessible to the genre are organically interrelated. But we have seen that the reality of the genre is the social reality of its realization in the process of artistic intercourse. Therefore, genre is the aggregate of the means of collective orientation in reality, with the orientation toward finalization. This orientation is capable of mastering new aspects of reality. The conceptualization of reality develops and generates in the process of ideological social intercourse. Therefore, a genuine poetics of genre can only be a sociology of genre.

A Criticism
of the Formalist Theory of Genre

How do the formalists approach the problem of genre?

They separate genre from contact with its two determining poles. They separate the work from both the reality of social intercourse and the thematic mastering of reality. They make genre the fortuitous combination of chance devices.

Shklovskii's works "The Construction of the Story and Novel" and "How *Don Quixote* Is Made" are extremely typical in this respect.[4] He writes that

> The predecessor of today's novel was the collection of novellas. This may be stated as a simple chronological fact, with no need to prove a causal connection.
>
> Collections of novellas were usually such that the separate parts were connected, even if only formally. This was done by placing the separate novellas into a common frame.[5]

Further on, Shklovskii determines several types of frame. He considers *The Decameron,* with its motivation of narration for the sake of narration, to be the classic European type of frame.

The Decameron only differs from the European novel of the eighteenth century in that its episodes are not connected by a unity of characters. Shklovskii views the character as a playing card which makes the plot manifest. Gil Blas is such a character, which Shklovskii likens to an indifferent thread for stringing together the episodes of the novel.

Shklovskii considers the device of "stringing together" [*nanizyvanie*] another way to sew novellas into a novel. The further history of the novel, according to Shklovskii, merely amounts to finding more substantial, although no less superficial, means of sewing novellas together. "In general," he concludes, "one may say that in the history of the novel both the framing device and the device of stringing together developed toward the tighter and tighter inclusion of previously dispersed material into the body of the novel."[6]

Shklovskii analyzes *Don Quixote* from this point of view.

It turns out that this novel is nothing but the amalgamation, achieved through framing and stringing together, of diverse materials intrinsically alien to each other—novellas, the speeches of Don Quixote, scenes from everyday life, etc.

According to Shklovskii, the figure of Don Quixote himself is merely the result of the novel's construction. Here are his conclusions:

1) The type of Don Quixote, so glorified by Heine and beslobbered by Turgenev,[7] was not the primary aim of the author. This type was the result of the process of constructing the novel, just as the mechanism of performance often creates new forms in poetry.

2) In the middle of his novel, Cervantes was already aware that in loading his wisdom on Don Quixote he had made him a duality. Subsequently, he used or began to use this fact for his artistic ends.[8]

In all of this Shklovskii ignores the organic nature of the novel genre.

It will be clear to any open-minded reader that the unity of *Don Quixote* is not achieved through the devices of stringing together and framing. If we ignore these devices and the motivation for the introduction of material, the impression of the inner unity of this novel's world remains with us.

This unity is not created by external devices as Shklovskii understands them. On the contrary, the external devices are the result of this unity and the necessity to locate it in the plane of the work.

This is where the struggle for a new genre takes place. The novel is still in the process of formation. But a new vision and conceptualization of reality is at hand and, together with this, a new conception of genre.

Genre appraises reality and reality clarifies genre.

If no unit of life incapable of being fit within the framework of the novella enters the artist's horizons, he will confine himself to the novella or collection of novellas. And no external combination of novellas can replace the inner unity of reality adequate to the novel.

Sometimes the novellas of *Don Quixote* are insufficiently connected from a compositional point of view. In these cases one finds a new conception of reality that cannot fit within the genre framework of the novella. One perceives connections and relationships which break open the novella and force its subordination to the higher unity of the work.

These connections are formed in the unity of the epoch and not within the unity of the event that enters the framework of the novella. Just as we cannot create the unity of the social life of an epoch out of separate episodes and situations, the novel's unity cannot be created by stringing together novellas.

The novel reveals a new, qualitative aspect of the thematic conceptualization of reality, an aspect connected with the new, qualitative construction of the genre reality of the work.

The Problem of the Hero

Let us now turn to the theory of the hero.

Shklovskii's conception of Don Quixote is typical of formalism as a whole.

Here is Tomashevskii's definition of the constructive function of the hero:

> The hero is not necessary to story [*fabula*]. Story, as a system of motifs, can even do completely without the hero and his personality. The hero is the result of the plot development of the material and is, on the one hand, the means for the stringing together of motifs and, on the other hand, the personified or, as it were, the incarnate motivation of the connection of motifs.[9]

Thus the hero turns out to be simply one of the elements of composition, and of the external construction at that.

But the hero is only able to perform compositional functions if he is a thematic element. The thematic significance of the hero is, of course, different in the various genres. In a novel such as *Gil Blas,* the characterization of the hero is of particularly little importance. The genre of this novel, genre understood as the aggregate of the means for seeing and conceptualizing reality, is not directed toward character, but toward the adventure.

But even here the hero is not a thread for the stringing together of separate episodes. All these episodes are, nevertheless, formed within the significant unity of one life, lived by one and the same hero. The unity of the hero is thematically necessary in the picaresque novel, as it is in the adventure novel, but this unity is not one of character.

Don Quixote is different. It is no accident that its hero was "glorified by Heine and beslobbered by Turgenev." It is possible to disagree with the concrete thematic elaboration and interpretation of this image of the hero. All interpretations of artistic images are relative and conditional. But the very fact that such interpretations are possible and necessary is important. It is evidence that this hero bears deeper thematic functions in the work.

According to Shklovskii all that Cervantes needed at the start was Don Quixote's madness or even, more precisely, his stupidity as motivation for a succession of adventures. The author subsequently began to use his character as motivation for the introduction of his own views, which were far from stupid and often exceptional. The result was that Don Quixote became simultaneously motivation for insane acts and wise speeches. In what followed, according to Shklovskii, Cervantes consciously made use of this accidental aspect of Don Quixote.

This is primarily a specific hypothesis about the genesis of this novel. It has absolutely no factual basis. Shklovskii provides no solid evidence to support his interpretation of the author's original intention or the changes which followed it. He simply ascribes his own ideas to Cervantes.

But this is not what is important to us.

Leaving aside the genesis of the novel and its hero, the real constructive significance of the figure of Don Quixote is absolutely clear, and no such theses about its origin are needed.

First of all, the figure of Don Quixote is not motivation for anything—not for wise speeches or insane situations. It is an end in itself, as are all essential constructive elements of the work.

Don Quixote is juxtaposed to Sancho, and this pair implements the basic thematic plan of the novel: the ideological conflict, the inner contradiction of the ideological horizon of the epoch. The speeches and adventures of Don Quixote are subordinate to this plan, as are the speeches and adventures of his armorbearer.

The novellas not directly connected with Don Quixote or Sancho are also subordinate to this plan, and there are a considerable number of these.

The inner thematic unity of the novel causes its several external flaws to be forgotten.

Theme, Story, and Plot

The real constructive significance of story and plot can now be understood against the background of thematic unity and its realization in genre.

Story (when present) characterizes genre from the point of view of its thematic orientation in reality. Plot does the same, but from the point of view of the actual reality of genre in the process of its social realization. It is impossible to distinctly separate the two and to no purpose to do so. An orientation toward plot, i.e., toward the definite and actual development of the work, is necessary to master the story. Even in life we see the story with the eye of the plot.

At the same time, no plot can be indifferent to the importance of the story in life.

Thus story and plot are essentially the same constructive element of the work. As story, this element defines the reality being finalized in terms of thematic unity, while, as plot, it determines the finalization of the actual reality of the work.

Every element of the artistic structure is located in an analogous position. Thus the hero may be defined within the thematic unity of the work, but his compositional functions may also be defined within the actual development of the work. The thematic and compositional functions of the hero merge inseparably in him: only as the hero of an event of life is he able to enter the work. On the other hand, certain aspects of his reality in life can only be seen and understood through the prism of his possible role in the artistic unity of the work (and, consequently, through the prism of his compositional role).

The artist can also view a human being from the point of view of his possible artistic functions; he can find a hero in life. In this view of a human being as a possible hero, cognitive determinations and ethical evaluations are found in chemical combination with artistic development.

If all there is to a hero are his compositional functions, he could not be perceived outside the work, in life. The imitation of a literary hero in actual life would be impossible. But it is a fact that there have been cases of such an influence of literature on life. Byronic heroes appeared in real life and were everywhere recognized as such.

What is more, a real life can be made into an artistic story. It is true that such heroes without works and stories without plots are strange phenomena. For they do not attain the reality of life because their orientation toward the work is too strong, as is, consequently, their orientation toward finalization, which is alien to life. But, on the other hand, they do not acquire artistic reality either, for this is only realized within the work. The artistic theme severed from the actual reality of the work is the unique antipode of the transrational word torn from thematic reality.

In addition to the problems of the story, plot, hero (and, of course, elements of the story-plot), the thematic problem has great constructive significance. And this problem can be understood both in reference to thematic unity and in reference to the actual realization of the work (the compositional functions of the problem). Outside of art any cognitive problem can be interpreted in reference to its possible finalization in the plane of the work of art. This is quite common in philosophy. The philosophical formulations of Nietzsche, Schopenhauer, etc., are semi-artistic in nature. For these philosophers problem becomes theme and functions compositionally in the plane of their actual literary works.

This is the source of their great artistic perfection. On the other hand, in the novel, where the thematic problem is usually of great significance, the opposite phenomenon may occur: the problem may be detrimental to the artistic worth of the work, may break out of its plane and acquire a purely cognitive significance, with no orientation toward finalization. The result is a hybrid, analogous to an artistic philosopheme.

We will not concern ourselves with other constructive elements here, for instance elements of the lyric theme. We will exclude questions of rhythm (poetic and prosaic), questions of style, etc. The methodology for solving all these problems is the same. What is important for us is the construction of a sociological poetics and not the concrete solution of its problems.

In any case, in the tiniest element of the poetic structure, in every metaphor, in every epithet we find the same chemical combination of cognitive definition, ethical evaluation, and artistically developed conclusion. Every epithet has a place in the actual realization of the work, resonates in it, at the same time as it is directed toward the thematic unity which is the artistic definition of reality.

It might be useful to glance back from our point of view toward the usual division of the work into form and content. This terminology can only be accepted under the condition that form and content are thought of as limits between which all the elements of the poetic construction are situated. Then content will correspond to thematic unity, and form to the actual realization of the work. But it is necessary to bear in mind here that every element of the work is a chemical combination of form and content. There is no formless content and there is no contentless form. Social evaluation is the common denominator of the content and form of every element of the construction.

Conclusions

In our survey of the formalist view of genre and its constructive elements the formalists' basic tendency to see creativity as the recombination of ready-made elements stands out in sharp relief. A new genre is made from genres at hand; within every genre a regrouping of already prepared elements takes place. Everything is provided the artist—all that remains is to combine the ready material in a new way. The story is given; all that is necessary is to combine it into a plot. The devices of the plot are also given and only need to be rearranged. The hero is given, and it is only necessary to string the ready-made motifs on him.

The first part of Shklovskii's "How *Don Quixote* Is Made" is entirely devoted to an analysis of the motivations of the speeches of Don Quixote (and in part of Sancho and other characters), which, as is known, occupy a very large place in the novel. But when Cervantes puts these speeches into the novel, it is hardly for the sake of their motivation. But this is what Shklovskii contends. It is clear that Cervantes poured his creative energy into the creation of the speeches, not into their motivation. And what are the devices of the speeches? What is the significance of their content? Shklovskii does not even ask these questions, for all that is involved are ready-made elements. He only looks for artistic creation in the combination of these elements.

The formalists assume that all the elementary and basic creative work of the artistic seeing and conceptualizing of life has already been done; that is, they presuppose a ready-made story, hero, problem. They ignore the intrinsic content of this ready material and are only interested in its external distribution in the plane of the work. But they sever this plane from the real social conditions of realization. Within the work an empty game is played with material with no regard to its meaning. Shklovskii describes this very well:

> I have decided upon this analogy: The action of the literary work takes place in a definite field; let the types and masks, the cast of the contemporary theater, correspond to chess figures. Plots will correspond to gambits, i.e., to the classic options, variations of which are played by the players. The tasks and peripeties correspond to the opponent's moves.[10]

The question arises: why not replace all the material once and for all with ready conventional figures, as in chess? Why waste so much creative energy on the creation of material? We will see that in their works on literary history the formalists are as close as possible to the most radical answer to this question. They consistently regard the material as being composed of a limited number of definite elements which remain unchanged in the course of the historical development of literature (for there are no impulses for the bringing in or creation of new material). These elements are merely distributed and combined in different ways in various works and schools. Only recently have the formalists begun to revise this absurd theory somewhat. But this revision cannot be deep. To be truly productive it must begin at the foundation of the formalist edifice, i.e., at the basic points of their theory which we have surveyed.

PART FOUR
The Formal
Method in Literary History

CHAPTER EIGHT
The Work of Art
as a Datum External to Consciousness

The Formalist View of the Work
as Extrinsic to the Ideological Horizon

The formalists insistently emphasize that they study the artistic work as an objective datum which is independent of the subjective consciousness and subjective psyche of the creator and perceiver. Therefore, for them literary history is the history of works and those objective groups —movements, schools, styles, genres—in which these works are combined according to intrinsic and immanent indices.

To the extent that this formalist position is pointed against psychological esthetics and the naive, psychologically subjective interpretation of the artistic work as the expression of the inner world or "soul" of the artist, this formalist thesis is quite acceptable.

For subjective psychological methods are completely unacceptable in both poetics and literary history.

This does not, of course, mean that the individual consciousness can be ignored. It only means that it must be taken in its objective manifestations. The individual consciousness is only suitable for appraisal and study to the extent that it is objectively, materially expressed in some definite aspect of the work. In this regard objectivism must be carried through to the end.

However, this formalist thesis does not result in the proper negation of subjective psychologism in literary scholarship.

While liberating the work from the subjective consciousness and psyche, the formalists at the same time estrange it from the whole ideological environment and from objective social intercourse. The work is cut off from both real social realization and from the entire ideological world.

The formalists, while criticizing psychological esthetics and the idealist conception of consciousness, at the same time made the errors of these movements their own. Together with the idealists and psychologists they projected everything ideologically meaningful into the individual subjective consciousness. Idea, evaluation, world view, mood, etc.—for them all these things were the content of the individual consciousness, the "inner world" of the "soul." In cutting off the subjective consciousness, the formalists also cut off the ideological content they had improperly located in it. As a result, the work ended up in a complete ideological vacuum. Objectivity was purchased at the price of meaning.

But, in fact, we know that the content of consciousness may be presented just as objectively as the work of art.

The objectivity the formalists ascribe to literature can just as properly be attributed to all ideological signification, no matter how insignificant or short-lived external appearances may be. For even the most primitive expression of an evaluation (emotion) in the utterance or even the gesture is the same sort of "fact external to consciousness" as the literary work, although its significance and influence on the whole of the ideological environment is negligible.

What is involved here, consequently, is the juxtaposition of one ideological formation (literature) to other ideological formations (ethical, cognitive, religious, etc.), i.e., the juxtaposition of various aspects of the materially objectified ideological environment and not the juxtaposition of literature to the subjective psyche. "Those fond of biography," says Eikhenbaum,

> are puzzled by the "contradictions" between Nekrasov's life and his poetry.[1] This contradiction cannot be smoothed over, and is not only legitimate, but absolutely necessary, for "soul" or "temperment" is one thing, and the creative work is something altogether different.[2]

This is a typical statement.

If we assume that life is one thing and creative work another, quite different thing, it nevertheless does not at all follow that a contradiction between them is necessary or legitimate. And completely different things cannot contradict one another. Contradiction is only possible where two phenomena meet on the same plane and are both subordinate to a higher unity. Where two phenomena have nothing in common semantically, where both do not relate to the same meaning, there cannot be a contradiction.

Furthermore, where contradiction is possible, so is agreement. If there is a contradiction between life and work, then it necessarily follows that life and work are not simply different things, but lie in the same plane and are therefore able to interact and clash. And, in fact, life and creative work both belong to the unity of the ideological world, and conflicts between them are not only possible, but sometimes even necessary.

For that reason the equation of life with "soul" or "temperment" is absolutely inadmissible. This is just as false as the equation of artistic creation with soul or temperment, which Eikhenbaum is completely correct in rejecting.

In the discussion of the contradictions between the life and work of Nekrasov, life is understood as the aggregate of his objectified life—his career as an editor, as a publisher, the social and class orientation of his practical affairs, and, finally, a number of intimate, personal phenomena. The discussion compares these things with his poetic objectification in the unity of the ideological environment, and, in this case, a contradiction is found.

We are, of course, not concerned with whether there was, in fact, a contradiction here, how deep it was, how it might be explained, and so on. We are only interested in showing that it is methodologically incorrect to juxtapose life and creative work.

It is true that the very concept of "life" is too vague and general, but in the given context it is at least clear that a number of objectifications come under the heading of "life"—ethical, practical, socioeconomic, world view—which are just as objective as Nekrasov's poetic observations, although lacking their historical significance.

Eikhenbaum continues:

> The role Nekrasov chose was prompted by history and undertaken as a historical act. He played his role in a play composed by history, and played it "sincerely," to the same extent and in the same sense as one might speak of the "sincerity" of an actor.[3]

Eikhenbaum puts Nekrasov's career as a poet in the category of a historical act. But Nekrasov's publishing activities, his commercial speculations, and his socioeconomic position in property dealings can and should be put in the same category. The point here is not the scale of the historical act, not the degree of significance, but the content of the act. Once the category of a historical act exists, not only poetic activity belongs in it but also all the other objectifications of the given individual, and there can be contradictions between them.

If Eikhenbaum calls poetic activity "a role composed by history," it seems just as correct to assign the same role to all the other aspects of Nekrasov's activity. And if the sincerity of an individual's poetic objectification is equated with the sincerity of an actor upon the stage, it is no less correct to do this with every other objectification of an individual—cognitive, world view, life, etc.

Thus all of man's objectifications, without exception, belong to one world of sociohistorical reality and therefore interact and are able to form contradictions or agreements.

There are no grounds to build a Chinese wall between them. All that follows from the point that life is one thing and literature another is that life is not literature; it does not at all follow that there can be no interaction between them. The difference between the two phenomena, on the contrary, is one of the necessary conditions of their interaction. Only differences can interact.

The following excerpt from Eikhenbaum's "How Gogol's *The Overcoat* Is Made" is no less illustrative. Eikhenbaum, interpreting the famous "humane passage" of *The Overcoat* as a grotesque device ("I am your brother"), states:

> Starting from the basic premise that no one phrase of the artistic work can in itself be the simple "reflection" of the personal feelings of the author, but is always a construction and a performance, we cannot and have no right to see in such a passage anything other than a definite artistic device. The usual manner of identifying some particular opinion with the psychological content of the author's soul is a false path for scholarship. In this sense, the soul of the artist as an individual who experiences various moods is and should always remain outside the limits of his creation. The artistic work is always something made, designed, invented—not only artful, but also artificial in the good sense of the word; and therefore there is not, nor can there be, a place in it for the reflection of spiritual data.[4]

This whole passage is extremely typical of formalism's conception of the objective nature of the literary work as a datum external to subjective consciousness.

The external nature of the work to the subjective consciousness is constantly shuffled around in the most false and naive way until the work becomes external to the whole ideological horizon. We know that everyone interprets and understands the "humane passage" in *The Overcoat* as a socioethical, "confessional" objectification. If it is considered the interference of the soul and the reflection of the personal feelings of the author, the same grounds compel us to also place the esthetic objectification as Eikhenbaum understands it, i.e., the grotesque device, in this category.

This is what the psychologist does. His psychological orientation does not contradict his acknowledging that in the given case we actually have a conventional device, not an ethical appeal. But he will also explain this artistic device with subjective, psychic mechanisms, as he would the ethical appeal.

If we fence off literature from "the soul," it is necessary to do the same with the ethical confession. As a definite ideological objectification, the latter is no less objective and, like the literary work, does not lend itself to subjective psychological explanations. And if "soul" is going to be sought, where else shall we seek it but in artistic works?

This is what those inclined to psychologism have always done. So, if an objective method is going to be followed, it must be followed in all spheres of ideological creation without exception.

The matter under consideration does not involve the interference of "the soul" or the reflection of spiritual facts, but the entrance of direct socioethical evaluations into the artistic work. We already know that, just as it enters the epistemological work, such evaluation enters the poetic construction without losing its individuality and seriousness and without destroying the construction. And in the present case ethical pathos is found in chemical combination with artistic finalization. To exclude the ethical aspect from the artistic construction of *The Overcoat* is to misunderstand this construction.

The formalists always act in an analogous way: in excluding "the soul," the formalists actually exclude all ideological meaning from the work. As a result the work does not turn out to be a datum external to the subjective consciousness, but a datum external to the ideological world.

The Formalist Theory of Perception

As for psychological subjectivism—it is the very thing the formalists were unable to overcome. On the contrary, in severing literature from the ideological world, the formalists turned it into some kind of stimulus for relative and subjective psychophysical states and perceptions.

For their basic theories—deautomatization, the perceptibility of the construction, and the others—presuppose a perceiving, subjective consciousness.

What is more, in its vital aspects formalist theory amounts to a unique psychotechnics of artistic perception, i.e., to the explanation of the general psychotechnical conditions in which the artistic construction is perceptible.

We have criticized the formalists' theories of the made-difficult form and deautomatization in a different context. It is now necessary to focus on these same theories in connection with the formalist theory of perception, since this theory is at the foundation of their conception of the historical development of literature.

We have seen that the concept of "perceptibility" is absolutely vacuous. What is supposed to be perceptible is not even known. It is not the ideological material as such that must be perceived, and the device itself cannot be the content of perception, since its purpose is to create perceptibility. In this way, perceptibility as such is completely indifferent to what exactly is perceived, and itself becomes the only content of artistic perception, and the work turns into an apparatus for the stimulation of this perceptibility. It is clear that under such a condition perception becomes completely subjective and dependent on a series of accidental situations and conditions. It will express the subjective condition of consciousness, not the objective datum of the work.

It seems to us that Zhirmunskii is completely correct in the following excerpt:

> It seems to me that the principle of rejecting basic stereotypes, the device of "making it strange," and the device of the "made-difficult form" are not organizing or moving factors in the development of art, but only secondary factors expressing the evolution taking place in the consciousnesses of readers whose artistic demands have been left behind. Goethe's *Goetz* did not seem difficult, obscure, or strange to the admirers of Shakespeare from the circle of "stormy geniuses," but to the reader brought up on French tragedies and the dramatic practice of Gottsched and Lessing; for Goethe himself the form of *Goetz* was not "braked" or "made-difficult" in contrast to something conventional, but rather the simplest and most adequate expression of his artistic tastes and world view....
>
> Blok's metaphors or Maiakovskii's rhythms really do produce the impression of "braked" or "distorted" poetic speech, but only to the reader who was brought up on, say, A. K. Tolstoi,[5] Polonskii,[6] or Balmont, the reader who is, as it were, unenlightened, unused to the new art; or, in what is the opposite case, these rhythms only make this impression on a reader of the younger generation, who experiences this art as a convention which has ceased to be intelligible and expressive. Thus the sensation of "making it strange" and "making it difficult" precedes esthetic experience and signifies the inability to construct an unusual esthetic object. At the moment of experience this sensation disappears and is replaced by the feeling of simplicity and usualness.[7]

The orientation of the work toward perceptibility is the worst kind of psychologism, since it makes the psychophysical process into something self-sufficient and empty of all content, i.e., something lacking any connection with objective reality. Neither automatization nor perceptibility are objective features of the work; neither exists in the structure of the work. While ridiculing those who seek "soul" and "temperment" in the artistic work, the formalists search it for psychophysiological stimuli at the same time.

The Formalist
Theory of Perception and History

The formalists' theory of perception suffers from yet another serious methodological defect, one which is quite typical of psychologism and biologism: they make a process which is able to take place within the bounds of the individual life of a single organism into the blueprint for the conceptualization of a process which extends over a series of successive individuals and generations.

Indeed, automatization and deautomatization (i.e., perceptibility) must come into contact within a single individual. Only a person for whom a given construction is automatized can perceive against its background the other construction which must replace it according to the formalist law of the succession of forms. If the work of the "senior line" [*starshaia liniia*], let us say Pushkin's work, is not automatized for me, then it will not serve as the background for me, will not serve as the background for my perception of the perceptibility of the work of the "junior line" [*mladshaia liniia*], let us say the work of Benediktov.[8] It is absolutely necessary that the automatization of Pushkin and the perceptibility of Benediktov come together in the single consciousness. If they do not, the whole mechanism becomes meaningless.

If Pushkin is automatized for one person, while another is in raptures over Benediktov, there can be absolutely no connection between the automatization and the perceptibility of these two temporally successive objects, just as there can be no connection between one person's upset stomach and another's overeating.

Such processes are fundamentally nonhistorical. They cannot go beyond the bounds of the individual organism. But the formalists make the opposition between "automatization" and "perceptibility" the foundation of their explanation of the historical succession of literary forms. This is to fundamentally ignore the qualitative individuality of the historical, the fundamental fact that it cannot be confined within the limits of the life of a single subject. This is to biologize and psychologize history.

We shall return to problems of literary history in the next chapter. Here we only want to point out the presence of primitive psychologism in formalist concepts. Estranging the work from the ideological horizon, the formalists connected it all the more tightly with the fortuitous subjective conditions of perception. The one was the inevitable consequence of the other.

The Formalists' Severing of the Work from Real Social Intercourse

The theory of the work as a datum external to consciousness has yet another extremely important negative aspect.

Attempting to separate the work from the subjective consciousness, the formalists at the same time sever it from the objective fact of social intercourse, with the result that the artistic work turns into a meaningless thing analogous to a commodity fetish.

Every utterance, including the artistic work, is a communication, a message, and is completely inseparable from intercourse. At the same time, the work is never a ready message given once and for all.

What is communicated is inseparable from the forms, means, and concrete conditions of communication. Communication itself is generated together with generating intercourse. In their interpretation, the formalists tacitly presuppose a completely ready and static intercourse and communication that is just as static.

This can be schematically expressed thus: given are two members of society, A (the author) and R (the reader); the social relations between them are constant and stable at the given moment; also given is the ready communication X, which will simply be transmitted from A to R. The "what" (content) of this message X differs from its "how" (form), and the "orientation toward expression" ("how") is characteristic of the artistic word.

This scheme was shaped in the first period of formalism, when the poetic work was opposed to the practical, ready-made, and automatized utterance. The work became the converse of such an utterance.

This scheme is radically incorrect.

In real fact, the relationship between A and R is constantly changing and generating, and itself changes in the communicative process.

And there is no ready-made communication X. It is generated in the process of intercourse between A and R.

Furthermore, X is not transmitted from one to the other, but is constructed between them as a kind of ideological bridge, is built in the process of their interaction. And this process causes both the thematic unity of the generating work and the form of its actual realization. These cannot be separated, just as the core of an onion cannot be found by peeling off its layers one after another.

If we separate ready-made work-objects [*proizvedeniia-veshchi*] from this living and objective social process, we find ourselves with abstractions which in themselves lack any movement, generation, and interaction.

Nevertheless, the formalists try to endow these abstractions with some life, force them to interact and condition each other.

Works can only enter into real contact as inseparable elements of social intercourse. This interaction has absolutely no need for the mediation of subjective consciousnesses, since, outside of their material manifestations, these are not given in objective intercourse. It is not works that come into contact, but people, who, however, come into contact through the medium of works and thereby bring them into reflected interrelationships.

The formalists do not make the work external to the subjective consciousness, but rather to the interrelationships and interactions of people, between whom the work is constructed ("created") and continues to live in the process of their historical succession. Every element of the work can be compared to a thread stretching between people. The whole

work is a network of such threads, which creates a complex and differentiated social interrelationship between the people who have access
to it.

The ideological utterance between people, and, consequently, the
poetic work, primarily depend on the most intimate relations and the
most immediate forms of social similarity or difference between people.
These direct and individualized interrelationships determine the most
changeable and individual aspects of the utterance, its expressive intonations, individual word and phrase selection, and so on.

Further, in its typical and essential aspects, the utterance is defined
by the constant and more general interrelationships of the speakers as
representatives of definite social groups, social interests, and, in the final
analysis, definite social classes.

The deepest levels of these interrelationships can be outside the
subjective consciousness of the speakers and, none the less, still define
the deep structural aspects of their utterances.

The work cannot be understood, nor can even one of its functions be
studied outside of the organized interrelationships of the people between
whom the work is situated as the ideological body of their intercourse.

The crux of the matter is not in the subjective consciousnesses of the
speakers or the artists, or in what they think, experience, or want, but in
what the objective social logic of their interrelationships demands of
them. In the final account, this logic defines the very experiences of
people (their "inner speech"). These experiences are only another, less
essential, ideological refraction of the same objective logic of organized
social interrelationships.

The formalists sever the work from the interrelationships between
people, of which it is an aspect. In doing so they destroy all the
connections essential to the work. They relate the work to something
extrahistorical, something unchanged by man which only demands the
periodic replacement of automatization with perceptibility. The perceiver
does not sense another person behind the work, or other persons, friends
or enemies; all that he senses is a thing—more precisely, his own empty
sensation stimulated by the thing.

The Dialectic of "Extrinsic" and "Intrinsic"

The generation of social intercourse conditions the generation of all
aspects of literature and how every separate work is created and perceived. On the other hand, the generation of intercourse is dialectically
conditioned by the generation of literature as one of its factors. In the
process of this generation, it is not the combination of unchanging

elements that changes. The elements themselves change, as do their combinations, and the whole configuration.

The generation of literature and the individual work can only be understood within the whole ideological horizon. To the extent that it is estranged from this horizon, it becomes stagnant and dead inside.

As we know, the ideological horizon is constantly generating. And this generation, like all generation, is a dialectical process. Therefore, at every point of this generation we will find conflicts and inner contradictions within the ideological horizon.

The artistic work is also drawn into these conflicts and contradictions. It is penetrated by and absorbs some elements of the ideological environment and turns away other elements external to it. Therefore, in the process of history, "extrinsic" and "intrinsic" dialectically change places, and, of course, do not remain unchanged as they do so. That which is extrinsic to literature today, is an extraliterary reality, can enter literature as an intrinsic constructive factor tomorrow. And that which is literature today may turn out to be an extraliterary reality tomorrow.

The formalists themselves know that everyday life can become literature, and literature can become life. They also know that, at the same time, literature does not cease being literature, and life does not stop being life, that in changing places these areas retain their identity.

Tynianov writes:

> Where everyday life enters literature, it itself becomes literature, and must be evaluated as a literary fact. It is interesting to keep track of the meaning of artistic life in an epoch of great literary change and revolution, when the literary line acknowledged by everyone breaks up and is exhausted—and another movement is not yet felt. In such periods artistic life becomes literature, takes its place for a while. When the elevated line of Lomonosov fell to the epoch of Karamzin,[9] the literary fact became the petty detail of everyday domestic life: the friendly letter, the passing joke. The essence of the thing was that the everyday fact was raised to the level of a literary fact. In the epoch ruled by the elevated genres, such domestic correspondence was a fact of life, having no direct relationship to literature.[10]

Unfortunately, the formalists interpret the interrelationship of literature with extraliterary reality, in the given case with literary life, as the one-sided absorption of the one by the other. While admitting that life can enter literature, that it may be "raised to the level of a literary fact," they suppose that it thereby ceases to be life, that life acquires its literary, constructive significance at the expense of its meaning as life, indeed, that the latter meaning is annulled.

In real fact, what occurs here is not the substitution of one type of significance for another, but the superimposition of one significance on another (and not, of course, mechanistically). Literary, constructive significance is added to the significance of the fact as life. If the fact had no life significance, or had lost this significance upon entering literature, it would have been uninteresting and useless for literature.

The same is true of all other extraliterary phenomena. The philosophical idea, entering literature from philosophy or leaving literature for philosophy (as did many of Dostoevskii's ideas) does not lose its ideological essence in the course of its wanderings. But even when the given fact of life or the given idea is situated outside of literature, there is àn active and essential interaction between it and literature. For if the given fact of life remains outside of literature, then another fact of life is present within literature, and is in some interrelationship (for instance, contradiction) with the first. But, beyond this, literature as such is both oriented toward life as a whole, and toward its particular manifestation.

When literature perceives some social factors or demands as being external to it, as alien to its nature, it does not at all follow that the social factor as such is alien to literature. In fact, the social factor is only a genuine extrinsic factor when literature itself contains another factor which is social but of another class orientation.

It is not the nature of literature that is antagonistic to the given social factor, but the other, hostile social factor which has become an inner factor of literature in the given period.

This struggle between two social orientations takes various forms, such as the proclamations of "art for art's sake," "the autonomous nature of art," etc. At the bottom of all these theories lies the actual fact of a contradiction between the given art and the given social conditions. But the intrinsically social nature of art is no less sharply evident in these formulations than it is in cases of direct agreement between art and the social demands of the epoch. A dialectical conception of the "intrinsic" and the "extrinsic" of literature and extraliterary reality (ideological and otherwise) is an obligatory condition for the formulation of a genuine Marxist literary history.

The Problem of Artistic Convention

The concept of artistic convention is widespread in *Kunstwissenschaft* and *Literaturwissenschaft*. The formalists also make use of it.

This concept does actually correspond to a certain artistic phenomenon. Sometimes the ideological material brought into the artistic construction actually does become conventional. The conventions of various schools, movements, or individual artists are of this nature. But it is completely inadmissible to extend this conventionality to art as a whole.

It is typical that where an ideological value becomes an artistic convention, it becomes conventional for the given movement outside of art as well. The material usually becomes conventional just before it is replaced, i.e., at the end of the given movement's life, in the hands of epigones. Thus ideological material introduced by classicists only becomes conventional in the period of classicism's dissolution. The same is true of romanticism. The ideological material introduced by the symbolists was taken seriously in art, in philosophy, and in life, and only became conventional for the acmeists. But since life did not provide any new material or a new ideological spirit, acmeism only provided a basis for a doctrine of the fundamental conventionality of the artistic material (in a moderate form, it is true); the spirit was not wholly stifled.

This process is reflected in literature. Material is not abandoned because it has become automatized in the artistic construction for psychotechnical reasons, but because it has ceased to be important in the ideological horizon and, consequently, in the socioeconomic conditions of the given epoch. If the material is important and timely, it has nothing to fear from repetition.

If the formalists, in trying to clarify the psychotechnical conditions of perception, had consulted real psychotechnics, they would have discovered an elementary principle: the more vital and substantial interest in something is, the more distinctly and completely it is seen and experienced.

When material that has lost its full weight in the ideological horizon enters art, it must somehow compensate for the loss of its direct ideological importance. This compensation takes the form of a more intense and extensive orientation toward the purely literary context. The material is surrounded as densely as possible by the purely artistic reminiscenses of other literary works, movements, schools, epochs. The material acquires purely artistic associations, echoes, allusions. The perceptibility of its literary nature is consequently particularly sharp.

This most intense orientation of ideologically weakened material toward the literary context can develop in two directions. The artist may follow the positive route, selecting the correspondences between his material and other literary works on the basis of positive reminiscences and associations. But he may also try to make differences perceptible, to create the so-called "quality of divergence" [*Differenzqualität*].[11]

Both directions lead to the same end: the given material is more firmly rooted in the purely literary context through the general expansion of this context. It is through such compensation that the ideologically weakened material becomes conventional.

It is true that this conventionality differs somewhat from the flat conventionality of epigones. Here there is an attempt to revive the ideological spirit of the material, to strengthen its accents by reference to the literary past and by changing and renewing its context, while the conventionality of epigones is the result of the mere reproduction of literary stereotypes with ideologically dead material.

The cases of the renewal of the material by the intentional creation of "divergent qualities" should be strictly distinguished from cases in which the "divergent qualities" which register in the consciousness of some group of readers do not enter the plan of the artist or serve other ends. The sentimentalists, for instance, did not strive to create "divergent qualities" with regard to classicism, and if they did sometimes create them with artistic intention, their goal was not only a hostile literary contrast, but a contrast to the general ideology of classicism. The sentimentalists' material possessed a full measure of ideological timeliness and importance and had no need for special artistic reminiscences of the negative type.

Usually the formalists did not distinguish between these cases, nor could they if they were to remain true to themselves and their theory, which rejected the ideological import of the material.

The Value Center
of the Ideological Horizon
of an Epoch as the Basic Theme of Literature

There is still another problem connected with the formalists' theory of the work as a datum external to consciousness.

In isolating the work, cutting it off on all sides from the ideological horizon, they deny themselves access to a very important feature of the ideological material.

The artist seeks that material which lies at the point where several ideological series intersect. The greater the number of intersecting ideological paths, and the more varied their ideological interest, the more sharply the material is perceived.

Within the ideological horizon of every epoch, there is a value center toward which all the paths and aspirations of ideological activity lead. This value center becomes the basic theme or, more precisely, the complex of themes of the literature of a given epoch. The thematic dominants are also connected, as we know, with the specific repertoire of genres.

The ruling themes of every literary epoch are always those which pass through all the spheres of ideological creation. Against this background of the problematic unity of all the spheres of ideology the individuality of each of these spheres stands out with particular sharpness.

Art, in being oriented toward the common value center of the ideological horizon of the epoch, not only does not loose its specificity and individuality as a result, but, on the contrary, only reveals its full power in this way. The aim of the artistic finalization of the historically actual and important is the most difficult aim of art, and its attainment is art's greatest triumph.

That which has already lost its historical timeliness and importance, that which has already been finalized or, more precisely, has been repealed by history itself, can easily be finalized, but this finalization will not be perceptible. This is the reason that, if the artist chooses historical material, he makes it ideologically timely by a valuational connection with the contemporary.

If this connection is not perceptible, then the given historical material cannot become the object of artistic finalization. For while it is possible to remove thematic unity to any far-off time or place, the development of the real body of the work takes place under the contemporary conditions of social intercourse. The goal of the artistic structure of every historical genre is to merge the distances of space and time with the contemporary by the force of all-penetrating social evaluation.

Summary

In asserting that the literary work is external to consciousness, the formalists did not cleanse it of the subjectivity and fortuitousness of individual perceptions. Instead, they severed it from all those spheres in which the work becomes historically real and objective—from the unity of the ideological horizon, from the objective reality of social intercourse, and from the historical timeliness and importance of the epoch contemporary to the work.

As a result, the work is locked into a closed circle of subjective, empty sensations. The participants in artistic creation and perception lose their historicity and turn into psychophysiological apparatuses for perception.

This theory of perception, the inevitable result of formalist poetics, predetermines the absolute fruitlessness of formalist literary history.

CHAPTER NINE
The Formalist Theory
of the Historical Development of Literature

The Formalist Conception
of Literary-Historical Change

The formalist theory of the development of literary history completely follows from the theory of the work as a datum external to consciousness and from the formalist theory of artistic perception.

The formalists consider the series of literary history, the series of artistic works and their constructive elements, to be completely independent of the other ideological series and of socioeconomic development. The formalists try to reveal the intrinsic, immanent laws of the development of forms within a closed, purely literary series.

The unbroken and self-sufficient path of the historical development of literature leads from work to work, from style to style, from school to school, from one constructive dominant to another, bypassing all extraliterary instances and forces. No matter what may take place in the world, no matter what economic, social, or general ideological changes may come about, the literary series moves with iron inner necessity from one developmental link to another, ignoring everything else.

This series can be broken, or can come under the influence of external factors. Extraliterary reality can slow its development, but, according to formalist theory, cannot change the inner logic of this development and cannot add even one new and important aspect of content to it. The very category of interaction is unknown to the formalists. At best they only know the partial interaction of simultaneous lines within the literary series. They only know the evolutionary movement of one stage after the other.

However, the formalist view of the nature of the changing of the links of the chain of development sharply differs from the usual notions of evolution. In the precise and strict sense of the word, there is no continuity between a given link and the one which precedes it. Unlike evolution in natural science, the link that follows does not arise as the further development of what preceded it, is not the further elaboration and complication of preceding potentials.

Strictly speaking, the formalist conception of the development of literary history cannot be called evolutionary without giving rise to ambiguities. The formalists see literary succession as being subject to a specific law, but this succession is not evolutionary. As Shklovskii puts it: "Literary history moves forward along a broken, suddenly changing line." This is explained by the fact that the literary inheritance of schools and movements is transferred "not from father to son, but from uncle to nephew." There takes place what the formalists call the "canonization of the junior line."

This theory of literary succession was formed once and for all between the end of the first and the beginning of the second period of formalism. Shklovskii provided the first complete formulation of the theory in his book *Rozanov* (1921). His formula was subsequently supplemented and further detailed and shored up, but its essence remained and continues to live as the basis for formalist works in literary history to the present time. In view of the historical and theoretical importance of Shklovskii's original formulation, we will cite it in full.

> In every literary epoch there is not one but several literary schools. They exist in literature simultaneously, but one of them represents the canonized crest. The others are not canonized and exist obscurely, as, for example, the Derzhavin tradition existed during the Pushkin period (the poetry of Kiukhel'beker and Griboedov),[1] simultaneously with the tradition of Russian vaudeville verse and with other traditions, such as the pure tradition of the adventure novel in Bulgarin.[2]
>
> Pushkin's tradition did not continue after him; i.e., a situation arose similar to that caused by a genius's failure to have brilliant and gifted children.
>
> But at the same time, on the lower level, new forms were being created to replace the forms of the old art, which were already no more perceptible than grammatical forms in speech, and which had changed from artistically oriented elements to auxiliary and imperceptible phenomena. The junior line bursts into the place of the old, and the vaudeville writer Belopiatkin becomes Nekrasov (see the work of Osip Brik),[3] Tolstoi, the direct descendant of the eighteenth century, creates a new novel (see Boris Eikhenbaum), Blok canonizes the themes and tempos of the "gypsy romance," and Chekhov brings *The Alarm Clock*[4] into Russian literature. Dostoevskii raises the devices of the boulevard novel to a literary norm. Every new literary school is a revolution, something like the appearance of a new class.
>
> But, of course, this is only an analogy. The defeated "line" is not destroyed, does not cease to exist. It is merely brought down from the crest, comes down to lie fallow for a while, and, as an eternal pretender to the throne, can rise again. In addition, the matter is in reality more complex, due to the fact that the new hegemon is usually not a pure restorer of the

previous forms, but is complicated by features of other junior schools and by features inherited from the previous occupant of the throne, although these play an auxiliary role.[5]

What are the preconditions of this conception?

The Psychophysiological
Preconditions of Literary Development

The basic precondition is the formalist law of "automatization-perceptibility."

Let us suppose that such a psychophysiological law (it cannot be defined otherwise) does indeed exist. Let us even suppose that it is suitable to explain literary phenomena. Even so, this law is quite unfounded and does not explain the succession of literary schools that Shklovskii describes.

Indeed, we already know that this law can only be applied within the bounds of the life of a single, individual organism. Consequently, the movement from old form to new form must be automatized for the father, and the new form that replaces it must be maximally perceptible and, consequently, artistically justified for the father.

But in such a case the law of "automatization-perceptibility" can substantiate and explain only the simultaneity of the old and new forms, i.e., the coexistence of the senior and junior lines, but not their succession.

This succession requires that the following generation, the generation of the children, side with the junior line and perceive its forms more sharply than the generation of the fathers does. But the law of "automatization-perceptibility" gives absolutely no grounds for this. The childrens' generation finds itself in the position of Buridan's mule between the old and young lines.[6] For the children the psychological preconditions for the perceptibility of the one or the other are completely equal, and only an accidental shove can send Buridan's mule in one direction rather than the other. Therefore, the chances for the canonization of the junior line are exactly equal to those for the further prosperity of the senior, canonized line.

It might be possible to suppose that the old form is more automatized for the children because they were nourished on it, that it was their school book, that for them it was a sort of preexisting form.

However, such a supposition is absolutely incorrect.

Schoolbooks contain so-called "classical models." Schoolbook literature is generally a special, organic world which does not coincide with the world of even one of the artistic movements existing in the history of the given literature. Children are never brought up on the literature which their fathers actively live. In the great majority of cases the childrens' school is separated from contemporary literature.

In relation to school children, contemporary literature is the literature of the fathers. "Preexisting literature"—the literature of education, upbringing, and individual growth—is a special and extremely important category of literary history, radically different from such categories as "artistic movement," "artistic school," "artistic taste." "Preexisting literature" partially coincides with the category of "classics" (in the nonpartisan sense of the word). In "preexisting literature," Pushkin coexists with Nekrasov, Pushkin's prose lives together with that of Turgenev, Turgenev's with Tolstoi's, and so on.

The artistic movement or school begins to be perceived as a definite artistic reality comparatively late, when the person is already completely formed. The person meets the senior and the junior lines in the same way, and the law of "automatization-perceptibility" creates absolutely no preconditions for the preference of one over the other. The real preconditions of this choice are completely different.

Thus the formalists cannot explain the historical succession of literary movements.

This is not surprising. No psychophysiological principle is able to be the basis for historical explanations and interpretations. Nor can it be the basis for the explanation and interpretation of history itself.

The Scheme of Literary Evolution

The passage from Shklovskii's *Rozanov* contains yet another principle highly typical of formalism.

In the majority of cases, the junior line is not something absolutely new, but the predecessor of the given canonized line, i.e., is the old line of the preceding period. Thus, during the Pushkin period, the Derzhavin tradition continued to live in the poetry of Kiukhel'beker. And Tolstoi, the heir of the eighteenth century, created a new novel.

It is true that the formalists also permit the existence and subsequent canonization of junior lines that are new and created for the first time, but the scheme itself does not demand this. As far as the scheme is concerned, such a novelty is accidental and inexplicable. It is not the result of the demands of the immanent development of literature.

The following statement by Eikhenbaum is quite characteristic:

> The creation of new artistic forms is not an act of representation, but of discovery, because these forms are hidden in the forms of preceding periods. Lermontov had to discover the poetic style needed for an escape from the poetic dead end that took shape after the 1820s. This style already existed potentially in some poets of the Pushkin period.[7]

Actually, the formalist law of the immanent development of literature has no need for the invention of new forms.

All that the formalist system needs is the existence of two mutually contrasting artistic trends, let us say the Derzhavin and the Pushkin traditions. Let us find them in the required situation of mutual contrast. The Pushkin tradition succeeds the Derzhavin tradition, and the latter tradition becomes the junior line. After a certain time the Derzhavin tradition succeeds the Pushkin tradition, which now takes the position of the junior line. This process can continue to infinity. No new forms are needed. If new forms appear, they do so for reasons completely incidental to literary development.

No matter how absurd this *perpetuum mobile* of two trends might be, the formalists strive to use it in as pure a form as possible and are extremely unwilling to admit the manifestation of new forms, although, of course, they cannot do without them, particularly because they must combine not two, but several trends.

Furthermore, according to the formalist scheme, the order in which the elements succeed one another is completely random.

Of course, if the first line canonized was really the Derzhavin tradition, the Pushkin tradition must follow it. But from the point of view of the scheme as such, it might have been the opposite: first the Pushkin, then the Derzhavin tradition. In terms of the scheme itself, the location of the Derzhavin tradition in the eighteenth century and the Pushkin tradition in the early nineteenth century is absolutely accidental.

It is necessary to go beyond the bounds of the purely literary series in order to explain the necessity of this connection with the epoch. In the literary series, the elements are interchangeable: no matter how they are arranged, they will contrast with each other.

Let us again add that this scheme presupposes the existence of a single individual for whom the Derzhavin tradition is succeeded by the Pushkin tradition. If this person dies, the Pushkin period might be repeated again—it is all the same to his son. Of course, there can be a countless number of individuals like the one we have proposed; a generation is represented by a great many people. But the contemporaries of one generation do not comprise the history of man.

We are not at all exaggerating the formalist scheme of evolution; we are merely giving it logical precision. In the works of the formalists themselves, it is filled out with historical material that is interesting in itself. But the order of an incorrect scheme will not correspond to reality and can only give a false impression of it. What is more, unimportant material will be selected or, if important, will be selected fortuitously and in spite of the scheme.

Incidently, the formalists do not shun consistency and formulate their scheme of literary history distinctly enough themselves, as in the statements from Shklovskii that we have cited.[8]

The Absence of Real Evolution
in the Formalist Theory of Literary History

We have already stated that the term "evolution" does not apply to the formalist theory of literary development.

But can the given scheme be considered that of immanent literary evolution? Of course not. The preceding form contains no potential for the following form and no indications or hints of it.

There can be any number of contrasting forms satisfying the law of "automatization-perceptibility." Therefore, a preceding form does not presuppose a following form. It is, therefore, possible that the following, contrasting form will be some form that has already existed in the historical development of literature.

If the Derzhavin tradition predetermined the Pushkin period, then it could not reappear following the Pushkin period. And the reverse: the Pushkin period could not determine the Derzhavin period, because the Derzhavin period existed first. Thus, according to the formalist conception, there can be no evolutionary connection between literary forms, no matter how broadly we understand the words "evolution" and "development."

In his programmatic article "On the Literary Fact," which is very important for the understanding of contemporary formalism, Tynianov makes the following, exceedingly precise declaration:

> In constructing a "solid," "ontological" definition of literature as "essence," literary historians had to consider phenomena of historical succession to be phenomena of peaceful continuity, of the peaceful and regular development of this "essence." A harmonious picture is obtained: "Lomonosov begat Derzhavin, Derzhavin begat Zhukovskii,[9] Zhukovskii begat Pushkin, Pushkin begat Lermontov." Pushkin's unambiguous remarks about his literary ancestors were overlooked (Derzhavin: "an eccentric who didn't know Russian grammar;" Lomonosov: "a bad influence on literature"). It was not noticed that Derzhavin was the heir of Lomonosov by making the latter's ode a hybrid, or that Pushkin inherited the large form of the eighteenth century and used it for the little themes of the Karamzin school. It was overlooked that these writers were only able to be the heirs of their predecessors because they made hybrids of their styles and genres. It was not noticed that the composition of every new phenomenon of succession is exceptionally complex, and that it is only fitting to talk about continuity in connection with the phenomena of the school, of epigonism, and not in connection with the phenomena of literary evolution, the principle of which is struggle and succession.[10]

Struggle and succession are not the principle of evolution.

It is true that struggle is possible in evolution, but in itself it does not make evolution. Parallel phenomena not involved in evolution can also struggle.

As for succession, the question is—what kind? Is it evolutional succession or some other kind, for instance, a mechanistic-causal succession, or the accidental, temporal succession of two phenomena that are unconnected or only connected extraneously and accidentally? An example of this latter kind occurs when two phenomena having nothing to do with one another are connected in a person's consciousness through some intimate associations.

Thus, neither succession nor struggle is at the bottom of evolution. To show that two phenomena struggle and are in succession is not to show that they are evolutionally connected. In order to reveal an evolutional connection, it is necessary to show something quite different: it is necessary to show that the two phenomena are connected in substance and that the first one essentially and necessarily determines the one that follows it.

This is just what Tynianov does not show. On the contrary, he strives to show that there is no evolution in literature and that another type of succession dominates. But, then, he uncritically and illogically calls this succession evolution.

And it is unclear why Tynianov believes that continuity must be peaceful. Continuity can be far from peaceful and still be continuity. What is more, all continuity is nonpeaceful to a certain degree. A dialectical connection may also be termed continuity (in reference to certain phenomena), and it is not a peaceful connection. The dialectical negation is born and ripens in the bosom of the negation itself. Thus socialism ripens in the bosom of capitalism. The phenomenon itself inevitably prepares its own negation, gives birth to it out of itself. If the negation is extrinsic, then it is not a dialectical negation.

Tynianov did not show and does not try to show that Derzhavin's hybridization of the Lomonosov ode was prepared within the Lomonosov ode itself, that it was intrinsically necessary for the Lomonosov ode to prepare this hybridization, that within the ode itself contradictions built up which inevitably led to its destruction and the creation of a new formation, the Derzhavin ode, in its place.

Of course, we do not assert here that such a dialectical continuity did in fact exist between the Lomonosov and Derzhavin odes. We will leave the question open. But if Tynianov had shown this, he would then have the right to speak of evolution and, precisely, of dialectical evolution. However, Tynianov and the other formalists not only do not do this, but they do not want to do it and cannot do it.

To do so would be incompatible with the basis of their conception of literary history. For then the historical series could not be reversible.

Besides, it would be imperative to show the necessity behind the hybridization of the given literary form. Formalism is not up to this.

The Law of
"Automatization-Perceptibility" as the Basis of Formalism

Literary evolution, in the formalist conception, is not an immanently literary phenomenon.

For we know that, according to their theory, the change from one form to another is not dictated by the specific nature of literature, but by the psychic law of "automatization-perceptibility," a very general law not at all connected with the specific nature of literature.

Derzhavin did not make a hybrid of the Lomonosov ode because the further development of the essence of the ode demanded it. This hybridization took place because the elevated ode had become automatized for Derzhavin and his contemporaries. The result of this psychological automatization was the lowering of the ode.

According to Tynianov,

> In the analysis of literary evolution we come across the following stages: (1) in connection with the automatized principle of construction we observe a dialectically opposite constructive principle; (2) this constructive principle seeks its easiest application; (3) it becomes widespread for the majority of phenomena; (4) it becomes automatized and elicits opposing constructive principles.[11]

It is quite unfortunate that Tynianov brings the word "dialectical" into the discussion. It is completely out of place here. All the stages of evolution Tynianov enumerates are neither stages of evolution in general, nor stages of literary evolution.

In fact, according to Tynianov, the opposite constructive principle "is observed in connection with the automatized principle of construction." Consequently, it is the "automatization" of the given artistic construction that gives birth to its negation. But it inevitably follows from this that the negation does not touch the inner essence of the given construction and is not given birth by this essence. For "automatized nature" [*avtomatizovannost'*] does not become part of the literary construction, does not become an element of it or its "perceptibility."

We must include in literature an artistic perception that is adequate to it, for without this literature would become a thing of nature. But the artistic perception of the construction that is being included in the given artistic construction is just as individual and important as the construction itself and corresponds completely to its uniqueness. The perception of Lomonosov's ode is qualitatively different from the perception of the Derzhavin ode.

Perception controls the intrinsic, immanent individuality of the artistic structure, that value which the latter helps realize.

This cannot be said of automatization and perceptibility. These are always the same thing, whether they pertain to the ode of Lomonosov or Derzhavin, and which ode will be automatized and which will be perceptible completely depends on who perceives them and when. Automatization and perceptibility are identically adequate to any given work. Or, more precisely, they are equally far from touching the actual intrinsic individuality of the work and only characterize something absolutely external to the work, the accidental subjective state of the perceiver.

If one and the same work can be perceptible today and automatized tomorrow, or can simultaneously be perceptible to some and automatized to others, then perceptibility and automatization absolutely cannot pertain to the intrinsic features of the given work, just as the poor hearing of the listener or the drowsiness or sharp attention of the perceiver cannot pertain to these intrinsic features.

The situation would have been otherwise if the formalists had connected perceptibility and automatization with the general ideological and socioeconomic conditions of the epoch. It is true that even then perceptibility and automatization would in themselves be only attendant phenomena. The historian's work would then amount to showing the real noncorrespondence of a given construction to the concrete and vital conditions of the epoch or, what is the opposite, to showing the real historical timeliness and importance of a given work in the whole ideological horizon. Consequently, even here perceptibility and automatization would remain formalistic and empty concepts.

But in any case they would have been brought out of the psychophysiological category into the category of the historical. However, this is completely alien to formalist theory.

Further, automatization and perceptibility apply not only to literary works, but to all objects and phenomena whatever. Perceptibility is the *conditio sine qua non* of all meaningful comprehension, not only of all ideological phenomena, but of natural phenomena as well. But it is precisely as a *conditio sine qua* that perceptibility does not touch the content of what would be comprehended.

Thus neither automatization nor perceptibility can be considered features of the artistic construction and are not immanent characteristics of the artistic construction as such. Consequently, Tynianov's first stage of evolution has no relation to the generation of literature. One construction merely replaces another in the plane of the extrahistorical perceptions of the subjective consciousness. Constructions come into contact in this plane, but, of course, there is no way to deduce the real evolution of literature itself from this extrahistorical and accidental contact.

The second stage of evolution, according to Tynianov, in which the constructive principle seeks its easiest application, is no less extrahistorical and accidental in terms of the individuality of literature. The concept of "the easiest" is just as relative and just as psychotechnical as the concept of perceptibility.

The third stage concerns the spreading of the already created phenomenon within the bounds of actual, present time. It also has no relationship to history and evolution.

The fourth stage returns us to the beginning of the whole "evolution." And, of course, in agreement with Tynianov's scheme of evolution, the link preceding the given link can return, i.e., the evolution can be left with just two links.

Tynianov's evolutional scheme provides no basis for understanding the necessity or even the possibility of the appearance of a completely new third line. If two mutually contrasting trends are already present in literature, then no impulses for the creation of a third trend can be born if literature is as the formalists conceive it to be. Only the alien interference of extraliterary reality can lead to such creation.

It is surprising that the formalists themselves take no notice at all of the elementary and crudely psychologistic bases of all their theories. And they do not even conceal these bases: they use the terms "perceptibility" and "automatization" at every step of their formulations. An elementary methodological instinct should have turned their attention to the psychophysiological character of their terms and the meaning which is posited in them.

Even more striking are such statements as the following by Eikhenbaum. Criticizing Marxists, Trotskii in particular, he says:

> It is sometimes even unclear how a given phenomenon of culture should be defined — as answering the sociopolitical demands of the moment, or not. Thus, not only in art, but even in scholarship, Trotskii himself points out that the question of whether Einstein's theory of relativity is reconcilable with materialism or not is unclear and undecided, as is the same question with regard to Freud's psychoanalytic theories. If this is so, then it remains a question whether the facts of art still more complex in terms of their connection with society (for besides literature there is also music, painting, architecture, ballet) can be fruitfully considered from the point of view of their correspondence to socioeconomic theories. Would not this cause all concreteness and specificity to disappear? Instead of real evolution, would not what was obtained be a simple psychological genesis which explains nothing?[12]

But what does the formalist scheme of evolution provide if not the simple, psychological genesis of a new form from the psychophysiological conditions of perception?

Marxism constantly relies on historical categories. There is no basis for these categories in formalist theory. Eikhenbaum's critical observations, directed against Marxism and Freudianism, are correct only with regard to Freudianism. But they are most accurate with regard to the formal method itself.

It is necessary to state that the formalists' psychologistic premises are very deeply lodged in the foundations of their theory. Any revision or denial of these premises must result in the complete destruction of formalism.

Ideological Material in Literary History

When applied to the ideological material brought into the artistic construction, the formalist scheme of literary development leads to conclusions no less paradoxical: novelty of ideological material is not only unnecessary, but even harmful to the immanent development of literature.

Indeed, novelty of material can weaken the perceptibility of the contrast between the given literary trend and the preceding one. It binds the work with the epoch, with extraliterary reality, and will attract attention to this reality.

Therefore, in their works in literary history the formalists are particularly careful to exterminate the directly ideological nature of the material. For, if the material itself is important in its contemporary environment, then it is very difficult to contend that it is brought into the work only for the sake of contrast with the preceding line and still retain at least a shadow of verisimilitude. The extremes to which the formalists will sometimes go to remove the direct ideological significance of the material is evident in the following statement from Eikhenbaum's book *The Young Tolstoi.* Citing a program for life in the country that Tolstoi developed in his diary for 1847, Eikhenbaum arrives at this completely unexpected conclusion:

> It is clear [?] that this is not a real, serious program of actual undertakings, but rather a program as device, as an end in itself.[13]
>
> We will cite the first points of this "program-device."
>
> "What will be the goal of my life in the country for the next two years? (1) To study the complete course of jurisprudence needed for the final university examination; (2) to study practical medicine and some theoretical medicine; (3) to study languages: French, Russian, German, English, Italian, and Latin."[14]

One has just as much right to call someone's desk calander a "calander-device" because he sometimes does not live according to this calander. What is more, we must also consider Tolstoi's leaving home [10 November 1910] to be a device organically connected with his artistic manner.

Eikhenbaum's articles on Nekrasov are also directed toward excising the socioideological significance of the writer's themes. Thus Nekrasov's turn to popular, folk themes is explained this way:

> It was quite natural, given his polemical relationship to the canonized literary genres and forms, that Nekrasov had to turn to folklore. Folklore is an unfailing source for the renewal of artistic forms at times of sharp change in art, of battle with the canons. In our time, Maiakovskii used the street ditty [*chastushka*] in this way.[15]

The formalists do not admit fundamental renewal of the material for the sake of the material.

The Logical and Analytical Extremes of the Formalist Conception of Artistic Perception

It is here necessary to turn our attention to yet another aspect of the formalist doctrine of artistic perception which is particularly clearly evident in their works on literary history.

They reduce both contemplative and creative perception to acts of juxtaposition, comparison, difference, and contrast, i.e., to purely logical acts. These acts are treated as equally adequate to both the perception of the reader and the creative intention of the artist himself. Owing to this, artistic perception is rationalized in the extreme and becomes inseparable from the analysis of literary history "according to the formal method."

It is hardly necessary to say that such a conception of perception does not fit reality.

The formalists combine the logical and analytical nature of perception with the theory of "automatization-perceptibility." They produce the impression that both the reader and the author must convince themselves of the automatization or perceptibility of their devices by formal analysis and historical excursus.

Perceptibility is deprived of all immediacy and becomes a sort of well-grounded, deliberate perceptibility.

The Absence of the Category of "Historical Time" in Formalist Literary History

The formalist theory of literary evolution lacks the essential aspect of history: the category of historical time. This lack is the inevitable consequence of all the aspects of the theory we have examined.

The formalists, in essence, know only some "permanent present," some "permanent contemporaneity."

This is quite understandable. The law of "automatization-perceptibility" demands one life, one generation. Everything that takes place in formalist literary history takes place in some eternal contemporaneity. It is characteristic that they only know literary continuity as epigonism. Everything must fit within the framework of the contemporary. If the following epoch continues the business of the preceding in a positive manner, does not destroy or hybridize it, then it is a fruitless epoch of epigonism.

The question arises: what shall we do with tasks which can only really be accomplished over a long series of generations and a succession of epochs? For such tasks are the real, historical tasks. We find them in all areas of ideological creation and social life, and these are the most important and substantial tasks.

What is more, there exist organizations, such as parties, which work in a disciplined and strictly consistent manner to accomplish tasks which can only be achieved over a period of centuries. What would happen if parties evolved according to the formalists' idea of dialectical succession? What would happen to science if everything in it were only developed to counterbalance the old?

Of course, even in science there are revolutions. But, as is true of all revolutions, these have a purely positive program. From the formalist point of view, every scientist is an epigone, except for sensationalists.

Whatever area of creativity or life we choose, we nowhere find even a hint of the possibility of applying the formalist scheme of evolution. That alone should make the use of this scheme in literary history doubtful to say the least.

We suggest that the basic spirit of formalist literary history originates in futurism, in which extreme modernism and radical negation of the past is combined with complete absence of inner content. The impression is that futurism's vaudevillistic attacks on the past became the formalists' unconscious blueprint and prototype for all literary succession.

History as the Illustration of Theory

We may now sum up.

The conception we have examined deprives the formalists of all access to history as such. History for them is merely a warehouse for the storage of vast material for the illustration of their theoretical positions. The real aim the formalists brought to history was not to verify poetics by the facts of history, but to select from history material that could prove and illustrate poetics. It was not the theory that had to reflect historical reality—the formalists believe that only with the eyes of a theory, any theory, is it possible to discern any "material" whatsoever in history.

This statement of Eikhenbaum's, from his "Literature and Literary Life," is very clear:

> We do not see all facts at the same time, do not always see the same ones, and do not always need to have the same interrelationships revealed to us. But everything that we know or can know is connected in our perception by some intelligible sign, is changed from something random into a fact having a certain meaning. The vast material of the past which is found in documents and various memoirs only partially falls into the pages of history (and is not always the same then) to the extent that theory gives the right and makes it possible to introduce part of the material into the system under one or another sign. And there is no historical system outside of theory, since a principle for the selection and comprehension of facts is lacking.[16]

Here Eikhenbaum is defending patent historical relativism: the laws of the development of history itself cannot be discovered; only theory brings order and sense to the chaos of historical reality. But it follows from this that any theory is good, since any theory can fish out a sufficient number of historical facts. This is Eikhenbaum's line of reasoning.

It is, of course, faulty. We need not take the sign into historical reality. On the contrary, our own ideas only become meaningful if they are subordinated to the intelligible signs of historical reality itself. A historical meaning can only be that meaning which is objectively present in history as its meaning. It is the task of history and the historian to reveal this meaning.

This objective meaning of the historical process is what historical materialism has revealed. All branches of literary scholarship should give detail to this meaning as applied to the historical reality of literature. It is true that all the definitions and theories of poetics are primary, originating in poetics—but they are only preliminary. They receive their final justification and concretization in the historical material. To use history to illustrate a theory means to use history to consolidate mistakes and to scatter the historical material with false premises so that these are hard to detect.

In the same article Eikhenbaum freely admits:

> In overcoming this system in recent years, scholars have rejected the traditional material of literary history (including even biographical material) and have concentrated on general problems of literary evolution. One or another fact of literary history thus served to illustrate general points of theory.[17]

We suggest that this relationship to history made it significantly more difficult for the formalists to recognize their errors when they should have and harder for them to revise the bases of their original theory on time. It was as if they were sinking their theory by overloading it with a mass of historical facts. It was easy to collect facts, and they were new since the theory was new and history is inexhaustible. This seduced the formalists. Instead of bringing them back to reality, history made them more stubborn in their original opinions.

Formalism and Literary Criticism

Literary criticism was of great importance to the formalists in their first period. At that time, their research actually merged with timely and sometimes even journalistic literary criticism. In subsequent periods, the formalists also had high hopes for direct participation in literary life.

Boris Engel'gardt is completely correct in saying that

> For many of formalism's partisans active participation in literary contemporaneity was always in the foreground, and, while working out methods for the objective and abstract study of the so-called formal elements of poetry, they half-consciously carried these over into the sphere of criticism.[18]

The formalists gave their futuristic tastes the appearance of scholarly formulas and thereby brought criticism into scholarship—and bad scholarship into criticism.

But the essential element of formalist criticism is its fundamentally partisan nature.

In their opinion, criticism should be the organ of the writer, should express a definite artistic trend, rather than be the organ of the reader. This is to deprive criticism of its functions, its basic role of mediator between the social and general ideological demands of the epoch, on the one hand, and literature, on the other.

Instead of placing "social orders" in a language understandable and vital to the artist and critically evaluating orders that have already been filled, the formalist critics have taken an absurd and ambiguous position between scholarship and a militant literary movement. Accordingly, they have studied linguistics and have fastened themselves to a futurist program and use one to support the other.

Of course, such a situation is profoundly abnormal and cannot last for long. It is obvious at present that it is being overcome. The formalists are little by little beginning to take a position between the reader and literature, although they are still drawn to their former place between philosophy and futurism. This is the origin of "LEF." It should hardly be necessary to emphasize that the formalists do not possess the real sociological premises necessary to literary criticism.

Conclusion

Here, at the conclusion of this book, it is appropriate to ask: what is the historical significance of the formal method?

The present historical task with regard to formalism is clear. It involves merciless criticism by nonformalists and unflinching revision of their basic principles by the formalists themselves.

But what was the meaning of their theories in the past?

Here our answer will be different. In general, formalism played a productive role. It was able to formulate the most important problems of literary scholarship, and to do so with such sharpness that they can no longer be avoided or ignored. Granted, formalism did not solve these problems. But its very mistakes, in their boldness and consistency, did even more to focus attention on the problems that were formulated.

Therefore, it would be most incorrect to ignore formalism or to criticize it on grounds other than its own. Both paths only lead to compromise. This path was followed by academic scholarship, which at first ignored formalism and now seeks to do the same by half-heartedly acknowledging it. Some Marxists arrive at the same compromise by preferring to hit formalism in the back instead of meeting it face to face.

We believe that Marxist scholarship should even be grateful to the formalists, grateful that their theory can be the object of serious criticism, in the process of which the bases of Marxist scholarship will be clarified and strengthened.

Every young science—and Marxist literary scholarship is very young—should value a good opponent much higher than a poor ally.

Notes

Notes to Introduction

1. A. A. Leont'ev, *Psikholingvistika* (Leningrad, 1967), pp. 86-88.

2. *Voprosy iazykoznaniia* 2 (1971): 160-62 (report by O. G. Revzina).

3. Pumpianskii's discussion of dialogue in Tiutchev's "lyrical fragments" displays affinities with the discourse model presented in Voloshinov's "The Word in Life and the Word in Poetry" (1926); see the former's introduction to *Uraniia: tiutchevskii al'manakh*, ed. E. P. Kazanovich (Leningrad, 1928).

4. In August 1976, thanks to an IREX summer exchange, I was able to talk about Bakhtin with Vladimir Nikolaevich Turbin of Moscow University. Victor Ripp, Cornell University, also took part in these conversations, hereafter cited in the text.

5. *Philosophical Thought in the West Today*, mentioned in a footnote to *Freidizm: kriticheskii ocherk* (Moscow and Leningrad, 1927); subsequently pages from V. N. Voloshinov, *Freudianism: A Marxist Critique*, trans. I. R. Titunik, ed. Neal H. Bruss (New York and London, 1976), will be cited in the text. This reference is to page 14.

6. V. V. Ivanov, "The Significance of M. M. Bakhtin's Ideas on Sign, Utterance, and Dialogue for Modern Semiotics," *Soviet Studies in Literature* (Spring-Summer, 1975): 186-243; 242; this is a translation of "Znachenie idei M. M. Bakhtina o znake, vyskazyvanii i dialoge dlia sovremennoi semiotiki," *Trudy po znakovym sistemam* 6 (Tartu, 1973).

7. V. Kozhinov and S. Konkin, "Mikhail Mikhailovich Bakhtin, Kratkii ocherk zhizni i deiatel'nosti," *Problemy poetiki i istorii literatury (Sbornik statei)* (Saransk, 1973), p. 6.

8. V. Vinogradov, *Stil' Pushkina* (Moscow, 1941), p. 548.

9. On the relationship between Kantian esthetics and early formalism, see Ewa Thompson, *Russian Formalism and Anglo-American New Criticism. A Comparative Study* (The Hague, 1971), and, in this connection, Rudolf Lüthe, *New Criticism und idealistische Kunstphilosophie* (Bonn, 1975).

10. Voloshinov quoted from *Marxism and the Philosophy of Language*, trans. Ladislav Matejka and I. R. Titunik (New York and London, 1973), p. 95; pages cited in the text refer to this translation. The 1929 original is subtitled *Basic Problems of the Sociological Method in Linguistic Scholarship*. The passage is discussed in Samuel M. Weber, "Der Einschnitt. Zur Aktualität Voloshinovs," in Voloshinov, *Marxismus und Sprachphilosophie*, trans. Renate Horlemann (Frankfurt/M, 1975), pp. 13 f.

11. Derrida cautions that to free the signifier from subordination to the signified "does not, by simple inversion, mean that the signifier is fundamental or primary." *Of Grammatology*, transl. Gayatri Chakravorty Spivak (Baltimore and London, 1976), note, p. 324.

12. *Freudianism*, "Translator's Introduction," p. 4.

13. Ibid.

14. M. Bakhtin, *Problems of Dostoevskii's Poetics*, trans. R. W. Rotsel (Ann Arbor, 1973), p. 64.

15. Ibid., p. 71. I have made an adjustment in the translation, following a suggestion in Henryk Baran's review in *The Slavic and East European Journal* 18 (1974): 77-79.

16. Bakhtin, "Slovo v romane," *Voprosy literatury i estetiki* (Moscow, 1975), p. 86.

17. On Bakhtin's unsuccessful defense, see Kozhinov and Konkin, "Bakhtin," pp. 8-9; the study (finished 1940) was published in 1965 as *Tvorchestvo Fransua Rable i narodnaia kul'tura srednevekov'ia i Renessansa;* in English: *Rabelais and His World*, trans. Helene Iswolsky (Cambridge, Mass., and London, 1968).

175

18. Paul de Man, *Blindness and Insight: Essays in the Rhetoric of Contemporary Criticism* (New York, 1971); on Voloshinov and the nonverbal unconscious, see Neal H. Bruss, "V. N. Voloshinov and the Structure of Language in Freudianism," *Freudianism*, Appendix II.

19. Sergei Eisenstein, *Film Form*, trans. Jay Leyda (New York, 1949), pp. 16-17, writes of this period (1924-30): "We brought collective mass action onto the screen, in contrast to individualism and the 'triangle' drama of the bourgeois cinema. Discarding the individualistic conception of the bourgeois hero, our films of this period made an abrupt deviation—insisting on an understanding of the masses as hero."

20. Dorogov's paper is mentioned in the *Voprosy iazykoznaniia* report 2 (1971): 161.

21. Kozhinov and Konkin, "Bakhtin," p. 7.

22. Bakhtin, "Rabelais and Gogol (The Art of the Word and the Popular Culture of Laughter)," *Voprosy estetiki*, p. 492.

23. M. K. Dobrynin in *Literatura i marksizm* 1 (1929): 72; cited in A. Miasnikov, "Problemy rannego russkogo formalizma" ["Problems of Early Russian Formalism"], *Kontekst 1974: literaturno-teoreticheskie issledovaniia* (Moscow, 1975), p. 81.

24. Partially reprinted in P. N. Medvedev, *V laboratorii pisatelia* (Leningrad, 1971).

25. Miasnikov, "Problemy rannego russkogo formalizma," p. 82.

26. *Kratkaia literaturnaia entsiklopediia*, ed. A. A. Surkov (Moscow, 1962-67), 4: 723.

27. A. V. Lunacharskii, "O 'mnogogolosnosti' Dostoevskogo" ["On Dostoevskii's 'Multivoicedness'"], *Novyi mir* (1929), no. 10.

28. Kozhinov and Konkin, "Bakhtin," p. 8. All dates in Bakhtin's life cited in this introduction are taken from their biographical sketch.

29. Bakhtin, *Problemy poetiki Dostoevskogo* (Moscow: Sovetskii pisatel', 1963).

30. Five hundred copies of Lotman's book were printed then. It is available as Brown University Slavic Reprint V: *Lektsii po struktural'noi poetike: vvedenie, teoriia stikha*, intro. Thomas G. Winner (Providence, 1968).

31. Bakhtin, "K metodologii literaturovedeniia" ["Toward a Methodology of Literary Scholarship"], *Kontekst 1974* (1975), p. 206.

32. Bakhtin, "Problema soderzhaniia, materiala i formy v slovesnom khudozhestvennom tvorchestve," *Voprosy estetiki*, p. 9.

33. The most published information on Medvedev is found in E. Dobin's introduction to the selections in *V laboratorii pisatelia* (Leningrad, 1971).

34. Medvedev, "Sotsiologizm bez sotsiologii (O metodologicheskikh rabotakh P. N. Sakulina)," *Zvezda* (1926), no. 2: 267-71.

35. Medvedev, "Uchenyi sal'erizm (O formal'nom, 'morfologicheskom' metode)," *Zvezda* (1925), no. 3: 264-76; 275-76.

36. I. R. Titunik, "The Formal Method and the Sociological Method (M. M. Bakhtin, P. N. Medvedev, V. N. Voloshinov) in Russian Theory and Study of Literature," *Marxism and the Philosophy of Language*, p. 181, footnote.

37. Bakhtin, "Formy vremeni i khronotopa v romane. Ocherki po istoricheskoi poetike" ["Forms of Time and Chronotopos in the Novel"], *Voprosy estetiki*, p. 242.

38. Jacques Derrida, "Structure, Sign, and Play in the Discourse of the Human Sciences," *The Structuralist Controversy. The Languages of Criticism and the Sciences of Man*, ed. Richard Macksey and Eugenio Donato (Baltimore and London, 1970), p. 256.

39. Bakhtin, "Epos i roman (O metodologii issledovaniia romana)" ["The Epic and the Novel"], *Voprosy estetiki*, p. 482.

40. Apropos of "ahistoricism" in the passage cited in footnote 39, see D. S. Likhachev, *Poetika drevnerusskoi literatury* (2nd ed.; Leningrad, 1971), p. 167; for objections to Bakhtin's stress on Gogol's relationship to popular culture, see L. V. Zharavina, "Smekh Gogolia kak vyrazhenie ideino-nravstvennyx iskanii pisatelia," *Russkaia literatura* (1976), no. 2: 109-19; Leont'ev (*Psikholingvistika*) finds that Bakhtin/Voloshinov overstates the "purity" of linguistics' interest in the isolated word.

41. See "Discourse in Life and Discourse in Art," I. R. Titunik, trans., included in *Freudianism;* the original is "Slovo v zhizni i slovo v poezii: K voprosam sotsiologicheskoi poetiki," *Zvezda* (1926) no. 6: 244-67.

42. Compare and contrast the opening of Bakhtin's "The Problem of Content, Material, and Form" (1924), where he writes: "We have freed our work of the superfluous ballast of

citations and references. . . : they are not needed by the competent reader, and of no use to the incompetent." *Voprosy estetiki*, p. 7. Orientation toward speaker or receiver as a cultural mark is discussed in Lotman, Uspenskii, Ivanov, Toporov, Piatigorskii, "Theses on the Semiotic Study of Cultures (As Applied to Slavic Texts)," *The Tell-Tale Sign*, ed. Thomas A. Sebeok (Lisse/Netherlands, 1975), pp. 65 f.

43. Victor Erlich, *Russian Formalism. History–Doctrine* (2nd rev. ed.; The Hague, 1965), p. 115.

44. "Iz predystorii romannogo slova" ["From the Prehistory of the Word in the Novel"], *Voprosy estetiki*, p. 433.

45. Vadim Kozhinov informs me (correspondence) that *The Formal Method* has already been published under Bakhtin's name in Japan.

Notes to Chapter One

1. These founders of contemporary European artistic theory cannot be considered members of the formal movement, although they were strongly influenced by Hildebrand. They were specifiers in the best sense of the word, free from all partisan bias.

2. "Philosophy from below" [*von unten*] and "philosophy from above" [*von oben*] were Gustav Theodor Fechner's (1834-87) terms to describe the two trends in contemporary esthetics, the one relying on empirical experimentation, the other on idealist notions of "the soul." See the preface to his *Vorschule der Ästhetik*(1876). Also mentioned in Max Dessoir, *Aesthetics and Theory of Art*, trans. Stephen A. Emery (Detroit, 1970), pp. 33-34 (a translation of *Ästhetik und allgemeine Kunstwissenschaft*).–Trans.

3. See Gottfried Semper, *Stil in den technischen und tektonischen Künsten* (Munich, 1878-79).

4. See Alois Riegl, *Stilfragen. Grundlegung zu einer Geschichte der Ornamentik* (2nd ed.; Berlin, 1923); and August Schmarzow, *Grundbegriffe der Kunstwissenschaft* (Leipzig and Berlin, 1905), especially the introduction, "Gottfried Semper–Alois Riegl."

5. See Paul Bekker, *Die Symphonie von Beethoven bis Mahler* (Berlin, 1918); also Valentin N. Voloshinov, "Slovo v zhizni i slovo v poezii," *Zvezda*, 1926, no. 6, English translation I. R. Titunik, "Discourse in life and Discourse in Art," in Voloshinov, *Freudianism: A Marxist Critique* (New York, 1976).

Notes to Chapter Two

1. Subsequently, *siuzhet* will be translated as "plot" and *fabula* as "story."–Trans.

2. Pypin, Aleksander Nikolaevich (1833-1904). A biographer of the social critic Belinskii, this scholar combined social awareness with a cultural approach to literature.

Vengerov, Semen Afanasievich (1855-1920). Professor at Petersburg University, Vengerov, like Pypin, viewed literature as an aspect of cultural history.–Trans.

3. *Raznochinets:* a member of the "new class" which began to appear around the end of the eighteenth century to meet the needs of developing Russian capitalism. Their education set them off from the lower class of their origin.–Trans.

4. Jonas Cohn, *Allgemeine Ästhetik* (Leipzig, 1901).

5. Broder Christiansen, *Philosophie der Kunst* (Hanau, 1909).

6. Richard Hamann, *Ästhetik* (Leipzig, 1911). [Here Medvedev is singling out emphases of Hamann's esthetics, not his terminology; i.e., Hamann does not use *Dingheit* or *Dinglichkeit*, but refers to *das Ding* or to the *stofflichen Existenz* of the work, and to the *Autokratie des ästhetischen Objektes*, or to the *Selbstständigkeit, Formverhältnisse, Formengebilde* of works of art. Translator's note.].

7. In recent Russian criticism the feature of literature we are surveying has been brought up more than once in polemics with the formalists, but on a false basis and without

sufficient methodological precision. This is particularly true of A. A. Smirnov in his interesting article "The Aims of Literary Scholarship," *Literaturnaia mysl'*, 1923. He defines the poetic work as an indivisible unity of cognitive, ethical, and esthetic elements. However, the intuitive agnosticism of this author does not permit him to deal with concrete problems of poetic structure. According to Smirnov, all methods of study only lead the scholar to the threshhold of the "holy of holies" of poetic structure. Access to its depths is closed to scholarly methodology: it is only accessible to intuition.

The feature under discussion is also treated with particular immediacy in the works of A. Askol'dov, *Literaturnaia mysl'* and Sezeman, *Mysl'*, 1922, although extremely briefly in the latter. However there is no real methodological analysis in these studies either.

8. Veselovskii, Aleksander Nikolaevich (1838-1906). His vast comparative work showed the way from cultural history to historical poetics.—Trans.

9. Sakulin, Pavel Nikitich (1868-1930). Sakulin devoted a number of works to the problem of synthesizing Marxism and other views of literary history and poetics.—Trans.

10. P. N. Sakulin, *Sotsiologicheskii metod v literaturovedenii* (Leningrad, 1925).

11. Friche, Vladimir Maksimovich (1870-1929). A Marxist scholar, critic, and publicist who tried to show a direct correspondence between literature and the means of production. —Trans.

12. V. M. Friche, "Problemy sotsiologicheskoi poetiki," *Vestnik Kommunisticheskoi akademii* 17 (1926): 169.

13. Ibid., p. 171.

14. Ibid., p. 172.

Notes to Chapter Three

1. The first and only attempt of this kind is still B. M. Eikhenbaum's "Teoriia 'formal'nogo metoda'" [1926] in his collection of articles *Literatura (Teoriia, kritika, polemika)* (Leningrad, 1927). But this article does not satisfy the need for a wide orientation of the formalist method, nor is that its purpose. It is limited to a short historical sketch of formalism, and only a half-page is devoted to West European formalism.

2. See Julius Meier-Graeffe, *Hans von Marees. Sein Leben und sein Werk*, Book 3 (Munich and Leipzig, 1909-10), and Jonas Cohn's article in *Logos* (1911-12), nos. 2 and 3.

3. Fiedler's works are collected in *Schriften über Kunst* (2nd ed.; Munich, 1913-14), reprinted as *Schriften zur Kunst*, 2 vols. (Munich: Wilhelm Fink, 1971). In 1893 Hildebrand published *Das Problem der Form in der bildenden Kunst* (Strassburg, 1893); English translation *The Problem of Form in Painting and Sculpture* (New York and London, 1939).

4. The term is Jonas Cohn's [*Transgradient*].

5. Hildebrand, *Das Problem der Form* (3rd ed., Strassburg, 1914), p. 4.

6. See Fiedler's article "Ursprung der künstlerischen Tätigkeit," in *Schriften zur Kunst*, I: 266.

7. Fiedler, *Schriften*, I: 301. It is characteristic of our formalists that they began precisely with the contrast of artistic form to "the serious aims of cognition."

8. See Worringer's *Abstraktion und Einfühlung* (3rd. ed.; Munich, 1921); English translation *Abstraction and Empathy*, Michael Bullock, trans. (Cleveland and New York, 1967).

9. See Worringer's *Formprobleme der Gotik* (Munich, 1911), p. 69; English translation *Form in Gothic*, Herbert Read intro. and ed. (New York, 1957).

10. Eikhenbaum, Boris Mikhailovich (1886-1959). Eikhenbaum wrote something of importance about almost every classic Russian writer, with particular specialization on Tolstoi and Lermontov.—Trans.

11. Eikhenbaum, "Teoriia," *Literatura*, p. 118 (French translation in *Théorie de la littérature*, Tzvetan Todorov, ed. and trans., intro. Roman Jakobson [Paris, 1965], pp. 33-34.

12. G. T. Fechner's terms (*Vorschule der Ästhetik*, 1876).—Trans.

13. See V. M. Zhirmunskii's notes to O. Val'tsel, *Problema formy v poezii* (St. Petersburg, 1923).

14. On Sievers and Saran see Eikhenbaum, "Melodika stikha" ["The Melody of Verse"] [1921] in *O poezii* (Leningrad, 1969) and Zhirmunskii's notes to Val'tsel, *Problema formy v poezii.*

15. Eikhenbaum's use of Sievers' views is criticized in detail in Zhirmunskii's article "Melodika stixa," *Mysl'*, 1922, which is included in his *Voprosy teorii literatury* [*Problems of Literary Theory*] (Leningrad, 1928), reprint (The Hague, 1962).

16. For a typical example of this point of view see Emil Ermatinger, *Das dichterische Kunstwerk* (Leipzig, 1921).

17. Hermann Hefele's book *Das Wesen der Dichtung* (Stuttgart, 1923) is typical of this movement.

18. The Geneva School: Charles Bally and Albert Sechehaye.

Notes to Chapter Four

1. *Voskreshenie slova* (Petersburg, 1914). The importance of this brochure for OPOIAZ is debated by Victor Erlich and Richard Sheldon in *Slavic Review* 35 (1976): 111-12.—Trans.

2. Veselovskii's article "Iz istorii epiteta" [1895] in his *Istoricheskaia poetika* (Leningrad, 1940).—Trans.

3. Here is a statement of Shklovskii's that reflects this "escatological" motif: "The old has died and the new is not yet born; and things have died—we have lost the sensation of things; we are like a violinist who no longer feels the bow and strings; we have ceased being artists of everyday life: we do not like our houses and our clothes and we part easily with a life that is not perceptible to us. Only the creation of new forms can return the perceptibility of the world to man, can resurrect things and kill pessimism." *Voskreshenie slova* (Petersburg, 1914), p. 12; in *Texte der russischen Formalisten*, Jurij Striedter and Wolf-Dieter Stempel ed. and intros., 2 vols. (Munich, 1972), "Die Auferweckung des Wortes," 2: 13.

4. That is, in *Sborniki po teorii poeticheskogo iazyka I* (Petersburg, 1916); *Sborniki II* appeared in 1917, followed by *Poetika. Sborniki po teorii poeticheskogo iazyka* (Petrograd, 1919).—Trans.

5. "Po povodu 'zvukovyx zhestov' iaponskogo iazyka." Polivanov, Evgenii Dmitrievich (1891-1938): specialist on Eastern languages.—Trans.

6. Nyrop, Kristoffer (1858-1931): Danish linguist; the study is on sound in poetry. *Sborniki I* also includes work by the French linguist Maurice Grammont (1886-1946) on the same topic.—Trans.

7. Potebnia, Aleksander Afanasievich (1835-91). Professor at Kharkov University. His theories were developed and published by his students in *Voprosy teorii i psikhologii tvorchestva*, 8 vols. (Petrograd and Kharkov, 1907-23).—Trans.

8. Ivanov, Viacheslav Ivanovich (1866-1949). Leader of the Petersburg symbolists, Ivanov is one of the most erudite figures of Russian literature. He is perhaps best known in criticism for his study of Dostoevskii's "novel tragedies"; see his *Freedom and the Tragic Life* (New York, 1957). Briusov, Valerii Iakovlevich (1873-1924). Briusov is considered the founder of Russian symbolism. He is the author of important studies of Pushkin's verse and well-known articles on Tiutchev and Gogol. Belyi, Andrei (Bugaev, Boris Nikolaevich) (1880-1934). Poet, major novelist, and mystic, Belyi brought symbolism and mathematics to the study of poetry in *Simvolizm* (Moscow, 1910) and *Ritm kak dialektika* [*Rhythm as Dialectic*] (Moscow, 1929). Merezhkovskii, Dmitrii Sergeevich (1865-1941). Novelist, poet, and religious thinker, his best-known criticism is on Tolstoi and Dostoevskii. A translation of his article on Gogol and the devil is in *Gogol from the Twentieth Century*, Robert A. Maguire, intro., ed., trans. (Princeton, 1974). Chukovskii, Kornei Ivanovich (1882-1969). A writer of children's poetry and author of a book on language acquisition, Chukovskii's wide-ranging criticism includes *Litsa i masky* [*Faces and Masks*] (1914), a book of perceptive literary portraits.—Trans.

9. Eikhenbaum, "Teoriia," *Literatura*, p. 119; *Théorie de la littérature*, p. 35.

10. The formalists themselves do not deny their positivism. Eikhenbaum says: "It was important to oppose the subjective esthetic principles which inspired the symbolists' theoretical works with propaganda favoring the objective, scientific study of facts. This is

the source of the new spirit of scientific positivism characteristic of the formalists; the rejection of philosophical premises and psychological esthetics, and so on. This break with philosophical esthetics and with ideological theories of art was dictated by the state of affairs." "Teoriia," *Literatura*, p. 120; *Théorie de la littérature*, p. 39.

However the words which immediately precede the passage just quoted show that this formalist positivism was mixed with tendencies that were far from positivist. Eikhenbaum writes: "The schism between the theoreticians of symbolism (1910-11) and the appearance of the acmeists set the stage for a decisive revolt. All compromises were to be eliminated. History demanded of us a genuine revolutionary spirit: categoric theses, merciless irony, a bold rejection of any compromise." Ibid. This has little to do with positivism.

11. On this topic, see A. G. Fomm, "S. A. Vengerov kak professor i rukovoditel' pushkinskoi seminarii," in *Pushkinskii sbornik pamiati professora S. A. Vengerova* (Moscow and Petrograd, 1922).—Trans.

12. Peretts, Vladimir Nikolaevich (1870-1936). In his *Lektsii po metodologii istorii russkoi literatury* (Kiev, 1914) this literary historian distinguished between the "how" and the "what" of literature; see Erlich, *Russian Formalism*, p. 56.—Trans.

13. V. M. Zhirmunskii indicates the importance of Peretts in this regard in his article "Zadachi poetiki" ["The Aims of poetics"] [1921] in his *Voprosy teorii literatury* [*Problems of Literary Theory*] (Leningrad, 1928), reprint (The Hague, 1962), p. 19; *Texte der Formalisten*, 2: 138.

14. Another possible influence might have been Professor I. Mandel'shtam, that is, his book *O kharaktere gogolevskogo stilia. Glava iz istorii russkogo literaturnogo iazyka* [*The Nature of Gogol's Style*] (Helsingfors, 1902).

15. Khlebnikov, Velimir (1885-1922). Khlebnikov explored the linguistic history of words, looking for ways to link the primeval with the futuristic. His poem "Incantation to Laughter" (1910) is sometimes considered the beginning of Russian futurism; it is made of forms of one word, "smekh" [laughter].—Trans.

16. See "manifestos" by N. Gumilev and S. Gorodetskii, in *Apollon*, 1913, no.1. [Gumilev, Nikolai (1886-1921). One of the founders of acmeism, his verse features exotic and heroic themes. He was shot by the Bolsheviks. Gorodetskii, Sergei (1884-1967). Gorodetskii extolled the esthetics of Gautier and wrote poetry styled after Slavic folk literature. Translator's note.].

17. Balmont, Konstantin (1867-1943). One of the most musical of Russian poets, he was the author of an essay "Poeziia kak volshebstvo" ["Poetry as Magic"] (Moscow, 1915). Sologub, Fedor (Teternikov, Fedor Kuz'mich) (1863-1927). He expressed the ugliness of life in polished verse, but is perhaps better known for his novel *Melkii bes,* a tale of demonic banality; see *The Petty Demon,* Andrew Field, trans. (Bloomington, 1970).—Trans.

18. The acmeists did not produce theoretical works on poetics, aside from the book of rather random articles by the schoolmaster himself, N. Gumilev, *Pis'ma o russkoi poezii* [*Letters on Russian Poetry*] (Petrograd, 1923).

19. Akhmatova, Anna Andreevna (Gorenko) (1889-1966). The acmeist leader, Nikolai Gumilev, was her first husband. Her concise lyrics combine concrete detail and a deeply personal tone. Vinogradov, Viktor Vladimirovich (1895). His *Poeziia Anny Akhmatovoi* (Leningrad, 1925) in many ways anticipates his two studies of Pushkin's style. He is a specialist in stylistics and the development of the Russian literary language. Eikhenbaum's book on Akhmatova is *Anna Akhmatova. Opyt analiza* (Petersburg, 1923).—Trans.

20. Eikhenbaum, "Teoriia," *Literatura*, p. 120; *Théorie de la littérature*, p. 39.

21. Aleksander Blok, who is considered the greatest of the Russian symbolists, acknowledged the influence of Nietzsche on his understanding of "the spirit of music," which runs as a leitmotif through his essays entitled *Rossiia i intelligentsiia* (Petrograd, 1919).—Trans.

22. Baudouin de Courtenay, Jan (1845-1929). A professor at Petersburg University, he shifted attention from diachronic to synchronic aspects of language.—Trans.

23. Shcherba, Lev Vladimirovich (1880-1944). Baudouin de Courtenay's student, Shcherba continued the campaign against the neo-grammarians by studying the functional aspects of living speech.—Trans.

24. Shklovskii, "Iskusstvo kak priem" ["Art as Device"] [1917], in his *O teorii prozy* [*The Theory of Prose*] (2nd ed.; Moscow, 1929), p. 14; *Théorie de la littérature*, p. 85. In *Poetika* (1919), p. 126.

25. In particular, see Shklovskii's book, *Rozanov* (Petrograd, 1921).

26. *Skaz:* the formalist term for a manner of narration which draws attention to itself, creating the illusion of actual oral narration.—Trans.

27. Shklovskii, "Sviaz' priemov siuzhetoslozheniia s obshchimi priemami stilia" ["The Connection between the Devices of Plot Formation and General Stylistic Devices"], *Poetika* (1919): 115-50; also in *O teorii prozy*, pp. 24-67; *Texte der Formalisten*, 1, "Der Zusammenhang zwischen den Verfahren der Sujetfügung und den allgemeinen Stilverfahren."

28. Eikhenbaum, "Teoriia," *Literatura*, p. 132; *Théorie de la littérature*, p. 52.

29. Zhirmunskii, Viktor Maksimovich (1891-1971). His position *vis à vis* formalism is discussed by Erlich, *Russian Formalism*, pp. 96-98. His *Vvedenie v metriku. Teoriia stixa* (Leningrad, 1925) contains a critical account of the method Belyi uses in *Simvolizm;* see *Introduction to Metrics. The Theory of Verse*, C. F. Brown, trans. (The Hague, 1966), pp. 40-48 ff.—Trans.

30. "K voprosu o 'formal'nom metode,'" the introductory article to the Russian translation of Oskar Walzel, *Gehalt und Gestalt im Kunstwerk des Dichters* (Petrograd, 1923) and in Zhirmunskii's *Voprosy teorii literatury*.

31. Forsotsy: i.e., formalist-sociologists; see Erlich, *Russian Formalism*, pp. 110-14. Boris Ignatievich Arvatov's (b. 1896) article "O formal'no-sotsiologicheskom metode," *Pechat' i revolutsiia* (1927), Book 3, is an interesting contrast to Walter Benjamin's "The Work of Art in the Age of Mechanical Reproduction," *Illuminations*, Harry Zohn, trans. (New York, 1969).—Trans.

32. Articles by Sezeman and Askol'dov are cited in footnote 7 to Part One, Chapter Two.—Trans.

33. Smirnov, Aleksander Aleksandrovich (1883-1962). A specialist in European medieval and Renaissance literature. Engel'gardt, Boris Mikhailovich (1887-1942). Trained in philosophy in German universities, Engel'gardt wrote on a wide range of subjects and did some editing and translating.—Trans.

34. Third Section: Nicholas the First's secret police.—Trans.

35. See the articles by A. V. Lunacharskii, P. S. Kogan, V. Polianskii, P. N. Sakulin, and S. Bobrov in *Pechat' i revoliutsii* [*The Press and Revolution*], 1924, Book 5.

[Lunacharskii, Anatolii Vasilievich (1875-1933) was Commissar of Education 1917-29; Kogan, Petr Semenovich (1872-1932) was a professor at Moscow University and president of the State Academy of Arts; Valerian (P. I. Lebedev-)Polianskii (1881-1948) was president of the *Proletkult* and author of such works as *On the Literary Front* (1924) and "Motifs of Workers' Poetry" (1918); Bobrov, Sergei Pavlovich (b. 1889) was a poetic theorist associated with the Moscow Linguistic Circle and the "Centrafuge" poets. On the anti-OPOIAZ symposium held in the above-cited magazine, see Erlich, *Russian Formalism*, pp. 105-7 f.]

36. For instance Eikhenbaum's *Molodoi Tolstoi* (Petrograd and Berlin, 1922), *Lermontov* (Leningrad, 1924), "Nekrasov," *Nachalo* (1922, no.1), and in *Literatura*, pp. 77-115.

37. Eikhenbaum, "Teoriia," *Literatura*, p. 143; *Théorie de la littérature*, pp. 67-68.

38. See the above-cited article by Zhirmunskii, "K voprosu o formal'nom metode."

39. Eikhenbaum, *Lermontov*, p. 10.

40. Tomashevskii, Boris Viktorovich (1890-1957). A specialist on versification and an authority on Pushkin. Medvedev is probably referring to one of his studies of Pushkin here. Iakubinskii, Lev Petrovich (?-1945). In light of Bakhtin's emphasis on dialogue, the reference is probably to Iakubinskii's "O dialogicheskoi rechi," ["On Speech Dialogue"] *Russkaia rech'* (Petrograd, 1923), I.—Trans.

41. However, in his most recent work, a book on Tolstoi that is not yet published, it seems that Shklovskii too surrenders many formalist positions. [The reference is probably to *Material i stil' v romane L. N. Tolstogo Voina i mir* (Moscow, 1928).]

42. Eikhenbaum, "Teoriia," *Literatura*, pp. 116-17; *Théorie de la littérature*, p. 32.

Notes to Chapter Five

1. Eikhenbaum, "Teoriia," *Literatura*, p. 116; *Théorie de la littérature*, p. 31.

2. In his book *Formal'nyi metod v istorii literatury* (Leningrad, 1927) B. M. Engel'gardt is absolutely wrong in his interpretation of formalist assertions about the specific features of the literary work. He says these are conditional methodological orientations and holds to this interpretation from start to finish. As a result, he creates the false impression that formalism is a purely methodological system.

3. This transition was partly accomplished in Shklovskii's "Art as Device" (1917), but particularly in the last articles of *Poetika* (1919). The final article of this collection, Eikhenbaum's "How Gogol's *The Overcoat* Is Made," is the first formalist study of the construction of the poetic work.

4. Tynianov, Iurii Nikolaevich (1894-1943). His article "O literaturnom fakte," *LEF* (1924) reappeared in his *Arkhaisty i novatory* [*Archaists and Innovators*] (Leningrad, 1929); it is contained in *Texte der Formalisten*, 1, as "Das literarische Faktum." On "literary life," see Eikhenbaum, "Das literarische Leben," *Texte der Formalisten*, 1. — Trans.

5. Arnaut Daniel (fl. 1180-1200): Provençal poet. — Trans.

6. "Iskusstvo kak priem," *O teorii prozy*, pp. 21-22; *Théorie de la littérature*, "L'art comme procédé," pp. 95-96. Shklovskii originally expressed these views in "The Resurrection of the Word."

7. Ibid., p. 11; *Théorie de la littérature*, p. 81.

8. See Jakobson, *O cheshkom stikhe preimushchestvenno v sopostavlenii s russkim* [*On Czech Verse*] (Berlin, 1923).

9. Ibid., p. 17.

10. Iakubinskii, "O poeticheskom glossemosochetanii," *Poetika* (1919). — Trans.

11. Zhirmunskii, "Zadachi poetiki" [1921, 1923], in *Voprosy teorii literatury*, p. 39.

12. Shklovskii, *Poetika* (1919), p. 6.

13. Jakobson, *Noveishaia russkaia poeziia* [*The Latest Russian Poetry*] (Prague, 1921), p. 10.

14. Eikhenbaum, "Teoriia," *Literatura*, p. 121; *Théorie de la littérature*, p. 38.

15. Shklovskii, "Iskusstvo kak priem," *O teorii prozy*, pp. 21-22; *Théorie de la littérature*, pp. 94-96.

16. See Iurii Tynianov, *Problema stikhotvornogo iazyka* (Leningrad, 1924).

17. Shklovskii, "Iskusstvo kak priem," *O teorii prozy*, pp. 22-23; *Théorie de la littérature*, p. 97.

18. See Engel'gardt's *Formal'nyi metod v istorii literatury* (Leningrad, 1927).

19. Engel'gardt's term.

20. Shklovskii, "Sviaz' priemov siuzhetoslozheniia s obshchimi priemami stilia," *O teorii prozy*, p. 31; "Der Zusammenhang zwischen der Verfahren der Sujetfügung und den allgemeinen Stilverfahren," *Texte der Formalisten*, 1: 51.

21. Iakubinskii, "O dialogicheskoi rechi," *Russkaia rech'*, 1923.

22. In the article this sentence reads: "It is doubtful that there exists an area of speech *in which the relationship to the word could be totally mechanized,* in which the word could be exclusively a signal" [translator's italics]. — Trans.

23. Eikhenbaum, "Oratorskii stil' Lenina," *Literatura*, p. 250.

24. It is true that some poets' remarks on this subject are also cited, remarks mainly in poetic form, as in Lermontov's "Est' rechi . . ." or "Sluchitsia li tebe . . . ."

25. Iakubinskii's article "O zvukakh stikhotvornogo iazyka," *Poetika* (1919) opens with this contrast.

26. Ibid., p. 49.

27. It is true that the formalists subsequently abandoned such hypotheses and speculations. But the formalists never established a principled distinction between sound in language and sound in the poetic construction.

28. Of course, here too the phonetic whole is somehow regulated beyond its purely signifying meaning. Absolute disregard of this is not permissible. But we need not develop the point here.

29. Osip Brik, "Zvukovye povtory" ["Sound Repetitions"] in *Poetika* (1919).

30. Shklovskii, *Poetika* (1919), p. 24.

31. The present discussion leaves aside a series of problems connected with poetic sound. It goes without saying that a loud sound which is heard is not always organized, and a

sound which is pronounced and articulated can be organized. Finally, it is possible to organize the phonetic and articulatory possibilities of sound without intending to realize them. All of these points are very complicated and as tightly bound to the problem of the artistic audience as they are to the problem of social interaction. We have also not examined the problem of expressive intonation, which is conditioned by the nonrepeatable, unique meaning of the utterance, as distinct from syntactic intonation or intonation in general.

Notes to Chapter Six

1. For a discussion of *skaz*, see Martin P. Rice, "On *Skaz*," *Russian Literature Triquarterly* 12 (1975): 409-24.—Trans.

2. For an English translation, see Robert A. Maguire, "How Gogol's 'Overcoat' Is Made," *Gogol from the Twentieth Century. Eleven Essays* (Princeton, 1974).—Trans.

3. Eikhenbaum, "Kak sdelana *Shinel'* Gogolia," *Literatura*, pp. 151-52; *Théorie de la littérature*, pp. 215-16; Maguire, "Gogol's 'Overcoat,'" pp. 272-73.

4. Shklovskii, "Literatura vne siuzheta" ["Literature Outside Plot"], *O teorii prozy*, p. 237.

5. Shklovskii, "Parodiinyi roman. Sterne's *Tristram Shandy*," *O teorii prozy*, p. 177; *Texte der Formalisten*, 1: 245.

6. Eikhenbaum, "Literatura i kino," *Literatura*, pp. 297-98.

7. Shklovskii, "Parodiinyi roman," *O teorii prozy*, p. 204; *Texte der Formalisten*, 1: 299.

8. Ibid.

9. Teffi: penname of Nadezhda Aleksandrovna Buchinskaia (nee Lokhvitskaia) (1872-1952). Teffi is especially noted for her stories of emigre life in Paris in the twenties.—Trans.

10. Shklovskii, "Sviaz' priemov siuzhetoslozheniia...," *O teorii prozy*, p. 35; *Texte der formalisten*, 1: 58.

11. Ibid., p. 60; *Texte der formalisten*, 1: 107, 109.

12. For a discussion of the critical treatment of the "humane passages," see F. Driessen, *Gogol as a Short-Story Writer* (The Hague, 1965); in N. V. Gogol, *The Overcoat and Other Tales of Good and Evil*, David Magarshack, trans. (New York, 1957) these are the passages that begin: "Leave me alone, gentlemen. Why do you pester me?" (p. 236) and "And St. Petersburg carried on without Akakii, as though he had never lived there. A human being just disappeared and left no trace, a human being whom no one ever dreamed of protecting." (p. 265).—Trans.

13. Eikhenbaum, *"Shinel',"* *Literatura*, p. 162; *Théorie de la littérature*, p. 229; Maguire, "Gogol's 'Overcoat,'" p. 287.

14. Eikhenbaum, *"Shinel',"* *Literatura*, pp. 153-57; *Théorie de la littérature*, pp. 218-22; Maguire, "Gogol's 'Overcoat,'" pp. 276-80.

15. Shklovskii, "Literatura vne siuzheta," *O teorii prozy*, pp. 236-37.

16. Rozanov, Vasilii Vasilievich (1856-1919). Writer, publicist, philosopher, and critic, Rozanov's articles on Dostoevskii and Gogol are perhaps his best known criticism.—Trans.

17. Shklovskii, *Rozanov* (Petrograd, 1921), p. 8; [see also "Literatura vne siuzheta," *O teorii prozy*, p. 228].

18. Eikhenbaum, "O. Genri i teoriia novelly," *Literatura*, p. 195.

19. Ibid., p. 169.

20. Iurii Tynianov, *Problema stikhotvornogo iazyka* [*The Problem of Poetic Language*] (Leningrad, 1924), p. 7; reprint (The Hague, 1963).

21. Ibid., p. 8.

22. Jakobson, "Noveishaia russkaia poeziia," *Texte der Formalisten*, 2: 33.

23. Eikhenbaum, "Teoriia," *Literatura*, p. 148; *Théorie de la littérature*, p. 74.

24. For related elaboration of the difference between sign and signal, see V. N. Voloshinov, *Marxism and the Philosophy of Language*, L. Matejka and I. R. Titunik, trans. (New York and London, 1973), particularly pp. 68-69, 71, and 80.—Trans.

25. Shklovskii, *Rozanov*, p. 4; *O teorii prozy*, "Literatura vne siuzheta," p. 226.

26. Shklovskii, *Rozanov*, p. 5; "Literatura vne siuzheta," p. 226.

27. Even the majority of formalists do not deny this.

28. An instructive example of attempts to do this is Gustav Shpet's *Vnutrenniaia forma slova* [*The Inner Form of the Word*] Moscow, 1927). Shpet's attempt to bring in dialectics and history does not prevent him from seeking inner form in language and trying to substantiate it there. And, on idealist grounds, it could not be otherwise.

29. Of course, this is only a figurative analogy. The ideal space of the painting should not be equated with meaning in the literary work.

30. Eikhenbaum, *"Shinel'," Literatura*, p. 163; *Théorie de la littérature*, pp. 231-32; Maguire, "Gogol's 'Overcoat,'" p. 288.

Notes to Chapter Seven

1. In the second appendix to his and L. Matejka's translation of Voloshinov, *Marxism and the Philosophy of Language* I. R. Titunik refers to "zavershenie" as "finalized structured-ness." This seemed too cumbersome to sustain in the present translation. This "structuredness" is the topic of Barbara Herrnstein Smith's book *Poetic Closure. A Study of How Poems End* (Chicago and London, 1968), but it was felt that "closure," besides also being somewhat awkward, might be too "automatized," causing readers to overlook the technical meaning of "zavershenie." So "zavershenie" is translated here as "finalization," with its related forms. —Trans.

2. This aspect of genre was developed in the teachings of A. N. Veselovskii. He explained a series of elements of the artistic construction, for instance epic repetitions and rhythmic parallelisms, by the conditions of the social event of the realization of the work. He took account of the place which the work occupies in real space and time. It is true that this side of his work remained unfinished.

3. B. Tomashevskii, *Teoriia literatury* (Moscow and Leningrad, 1925), p. 131; reprint of 4th ed. (Ann Arbor: Ardis Publishers, n.d. [1971?]; *Théorie de la littérature,* "Thématique," p. 263. This book cannot be called "formalist" in the strict sense of the word. Its author has gone a long way from formalism in many respects. Tomashevskii revises many important formalist positions in his book. Nonetheless, his way of thinking is still quite formalist and he still holds to many basic formalist premises.

4. "Stroenie rasskaza" and "Kak sdelan *Don-Kikhot.*"—Trans.

5. Shklovskii, "Stroenie rasskaza," *O teorii prozy,* p. 83; *Théorie de la littérature,* p. 189.

6. Shklovskii, ibid., p. 90; *Théorie de la littérature,* p. 196.

7. The reference is to Turgenev's essay "Hamlet and Don Quixote" (1860) and pages in Heine's *Die romantische Schule* (1836).—Trans.

8. Shklovskii, "Kak sdelan *Don-Kikhot,*" *O teorii prozy,* pp. 100-01.

9. Tomashevskii, *Teoriia literatury,* p. 154; *Théorie de la littérature,* p. 296.

10. Shklovskii, "Sviaz' priemov siuzhetoslozheniia," *O teorii, prozy,* pp. 59-60; *Texte der Formalisten,* 1: 107.

Notes to Chapter Eight

1. Nekrasov, Nikolai Alekseevich (1821-78). A writer of "civic poetry," including verse that draws on Russian folklore, he was editor of the journal that was the mouthpiece of the radical critics Chernyshevskii and Dobroliubov. But he wrote an ode of praise to the tsar's hated enforcer Muravev. For more on this contradiction see Kornei Chukovskii, *The Poet and the Hangman* [1922] R. W. Rotsel, trans. (Ann Arbor, 1976).—Trans.

2. Eikhenbaum, "Nekrasov," *Literatura,* p. 96.

3. Ibid., p. 97.

4. Eikhenbaum, *"Shinel'," Literatura,* p. 161; *Théorie de la littérature,* p. 228; Maguire, "Gogol's 'Overcoat,'" pp. 286-87.

5. Tolstoi, Aleksei Konstantinovich (1817-75). A poet known for historical and dramatic verse, ballads, and humorous and satirical poems.—Trans.

6. Polonskii, Iakov (1819-98). A romantic, sentimental, melodious lyricist.—Trans.

7. Zhirmunskii, "K voprosu o formal'nom metode," *Voprosy teorii literatury,* pp. 165-66.

8. Benediktov, Vladislav Grigorievich (1807-73). His affected, ultra-romantic *Poems* (1835) enjoyed sensational, if short-lived, success.—Trans.

9. Lomonosov, Mikhail Vasilievich (1711-65). Called "the first Russian university," this many-sided genius decreed that Russian verse would be syllabo-tonic and legislated that genres would conform to three styles, the ode using the high style. Karamzin, Nikolai Mikhailovich (1766-1826). Historian and sentimentalist writer. Karamzin's school championed a Frenchified "middle style" as the language of literature.—Trans.

10. Tynianov, *Problema stikhotvornogo iazyka,* p. 123.

11. *Differenzqualität*—Broder Christiansen's term [in *Philosophie der Kunst* (Hanau, 1909); on the importance of this concept in Russian formalism, see Erlich, *Russian Formalism,* p. 178 and elsewhere. Translator's note.].

Notes to Chapter Nine

1. Derzhavin, Gavril Romanovich (1743-1816). Considered the greatest Russian poet before Pushkin, Derzhavin brought the subjective perception of the real world to the ode. Kiukhel'beker, Vil'hel'm Karlovich (1797-1846). Political activist (Decembrist), dramatist, and poet, this "archaist" favored the monumental poetic forms. Griboedov, Aleksander Sergeevich (1795-1829). Also classed as an "archaist" by Tynianov [*Arkhaisty i novatory* (Leningrad, 1929)], this poet and diplomat is best known for his play in verse *Gore ot uma* [*Woe from Wit*] (1924).—Trans.

2. Bulgarin, Faddei Venediktovich (1788-1859). Police spy and right-wing newspaper editor, Bulgarin wrote the moralistic melodramas *Ivan Vyzhigin* (1829) and *Peter Ivanovich Vyzhigin* (1831) and the didactic historical novels *Dmitrii the Pretender* (1830) and *Mazeppa* (1833-34).—Trans.

3. Brik, Osip Maksimovich (1888-1938). Brik wrote little, preferring to let his ideas stimulate others. He was intimately involved in the formation of Russian futurism and OPOIAZ, and in Maiakovskii's group The Left Front of Art (LEF). LEF reached its peak about 1923; Maiakovskii tried to revive it in 1927, renaming the group's journal *The New LEF,* but without success. Brik's article "Ritm i sintaksis" appeared in that publication, 1927, Nos.3-6, and is found in *Théorie de la littérature* and in *Texte der Formalisten,* 2.—Trans.

4. *The Alarm Clock* [*Budil'nik*] was one of the humorous magazines in which Chekhov published his first sketches and stories under various pseudonyms.—Trans.

5. Shklovskii, "Literatura vne siuzheta," *O teorii prozy,* pp. 227-28.

6. Buridan, Jean (Joannes Buridanus), 1300-58, Aristotelian philosopher and scientific theorist. In his commentary to Aristotle's *De caelo,* Buridan shows that if a dog must choose between two identical portions of food, he will do so randomly.—Trans.

7. Eikhenbaum, *Lermontov* (Leningrad, 1924), p. 12.

8. We will introduce more recent formulations by Tynianov below.

9. Zhukovskii, Vasilii Andreevich (1783-1852). Prolific translator of English and German romantic poets and an excellent elegist and ballad writer in his own right.—Trans.

10. Tynianov, "O literaturnom fakte" [1924] in *Texte der Formalisten,* 1: 400, 401.

11. Ibid., p. 413.

12. Eikhenbaum, "V ozhidanii literatury" ["In the Expectation of Literature"], *Literatura,* p. 285.

13. Eikhenbaum, *Molodoi Tolstoi* (Petrograd and Berlin, 1922), p. 19; *The Young Tolstoi,* Gary Kern ed. and trans. (Ann Arbor, 1972), p. 13.

14. "Dnevnik molodosti L. N. Tolstogo" in his *Polnoe sobranie sochinenii* (Moscow, 1937), 59: 28-29.

15. Eikhenbaum, "Nekrasov," *Literatura,* p. 106.

16. Eikhenbaum, "Literaturnyi byt" [1927] in *Texte der Formalisten,* 1, "Das literarische Leben," pp. 462, 463.

17. Ibid., pp. 470, 471.

18. B. M. Engel'gardt, *Formal'nyi metod v istorii literatury* (Leningrad, 1927), p. 116.

INDEX

Library of Congress Cataloging in Publication Data

Medvedev, Pavel Nikolaevich, 1891-1938.
    The formal method in literary scholarship.

    (The Goucher College series)
    Translation of Formal'nyi metod v literaturovedenii,
originally published in 1928 as a work of P. N. Medvedev;
also attributed to M. M. Bakhtin.
    Includes bibliographical references and index.
    1. Criticism. 2. Formalism (Russian literature)
3. Poetics. I. Bakhtin, Mikhail Mikhailovich.
II. Title.
PN98.F6M413 1977   801'.95   77-15529
ISBN 0-8018-2028-6